WORKBOOK

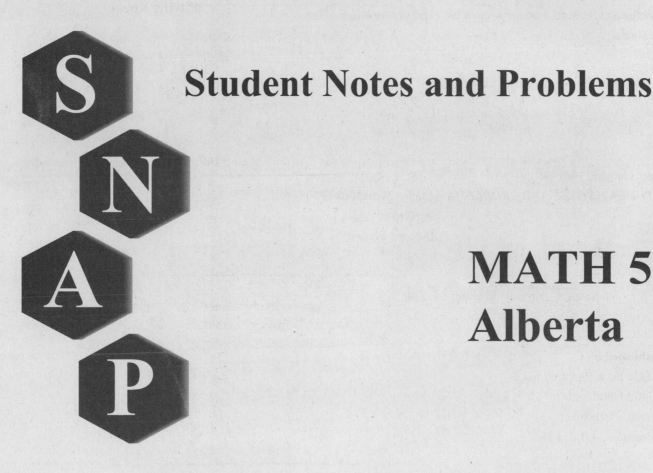

SNAP

Student Notes and Problems

MATH 5
Alberta

CASTLE ROCK
RESEARCH CORP

Publisher
Gautam Rao

Contributors
Phyllis Kozak

Rao, Gautam, 1961 –
STUDENT NOTES AND PROBLEMS – Math 5 Workbook
Alberta
(Second Edition)

1. Science – Juvenile Literature. I. Title

Published by
Castle Rock Research Corp.
2340 Manulife Place
10180 – 101 Street
Edmonton, AB T5J 3S4

1 2 3 FP 13 12 11

Dedicated to the memory of Dr. V. S. Rao

STUDENT NOTES AND PROBLEMS WORKBOOKS

Student Notes and Problems (SNAP) workbooks are a series of support resources in mathematics for students in grades 3 to 12 and in science for students in grades 9 to 12. SNAP workbooks are 100% aligned with curriculum. The resources are designed to support classroom instructions and provide students with additional examples, practice exercises, and tests. SNAP workbooks are ideal for use all year long at school and at home.

The following is a summary of the key features of all SNAP workbooks.

UNIT OPENER PAGE

- summarizes the curriculum outcomes addressed in the unit in age-appropriate language
- identifies the lessons by title
- lists the prerequisite knowledge and skills the student should know prior to beginning the unit

LESSONS

- provide essential teaching pieces and explanations of the concepts
- include example problems and questions with complete, detailed solutions that demonstrate the problem-solving process

NOTES BARS

- contain key definitions, formulas, reminders, and important steps or procedures
- provide space for students to add their own notes and helpful reminders

PRACTICE EXERCISES

- include questions that relate to each of the curriculum outcomes for the unit
- provide practice in applying the lesson concepts

REVIEW SUMMARY

- provides a succinct review of the key concepts in the unit

PRACTICE TEST

- assesses student learning of the unit concepts

ANSWERS AND SOLUTIONS

- demonstrate the step-by-step process or problem-solving method used to arrive at the correct answer

Answers and solutions for the odd-numbered questions are provided in each student workbook. A *SNAP Solutions Manual* that contains answers and complete solutions for all questions is also available.

CONTENTS

Estimation Strategies

Mental Strategies

Measurement

Multiplication of Two 2-Digit Factors

Data Management

Division of 3-Digit by 1-Digit Numbers

2-D Shapes and 3-D Objects

Fractions and Decimals

Transformational Geometry

Variables and Equations

Capacity and Volume

Addition and Subtraction of Decimals

Probability

Answers and Solutions

PATTERN RULES

When you are finished this unit, you will be able to…
- write a mathematical expression to represent a given pattern
- describe a given pattern using mathematical language
- use pattern rules to extend growing and shrinking patterns
- determine pattern rules for patterns in charts and tables
- use pattern rules to predict subsequent elements
- verify predictions visually
- use pattern rules to solve problems

PREREQUISITE SKILLS AND KNOWLEDGE

Prior to starting this unit, you should be able to…
- identify and describe growing patterns
- identify and describe shrinking patterns
- identify and describe patterns found in tables and charts
- translate among different representations of a pattern
- understand mathematical relationships in a pattern

Lesson 1 *UNDERSTANDING PATTERN RULES*

A pattern rule is a statement that describes how to find each succeeding term in a given pattern. It usually tells you what number the pattern starts with (the first term), what operation to use, and the number to use with that operation to get to the next term. Pattern rules are usually expressed in words.

When a pattern changes by the same number each time, the number is called a constant, because it never changes.

 Example

Jaymeson used the pattern rule "add 11 to each term to get the next term" to make this pattern: 8, 19, 30, 41, 53

Is Jaymeson's pattern correct or incorrect? Justify your answer.

Solution

Step 1
Verify the pattern.
Since the pattern rule says to add 11 to each term to get the next term, add 11 to each number in the pattern.
$8 + 11 = 19$
$19 + 11 = 30$
$30 + 11 = 41$
$41 + 11 = 52$

Jaymeson's pattern is incorrect.

Step 2
Justify your answer.

The pattern is incorrect because it does not follow the pattern rule for the whole pattern. When 11 is added to 41, the sum is 52, not 53.

 Time to Try 1

Dayton used the pattern rule "subtract 6 from each term to get the next term" to make this pattern: 54, 48, 42, 36, 32

Is Dayton's pattern correct or incorrect? Justify your answer.

PRACTICE EXERCISES

Use the following information to answer the next question.

Peter used the pattern rule "add 9 to each term to get the next term" to make this pattern:
12, 21, 30, 39, 48

1. Is Peter's pattern correct or incorrect? Justify your answer.

Use the following information to answer the next question.

Brett used the pattern rule "divide each term by 3 to get the next term" to make this pattern:
324, 108, 36, 12, 3

2. Is Brett's pattern correct or incorrect? Justify your answer.

Use the following information to answer the next question.

Olivia and Sam both made a pattern for the pattern rule "multiply each term by 2 to get the next term."
• Olivia's pattern: 12, 24, 48, 96, 192
• Sam's pattern: 14, 28, 56, 112, 224

3. Are the patterns correct or incorrect? Justify your answer.

3

Lesson 2 *EXPRESSING PATTERN RULES AS EXPRESSIONS*

NOTES

An expression of a pattern rule is a description of how to find each succeeding term, but it uses numbers and symbols of operations $(+, -, \times, \div)$ instead of words. It may use a letter to represent any given number in the pattern.

For example, a pattern rule like "start at 3 and multiply each term by 5 to get the next term" can be expressed as +5 or $n + 5$. The letter n represents any number in the pattern.

You can use any letter to represent the numbers in the pattern.

 Example

State the pattern rule for the pattern 87, 82, 77, 72, 67 as an expression.

Solution
Step 1
Determine the pattern rule.

Since the pattern of numbers is shrinking (decreasing), subtract two consecutive numbers to see how the numbers change from term to term.
$$87 - 82 = 5$$
$$82 - 77 = 5$$
$$77 - 72 = 5$$
$$72 - 67 = 5$$

The pattern rule used is to start at 87 and subtract 5 from each term to get the next term.

Step 2
State the pattern rule as an expression.

One way to express the rule is –5.

Another way to express the rule is to choose any one letter to represent each number in the pattern and then to use that letter in the expression: $n - 5$.

 Time to Try 1
State the pattern rule for the pattern 2, 4, 8, 16, 32 as an expression.

PRACTICE EXERCISES

For each of the following four patterns, describe the pattern rule as an expression in two ways, with and without a letter.

1. 55, 61, 67, 73, 79

2. 121, 111, 101, 91

3. 13, 130, 1 300, 13 000

4. 48, 24, 12, 6, 3

Lesson 3 USING MATHEMATICAL LANGUAGE TO DESCRIBE PATTERN RULES

NOTES

It is important to understand how a pattern is made so that you can identify the relationship between the figures or numbers used in the pattern. The relationship between the figures or numbers is the basis of the pattern rule.

This relationship or pattern rule can be expressed entirely in words. This is referred to as mathematical language.

Express the rule using phrases like "one more than," "three less than," "two times greater," "one-half the number." Express the number changes in words as well.

USING WORDS TO DESCRIBE VISUAL PATTERNS

To describe a visual pattern, start by identifying how each figure changes from the previous figure. You may need to count the number of items in each figure and then compare the numbers to determine how the pattern was made. The pattern rule indicates how the pattern was made.

✳ Example

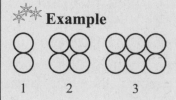

1   2   3

Use mathematical language to describe the pattern rule used in the given pattern.

Solution

Step 1
Determine how each figure changes from the figure before.

You can do this by counting the number of circles in each figure and comparing the numbers.

Figure	Number of Circles
1	2
2	4
3	6

Step 2
Express the pattern rule using mathematical language.

The pattern rule is that two more circles are added to each figure to make the next figure.

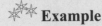 **Time to Try 1**

Row 1 ☆☆☆☆☆☆☆☆☆☆☆☆☆

Row 2 ☆☆☆☆☆☆☆☆☆☆☆☆

Row 3 ☆☆☆☆☆☆☆☆☆☆☆

Row 4 ☆☆☆☆☆☆☆☆☆

Row 5 ☆☆☆☆☆☆☆☆

Use mathematical language to describe the pattern rule used in the given pattern.

USING WORDS TO DESCRIBE NUMBER PATTERNS

To represent a number pattern, start by identifying how the numbers change from term to term. The pattern rule indicates how the pattern was made. Express the rule using words.

Example

117, 107, 97, 87

Use mathematical language to describe the pattern rule used in the given pattern.

Solution

Step 1
Determine how each number changes from term to term.

$117 - 107 = 10$

$107 - 97 = 10$

$97 - 87 = 10$

There is a difference of 10 spaces that are there between consecutive numbers in the pattern.

NOTES

Step 2
Express the pattern rule using mathematical language.
The pattern rule is that each term is ten less than the previous term.

 Time to Try 2

24, 30, 36, 42

Use mathematical language to describe the pattern rule used in the given pattern.

PRACTICE EXERCISES

Use the following information to answer the next question.

Layla makes this pattern out of square tiles.

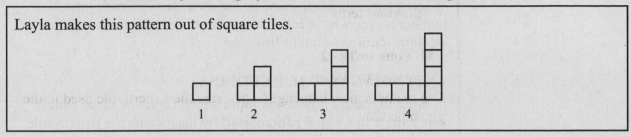

1. Use mathematical language to describe the pattern rule used in Layla's pattern.

Use mathematical language to describe the pattern rule used to make the following three patterns.

2. 95, 75, 55, 35

3. 4, 12, 36, 108

4. 24, 12, 6, 3

Lesson 4   USING PATTERN RULES TO EXTEND GROWING PATTERNS

A **growing pattern** increases in value or size with each term. When a pattern's terms grow by the same number each time, the number it grows by is called a **constant**. A pattern can grow through addition or multiplication.

EXTENDING VISUAL PATTERNS

In order to make a prediction about which figure or shape should appear next in a visual pattern, start by identifying the pattern rule being used. Continue applying the rule to determine how to make the next figure or shape.

✳✳✳ Example

First   Second   Third   Fourth

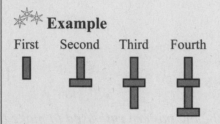

If this pattern is extended, how many rectangular bars will be needed to make the fifth and sixth figures?

Draw the shapes to verify your answer.

Solution

Step 1
Determine the pattern rule used to create each figure.

- The first figure uses one vertical bar.
- The second figure uses two bars. (One horizontal bar is added to the bottom of the first figure.)
- The third figure uses three bars. (One vertical bar is added to the bottom of the second figure.)
- The fourth figure uses four bars. (One horizontal bar is added to the bottom of the third figure.)

The figures grow by adding one more bar to each figure. The bars alternate from vertical to horizontal.

Step 2

Apply the pattern rule for the next two figures.

- The fifth figure should have five bars. Add one vertical bar to the bottom.
- The sixth figure should have six bars. Add one horizontal bar to the bottom.

This is what the extended figures should look like when you draw them:

Fifth   Sixth

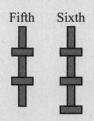

⚘ Time to Try 1

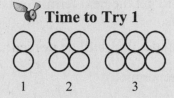

1   2   3

Extend the pattern by drawing figures 4 and 5.

EXTENDING NUMBER PATTERNS

In order to make a prediction about which number should appear next in a number pattern, begin by identifying the pattern rule being used. Continue applying the rule to determine the next term or terms. Number patterns can grow (increase) through addition or multiplication.

NOTES

EXTENDING PATTERNS THROUGH ADDITION

 Example

Kate writes this pattern of numbers: 75, 84, 93, 102

When the pattern is extended, what will the next two terms be?
Explain your answer.

Solution

Step 1

Determine how the numbers change from term to term.

One way to do this is to count up from any number to the
number on its right.

$$75 + 9 = 84$$
$$84 + 9 = 93$$
$$93 + 9 = 102$$

The pattern rule is to add 9 to each term to get the next term.
The rule can be expressed as +9 or $n + 9$.

Step 2

Apply the pattern rule of +9 for two more terms.

$$102 + 9 = 111$$
$$111 + 9 = 120$$

When the pattern is extended, the next two terms will be 111
and 120.

 Time to Try 2

Ethan writes this pattern of numbers: 7, 22, 37, 52

When the pattern is extended, what will be the next two numbers?
Explain your work.

EXTENDING PATTERNS THROUGH MULTIPLICATION

✳✳ Example

Emily writes this pattern of numbers: 2, 6, 18, 54

When the pattern is extended, what will be the next two numbers? Explain your work.

Solution

Step 1

Determine how the numbers change from term to term.

$2 \times 3 = 6$

$6 \times 3 = 18$

$18 \times 3 = 54$

Since each number is three times greater than the previous number, the pattern rule is to multiply each term by 3 to get the next term. The rule can be expressed as $\times 3$ or $n \times 3$.

Step 2

Apply the pattern rule of $\times 3$ for two more terms.

$54 \times 3 = 162$

$162 \times 3 = 486$

When the given pattern is extended, the next two terms will be 162 and 486.

🌱 Time to Try 3

Jacob writes this pattern of numbers: 3, 6, 12, 24

If this pattern is extended, what will be the next two numbers? Explain your work.

PRACTICE EXERCISES

Use the following information to answer the next question.

Jim uses square tiles to create this pattern.

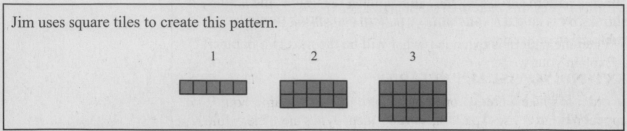

1. Extend the pattern by drawing figures 4 and 5.

Use the following information to answer the next question.

Julia makes this pattern of numbers: 56, 63, 70, 77

2. When the pattern is extended, what will be the next two terms? Explain your answer.

Use the following information to answer the next question.

Shane makes this pattern of numbers using a constant: 9, 18, 36, 72

3. When the pattern is extended, what will be the next two terms? Explain your answer.

Lesson 5 USING PATTERN RULES TO EXTEND SHRINKING PATTERNS

A **shrinking pattern** decreases in value or size with each term. When a pattern shrinks by the same number each time, the number it shrinks by is called a **constant**. A pattern can shrink through subtraction or division.

EXTENDING VISUAL PATTERNS

In order to make a prediction about which figure or shape should appear next in a visual pattern, start by identifying the pattern rule being used. Continue applying the rule to determine the next figure or shape.

✳ **Example**

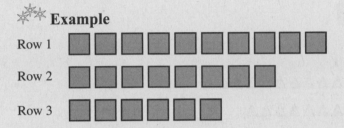

Row 1
Row 2
Row 3

When the pattern of squares is extended, how many squares will be in the next two rows?

Solution

Step 1
Examine how the number of squares changes from row to row.

- Row 1 has 10 squares.
- Row 2 has 8 squares, two fewer squares than row 1.
  $10 - 8 = 2$
- Row 3 has 6 squares, two fewer squares than row 2.
  $8 - 2 = 6$

Since there are two fewer squares in each row, the pattern rule is to remove two squares from each row to make the next row. The rule can be expressed as –2.

Step 2
Apply the rule of –2 for the next two rows.

• Row 4 will have four squares, two less than row 3.
  $6 - 2 = 4$
• Row 5 will have two squares, two less than row 4.
  $4 - 2 = 2$

When the given pattern of squares is extended, the next two rows will have four and two squares.

Row 4

Row 5

Time to Try 1

Row 1 △△△△△△△△△△△△△△

Row 2 △△△△△△△△△△△△

Row 3 △△△△△△△△△

When the pattern of triangles is extended, how many triangles will be in the next two rows?

EXTENDING NUMBER PATTERNS

In order to make a prediction about which number should appear next in a number pattern, begin by identifying the pattern rule being used. Continue applying the rule to determine the next term or terms. Number patterns can shrink (decrease) through subtraction or division.

EXTENDING PATTERNS THROUGH SUBTRACTION

 Example

Erica writes this shrinking number pattern: 111, 100, 89, 78

If the pattern is extended for two more terms, what will be the next two terms? Explain your work.

Solution

Step 1
Determine how the numbers change from term to term.

You can do this by subtracting each set of consecutive numbers.
$$111 - 100 = 11$$
$$100 - 89 = 11$$
$$89 - 78 = 11$$

Each number is 11 less than the previous number. The pattern rule used can be expressed as -11 or $n - 11$.

Step 2
Apply the pattern rule of -11 for two more terms.
$$78 - 11 = 67$$
$$67 - 11 = 56$$

If the pattern is extended for two more terms, the next terms will be 67 and 56.

 Time to Try 2

Greg writes this shrinking number pattern: 123, 117, 111, 105

If the pattern is extended, what will be the next two terms?
Explain your work.

NOTES

EXTENDING PATTERNS THROUGH DIVISION

 Example

Tyler writes this shrinking number pattern: 61, 32, 16

If the pattern is extended, what will be the next two terms?
Explain your answer.

Solution

Step 1
Determine how the numbers change from term to term.
$64 \div 2 = 32$
$32 \div 2 = 16$

Since each number is half of the previous number, the pattern
rule is to divide each number by 2 to get the next number.
The rule can be expressed as $\div 2$ or $n \div 2$.

Step 2
Apply the pattern rule of $\div 2$ for two more terms.
$16 \div 2 = 8$
$8 \div 2 = 4$

When the pattern is extended, the next two terms will be 8 and 4.

 Time to Try 3

Amanda writes this shrinking number pattern: 625, 125, 25

When the pattern is extended, what will be the next two terms?
Explain your work.

18

PRACTICE EXERCISES

Use the following information to answer the next question.

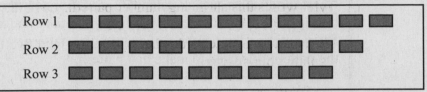

1. When the pattern is extended, how many shapes will be in the next two rows? Draw rows four and five.

Determine the next two terms for the following two patterns. Show your work.

2. 157, 137, 117, 97

3. 243, 81, 27

Lesson 6 DETERMINING PATTERN RULES FOR PATTERNS IN CHARTS AND TABLES

Charts and tables such as calendars, counting charts, and multiplication charts are often filled with many patterns of numbers. By examining the numbers of a particular pattern, you can determine the pattern rule used to make that pattern.

RELATIONSHIPS BETWEEN TERMS

In some number patterns, there is a relationship between the terms of the pattern. It is this relationship that will help you determine the pattern rule used.

To determine the pattern rule, identify what happened to the first number to result in the second number. Verify the pattern rule by determining if the same change occurred from the second number to the third number, and so on.

※※ Example

1	2	3	4	5	6	7	8	9	10
11	12	13	14	15	16	17	18	19	20
21	22	23	24	25	26	27	28	29	30
31	32	33	34	35	36	37	38	39	40
41	42	43	44	45	46	47	48	49	50
51	52	53	54	55	56	57	58	59	60
61	62	63	64	65	66	67	68	69	70
71	72	73	74	75	76	77	78	79	80

Starting at the number 8, what is the pattern rule for the circled numbers on the given chart? Express the pattern rule in words and as an expression.

Solution

Step 1
Determine how the numbers change from term to term.

Starting at the number 8, subtract two consecutive numbers to see how each number changes to result in the next number.
$17 - 8 = 9$
$26 - 17 = 9$
$35 - 26 = 9$
and so on.

Each number increases in value by 9. (8, 17, 26…)

Step 2
Express the pattern rule in words and as an expression.

In words: Start at eight, and add nine to each term (number) to get the next term (number).
As an expression: $+9$ or $n+9$ (using any letter)

Time to Try 1

JULY						
SUN	MON	TUE	WED	THUR	FRI	SAT
1	2	3	4	5	6	7
8	9	10	11	12	13	14
15	16	17	18	19	20	21
22	23	24	25	26	27	28
29	30	31				

Starting at the number 30, what is the pattern rule for the shaded numbers on the calendar chart? Express the pattern rule in words and as an expression.

RELATIONSHIPS BETWEEN TERM NUMBERS AND TERMS

Some patterns that are presented in charts or tables have a relationship with other numbers in the chart.

Example

The circled numbers in this chart form a pattern. Something was done to each top number to result in each circled number.

×	0	1	2	3	4
0	0	0	0	0	0
1	0	1	2	3	4
2	(0)	(2)	(4)	(6)	(8)
3	0	3	6	9	12
4	0	4	8	12	16

Express the pattern rule used in words and as an expression.

Solution

Step 1

Determine how each top number changes into its corresponding circled number.

Into Things	Out
7	15
3	11
13	21
9	17
24	32

$0 \times 2 = 0$
$1 \times 2 = 2$
$2 \times 2 = 4$
$3 \times 2 = 6$
$4 \times 2 = 8$

Each top number is multiplied by 2 to result in its corresponding circled number.

Step 2

Express the pattern rule in words and as an expression.

In words: Start with zero and multiply each top number by two to get the corresponding circled number.

As an expression: $\times 2$ or $n \times 2$ (using any letter).

 Time to Try 2

Marsha made the following In → Out chart. Each time she put a number in, she performed the same calculation to result in the corresponding out number.

Express the pattern rule used in words and as an expression.

PRACTICE EXERCISES

Use the following information to answer the next question.

AUGUST						
SUN	MON	TUE	WED	THU	FRI	SAT
1	2	③	4	5	6	7
8	9	⑩	11	12	13	14
15	16	⑰	18	19	20	21
22	23	㉔	25	26	27	28
29	30	㉛				

1. Starting at the number 31, what is the pattern rule for the circled numbers on the calendar chart? Express the pattern rule in words and as an expression.

Use the following information to answer the next question.

①	2	3	4	5	6	7	8	9	10
11	⑫	13	14	15	16	17	18	19	20
21	22	㉓	24	25	26	27	28	29	30
31	32	33	㉞	35	36	37	38	39	40
41	42	43	44	㊺	46	47	48	49	50
51	52	53	54	55	㊶	57	58	59	60
61	62	63	64	65	66	㊿	68	69	70
71	72	73	74	75	76	77	⑦⑧	79	80
81	82	83	84	85	86	87	88	⑧⑨	90
91	92	93	94	95	96	97	98	99	⑩⓪

2. Starting at the number 1, what is the pattern rule for the circled numbers on the given chart? Express the pattern rule in words and as an expression.

Use the following information to answer the next question.

Adam made the following In → Out chart. Each time he put a number in, he performed the same calculation to result in the corresponding out number.

In	Out
2	1
24	12
8	4
100	50

3. Express the pattern rule used in words and as an expression.

Lesson 7   USING PATTERN RULES TO MAKE PREDICTIONS

In order to make a prediction about which number or number of shapes should appear in a particular figure, you first need to identify the pattern rule being used. You then need to continue applying the rule in order to make the prediction.

An easy way to look at a pattern to see what might come next is to place the information presented in the pattern in a chart. You can then apply the pattern rule to predict subsequent figures. You can use the chart to verify your predictions.

MAKING PREDICTIONS FOR VISUAL PATTERNS

✸ Example

Jackson uses a particular pattern to build three consecutive figures out of square tiles.

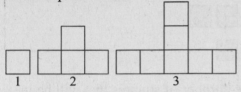

Complete a chart to predict the number of square tiles Jackson would need to build the sixth figure.

Solution

Step 1
Count the number of square tiles in each of the three figures. Enter the numbers in the chart.

Figure	Number of Tiles
1	1
2	4
3	7

Step 2
Determine the pattern rule.

Since each figure has three more square tiles than the previous figure, the pattern rule is to add 3 more squares to each figure to get the next figure. The rule can be expressed as +3 or $n + 3$.

NOTES

Step 3
Apply the pattern rule of +3 for the next three terms in the chart to determine the number of tiles needed to build the sixth figure.

Figure	Number of Tiles
4	$7+3=10$
5	$10+3=13$
6	$13+3=16$

Jackson would need 16 square tiles to build the sixth figure of his pattern.

Time to Try 1

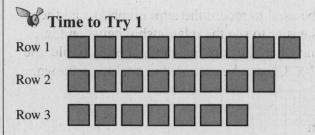

Row 1

Row 2

Row 3

Complete this chart to predict the number of squares that will be in row 7.

Row	Number of Squares
1	
2	
3	
4	
5	
6	
7	

MAKING PREDICTIONS FOR NUMBER PATTERNS

The first number of a number pattern is the first term, the second number of the pattern is the second term, and so on. For example, in the number pattern 1, 3, 4, 6, the first term is 1, the second term is 3, the third term is 4, and the fourth term is 6.

The term numbers are the sequential orders of the terms. Term numbers are usually ordered as 1, 2, 3…. Sometimes, they are ordered as 1st, 2nd, 3rd… or as *first, second, third….*

In order to make a prediction about a number pattern, it is helpful to transfer the numbers to a table of values.

A table of values can be used to record the term numbers and their terms. It is sometimes easier to see the relationship between the term numbers and terms when they are in a table. For example, the number sequence 12, 10, 8, 6 can be recorded in a table as shown.

Term Number	Term
1	12
2	10
3	8
4	6

You can then apply the pattern rule of −2 to predict subsequent terms.

USING ADDITION

You can make predictions about number patterns that grow through addition.

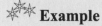 **Example**

Complete a table of values to predict the seventh term number of this growing number pattern: 28, 33, 38, 43

Solution

Step 1
Place the first four term numbers in the table of values to the right of their corresponding term numbers.

Term Number	Term
1	28
2	33
3	38
4	43

NOTES

Step 2
Determine the pattern rule.

Examine the numbers to see how they change from term to term.
$28 + 5 = 33$
$33 + 5 = 38$
$38 + 5 = 43$

Since each term is 5 more than the previous term, the pattern rule is to add 5 to each term to get the next term. The rule can be expressed as +5 or $n + 5$.

Step 3
Apply the pattern rule of +5 for the next three terms in the table of values to predict the seventh term.

Term Number	Term
5	$43 + 5 = 48$
6	$48 + 5 = 53$
7	$53 + 5 = 58$

If the pattern continues, the seventh term will be 58.

 Time to Try 2

Complete the table of values to predict the sixth term of this growing number pattern: 47, 60, 73

Term Number	Term
1	
2	
3	
4	
5	
6	

USING MULTIPLICATION

You can make predictions for number patterns that grow through multiplication.

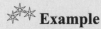 **Example**

Complete a table of values to predict the sixth term of this growing number pattern: 1, 4, 16, 64

Solution

Step 1

Place the first four terms of the pattern in the table of values to the right of their corresponding term numbers.

Term Number	Term
1	1
2	4
3	16
4	64

Step 2

Determine the pattern rule.

Examine the numbers to see how they change from term to term.
$$1 \times 4 = 4$$
$$4 \times 4 = 16$$
$$16 \times 4 = 64$$

Since each term is four times greater than the previous term, the pattern rule is to multiply each term by 4 to get the next term. The rule can be expressed as ×4 or $n \times 4$.

Step 3

Apply the pattern rule of ×4 for the next two terms in the table of values to predict the sixth term.

Term Number	Term
5	$64 \times 4 = 256$
6	$256 \times 4 = 1\ 024$

If the pattern continues, the sixth term will be 1 024.

NOTES

 Time to Try 3

Complete the table of values to predict the seventh term of this growing number pattern: 5, 10, 20, 40

Term Number	Term
1	
2	
3	
4	
5	
6	
7	

USING SUBTRACTION

You can make predictions about number patterns that shrink through subtraction.

 Example

Complete the table of values to predict the eighth term of this shrinking pattern of numbers: 380, 365, 350, 335

Solution

Step 1

Place a first four terms of the pattern in the table of values to the right of their corresponding term numbers.

Term Number	Term
1	380
2	365
3	350
4	335

Step 2

Determine the pattern rule.

One way to determine how the numbers change is to subtract
each set of consecutive numbers.

$380 - 365 = 15$
$365 - 350 = 15$
$350 - 335 = 15$

Since each term is 15 less than the previous term, the pattern rule
is to subtract 15 from each term to get the next term. The rule
can be expressed as -15 or $n - 15$.

Step 3

Apply the pattern rule of -15 for the next four terms in the table
of values to predict the eighth term.

Term Number	Term
5	$335 - 15 = 320$
6	$320 - 15 = 305$
7	$305 - 15 = 290$
8	$290 - 15 = 275$

If the given number pattern continues, the eighth term will
be 275.

 Time to Try 4

Complete the table of values to predict the sixth term of this
shrinking pattern of numbers: 139, 129, 119

Term Number	Term
1	
2	
3	
4	
5	
6	

USING DIVISION

You can make predictions about number patterns that shrink through division.

 Example

Complete a table of values to predict the fifth term of this shrinking pattern of numbers: 243, 81, 27

Solution

Step 1

Place the first three terms of the pattern in the table of values to the right of their corresponding term numbers.

Term Number	Term
1	243
2	81
3	27

Step 2

Determine the pattern rule.

Examine the numbers to see how they are decreasing in value.

$243 \div 3 = 81$

$81 \div 3 = 27$

Since each term is one-third the value of the previous term, the pattern rule is to divide each term by 3 to get the next term.

The rule can be expressed as $\div 3$ or $n \div 3$.

Step 3

Apply the pattern rule of $\div 3$ for the next two terms to predict the fifth term.

Term Number	Term
4	$27 \div 3 = 9$
5	$9 \div 3 = 3$

If the pattern continues, the fifth term will be 3.

Time to Try 5

Complete the table of values to predict the seventh term of this shrinking pattern of numbers: 256, 128 64, 32

Term Number	Term
1	
2	
3	
4	
5	
6	
7	

PRACTICE EXERCISES

Use the following information to answer the next question.

Row 1 ☆☆☆☆☆☆☆☆☆☆☆☆☆☆

Row 2 ☆☆☆☆☆☆☆☆☆☆☆☆☆

Row 3 ☆☆☆☆☆☆☆☆☆☆☆☆

Row 4 ☆☆☆☆☆☆☆☆☆☆☆

Row 5 ☆☆☆☆☆☆☆☆☆☆

1. Complete this table to predict the number of stars that will be in row 8.

Row	Number of Stars
1	
2	
3	
4	
5	
6	
7	
8	

Predict the seventh term of each of the following four patterns by completing each table of values.

2. 12, 19, 26, 33

Term Number	Term
1	
2	
3	
4	
5	
6	
7	

3. 1, 3, 9, 27

Term Number	Term
1	
2	
3	
4	
5	
6	
7	

4. 60, 56, 52, 48

Term Number	Term
1	
2	
3	
4	
5	
6	
7	

5. 320, 160, 80, 40

Term Number	Term
1	
2	
3	
4	
5	
6	
7	

Lesson 8   VERIFYING PREDICTIONS VISUALLY

USING PICTURES

One way to verify your predictions is to draw the figures that will represent the patterns or numbers. When you draw the figures, you need to apply the same rule that was used to create the number pattern.

Example

Tyler sees the number pattern 2, 4, 6… on the board. He predicts that the fifth term will be 10. Mr. Hudson, his teacher, asks Tyler to verify the prediction with a drawing.

Is Tyler's prediction correct?
Verify the prediction by drawing sets of circles to show the pattern.

Solution
Yes, Tyler's prediction is correct.

Step 1
Determine the pattern rule.
The pattern starts with 2, and each term increases in value by 2.

Therefore, the fourth term will be 8. (6 + 2 = 8)
The fifth term will be 10. (8 + 2 = 10)

Step 2
Verify the rule with a diagram.
This set of circles represents the pattern 2, 4, 6, 8, 10.

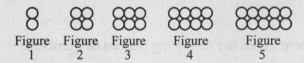

Figure 1   Figure 2   Figure 3   Figure 4   Figure 5

Time to Try 1

Kayla sees the number pattern 16, 14, 12… in her math book.
First, she determines the pattern rule, and then she predicts that the fifth term will be 8. To verify her prediction, she draws rows of stars.

Is Kayla's prediction correct? Verify the prediction by drawing rows of stars to show the pattern.

USING TABLES OF VALUE

Another way to verify your predictions visually is to represent the pattern in chart form, like a table of values. It is often easier to see relationships between numbers when you see them organized in a chart or table.

✳ Example

Lynette sees the pattern 3, 11, 19, 27. She predicts that the seventh term will be 51.

Is Lynette's prediction correct? Verify the prediction by making a table of values.

Solution

Yes, Lynette's prediction is correct.

Make a table of values for the given pattern, extending it for three more terms to verify Lynette's prediction.

Term Number	Term
1	3
2	11
3	19
4	27
5	$27 + 8 = 35$
6	$35 + 8 = 43$
7	$43 + 8 = 51$

🦋 Time to Try 2

David and Joshua were given the following pattern of numbers:
    1, 2, 4, 8, 16
• David predicted that the seventh term would be 56.
• Joshua predicted that the seventh term would be 64.

Whose prediction was correct? Justify your answer by representing the pattern in a table of values.

PRACTICE EXERCISES

Use the following information to answer the next question.

Kerrie sees the number pattern 1, 3, 5… in her math text. She predicts that the fifth term will be 9.

1. Is Kerrie's prediction correct? Verify the prediction by drawing figures of squares to justify your answer.

Use the following information to answer the next question.

Delia predicts that 25 will be the fifth term of this pattern: 5, 10, 15

2. List the next three choices.

Use the following information to answer the next question.

Marina predicts that 28 will be the seventh term of this pattern: 67, 60, 53, 46

3. Is Marina correct? Verify the prediction by making a table of values for the pattern rule.

2. Division is the opposite of _____.

Lesson 9   *USING PATTERN RULES TO SOLVE PROBLEMS*

PROBLEMS WITH PARTIAL PATTERNS

If you know only a few terms of a sequence of numbers, you can determine the pattern rule in order to complete the sequence and then predict subsequent events. You can use a table of values to verify your prediction.

✳ Example

The third, fifth, and sixth terms of a sequence are 4, 16, and 32. What is the tenth term of this sequence?

Solution

Step 1
Make a table of values to organize the numbers and to make it easier to see the given terms and their term numbers.

Term Number	Term
1	
2	
3	4
4	
5	16
6	32

Step 2
Determine the pattern rule.

Since only 16 and 32 are consecutive numbers, you can see that 16 is multiplied by 2 to get 32. That means that the pattern rule is to multiply each term by 2 to get the next term. The rule can be expressed as ×2.

Step 3
Verify the pattern rule by completing the given pattern.

Term Number	Term
1	1
2	2
3	4
4	8
5	16
6	32

NOTES

Step 4

Apply the pattern rule of ×2 to predict the tenth term.

Term Number	Term
7	32×2=64
8	64×2=128
9	128×2=256
10	256×2=512

The tenth term of the sequence will be 512.

 Time to Try 1

The third, fifth, and sixth terms of a sequence of numbers are 118, 124, and 127.

What is the tenth term of this sequence? Show your work.

PROBLEMS EXPRESSED IN WORDS

You can use pattern rules to predict subsequent events when the problems are expressed in words. First, you need to determine what the pattern rule is. Then, you need to apply the pattern rule to solve the problem. Organizing the work you do in a table of values will make it easier to verify your prediction.

✳✳ Example

On Monday, Kirby drew a square on a page in her math scribbler. Each day after, she drew four more squares on the same page. How many squares in total will Kirby have drawn on the page by Sunday? Use a table of values to help you solve this problem.

Solution

Step 1

Determine the pattern rule.

The pattern starts with one (square). For each day after Monday, the pattern grows by four (squares) for the remaining six days of the week.

The pattern rule is to start with 1 and add 4 to each term to get the next term for a total of 7 terms (Monday to Sunday).

The rule can be expressed as +4.

Step 2

Apply the rule of +4.

Make a table of values to help you predict the seventh term. The days of the week will be the term numbers. The number of squares drawn will be the terms.

Term Number	Term
1	1
2	5
3	9
4	13
5	17
6	21
7	25

On Sunday, Kirby will have drawn a total of 25 squares.

NOTES

 Time to Try 2

Jaz drew five squares of approximately the same size in his sketch book. He drew four circles inside the first square. Inside the next square, he drew three more circles than he drew in the first square.

Jaz continued this pattern, drawing three more circles in each square than he drew in the previous square.

How many circles did Jaz draw in the fifth square? Use a table of values to help you verify your answer.

DETERMINING THE TERM NUMBER OF A VALUE

You can predict all the terms in a sequence of numbers when you are given the pattern rule expressed in words. You can then determine which term has a particular value.

 Example

A pattern starts with 0 and continues by adding 3 to each successive term to obtain the next term.

Which term number has a value of 12? Show your work.

Solution

Step 1
Make a table of values.

The table of values will help you keep track of the term numbers and their corresponding terms as you apply the pattern rule of +3.

Term Number	Term
1	0
2	3
3	6
4	9
5	12

Step 2
The pattern generated by the given rule is 0, 3, 6, 9, 12,….

The fifth term of the pattern has a value of 12.

 Time to Try 3

A pattern starts with 5, and each term is multiplied by 2 to determine the next term.

Which term number in the pattern has a value of 160?
Show your work.

PRACTICE EXERCISES

Use the following information to answer the next question.

The second, third, and fifth terms of a sequence are 3, 9, and 81.

Term Number	Term
1	
2	3
3	9
4	
5	81

1. What is the seventh term of the sequence? Show your work.

Use the following information to answer the next question.

Angelina used building blocks to construct a tower that was 10 floors high. For the first floor, she used 18 blocks. She used 10 blocks for each of the other floors.

Use this table of values to help you organize your work.
• The term number will be the number of floors.
• The terms will be the number of blocks.

2. How many blocks in all did Angelina use to build the tower?

Term Number	Term
1	
2	
3	
4	
5	
6	
7	
8	
9	
10	

3. Make a pattern of numbers with six terms that follows this pattern rule: start with 100, and subtract 9 from each term to get the next term.

Use the table of values to show your work. Which term has a value of 73?

Term Number	Term

REVIEW SUMMARY

- A pattern rule usually tells you what number the pattern starts with, what operation to use, and what number to use with that operation to get the next term.
- When a pattern changes by the same number each time, the number is called a constant because it never changes.
- Pattern rules can be expressed as mathematical expressions with and without a letter.
- Pattern rules can be described in words using mathematical language
- Growing patterns can increase through addition or multiplication.
- Shrinking patterns can decrease through subtraction or division.
- Patterns in charts and tables can be represented by pattern rules.
- Pattern rules can be used to extend a pattern.
- Patterns rules can be used to predict subsequent elements.
- Predictions can be verified visually.
- Pattern rules can be used to solve problems.

PRACTICE TEST

Use the following information to answer the next question.

Adam used the pattern rule "add 13 to each term to get the next term" to make this pattern:
5, 18, 31, 44, 55

1. Is Adam's pattern correct or incorrect? Justify your answer.

Use the following information to answer the next question.

Brian is given the following pattern of numbers: 93, 101, 109, 117, 125

2. State the pattern rule for the given pattern as an expression. Express your answer with and without a letter.

Use the following information to answer the next question.

Marcia makes this pattern of numbers: 5, 25, 45, 65, 85

3. Express the pattern rule she used in mathematical language.

Use the following information to answer the next question.

Shelly's homework assignment was to make a growing pattern using a constant. This is the pattern she made: 61, 72, 83, 94

4. When the pattern is extended, what will be the next two terms? Show your work.

Use the following information to answer the next question.

Starting with the number 4, Clayton circles numbers on a calendar page to show a pattern of numbers.

JANUARY						
SUN	MON	TUE	WED	THU	FRI	SAT
					1	2
3	④	5	6	7	8	⑨
10	11	12	13	⑭	15	16
17	18	⑲	20	21	22	23
㉔	25	26	27	28	㉙	30
31						

5. Express the pattern rule used in words and as an expression.

Use the following information to answer the next question.

The second and third terms of a sequence are 6 and 18.

Term Number	Term
1	2
2	6
3	18
4	

6. What is the sixth term of the sequence? Show your work.

Use the following information to answer the next question.

Andrew used square tiles to build four figures.

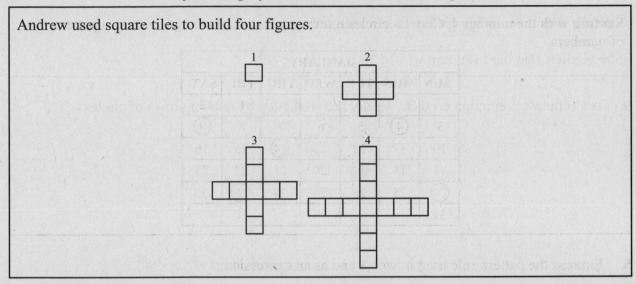

7. Complete this chart to predict the number of squares Andrew will need to create the sixth figure.

Figure	Number of Tiles
1	
2	
3	
4	
5	
6	

Use the following information to answer the next question.

A pattern of numbers starts with 5, and 7 is added to each term to get the next term.

8. Make a pattern that has six terms. Use the table of values to organize your work.

Term Number	Term
1	
2	
3	
4	
5	
6	

Use the following information to answer the next question.

Corinne sees this number pattern in her math text: 31, 24, 17

She predicts that the fifth term will be 3.

9. Is Corinne's prediction correct? Verify the prediction by drawing rows of circles.

Use the following information to answer the next question.

Miss Ames writes this pattern of numbers on the board at the front of the room:
1, 10, 100, 1 000

Hank predicts that the sixth number in the pattern will be 1 000 000.

10. Is Hank correct? Verify Hank's prediction by representing the pattern in a table of values.

Term Number	Term
1	
2	
3	
4	
5	
6	

REPRESENTING WHOLE NUMBERS TO ONE MILLION

When you are finished this unit, you will be able to…
- describe the pattern of adjacent place value positions, moving from right to left
- describe the meaning of each digit in a numeral
- express a given numeral in expanded notation
- write the numeral represented by a given expanded notation
- read and write numerals to 1 000 000
- compare and order numerals to 1 000 000
- understand the magnitude of 1 000 000

PREREQUISITE SKILLS AND KNOWLEDGE

Prior to starting this unit, you should be able to…
- understand place value to 10 000
- describe the value of each digit in a numeral to 10 000
- read and write numbers to 10 000
- compare and order numbers to 10 000
- understand the magnitude of numbers to 10 000

Lesson 1 PLACE VALUE AND PERIOD NAMES

NOTES

Numerals are organized into groups of three digits from right to left. These groups are called periods. From right to left, the names of the first three periods are ones, thousands, and millions. Each period is broken into ones, tens, and hundreds.

- Ones period (hundreds, tens, ones)
- Thousands period (hundreds, tens, ones)
- Millions period (hundreds, tens, ones)

In the following chart, base 10 blocks are used to show place value. The small cube (unit) can represent 1 in the ones period, and it can also represent 1 000 in the thousands period. The tens rod can represent 10 in the ones period and 10 000 in the thousands period. The hundreds flat can represent 100 in the ones period and 100 000 in the thousands period.

Thousands			Ones		
Hundreds	**Tens**	**Ones**	**Hundreds**	**Tens**	**Ones**
▦	▯	▫	▦	▯	▫
100 000	10 000	1 000	100	10	1

× 10   × 10   × 10   × 10   × 10   × 10

As you move from right to left in the place value chart, multiply the place value on the right by 10 to get the next place value immediately to the left.

- 10 ones make 1 ten.
  $1 \times 10 = 10$
- 10 tens make 1 hundred.
  $10 \times 10 = 100$
- 10 hundreds make 1 thousand.
  $100 \times 10 = 1\ 000$
- 10 thousands make 1 ten thousand.
  $1\ 000 \times 10 = 10\ 000$
- 10 ten thousands make 1 hundred thousand.
  $10\ 000 \times 10 = 100\ 000$
- 10 hundred thousands make 1 million.
  $100\ 000 \times 10 = 1\ 000\ 000$

Each digit in a numeral holds a place value position. The same digit can be used more than once in a numeral, but it will have a different value based on its position. A place value chart can help you see the different values.

 Example

The number 111 000 can be represented in this table of values.

Thousands			Ones		
H	T	O	H	T	O
1	1	1	0	0	0

What is the value of each digit 1 in the given number?

Solution

Remember: As you move from right to left on the place value chart, each place value is 10 times greater than the place value immediately before it.

- The digit 1 in the ones place in the thousands period has a value of 1 000.
- The digit 1 in the ten thousands place is one place value to the left. It has a value of $1\,000 \times 10 = 10\,000$.
- The digit 1 in the hundred thousands place is one place value to the left. It has a value of $10\,000 \times 10 = 100\,000$.

 Time to Try 1

The number 202 200 can be represented in this table of values.

Thousands			Ones		
H	T	O	H	T	O
2	0	2	2	0	0

What is the value of each digit 2 in the given number? Explain how you determined the value of each number.

PRACTICE EXERCISES

Use the following information to answer the next question.

The number 440 004 is represented in the following table of values.

Thousands			Ones		
H	T	O	H	T	O
4	4	0	0	0	4

1. How many times does the value of the digit 4 in the ones period need to be multiplied by 10 to equal the value of the digit 4 in the ten place in the thousands period?

Use the following information to answer the next question.

The number 110 011 is represented in the following table of values.

Thousands			Ones		
H	T	O	H	T	O
1	1	0	0	1	1

2. How many times does the value of the digit 1 in the tens place of the ones period need to be multiplied by 10 to equal the value of the digit 1 in the hundred place in the thousands period?

Use the following information to answer the next question.

The number 888 888 is represented in the following table of values.

Thousands			Ones		
H	T	O	H	T	O
8	8	8	8	8	8

3. How many times does the value of the digit 8 in the hundreds place in the ones period need to be multiplied by 10 to equal the value of the digit 8 in the hundreds place in the thousands period?

Lesson 2   USING PLACE VALUE CHARTS

A place value chart is an organized table that shows the positions of all the digits in a numeral. You can determine the value of each digit in a numeral by multiplying the given digit by the value of its position.

The zeros in a place value chart have no value. They are placeholders.

Following is an example of a place value chart.

Thousands			Ones		
H	T	O	H	T	O
4	0	5	0	2	7

 Example

Show the number 360 087 in a place value chart. Explain the value of each digit.

Solution

Thousands			Ones		
H	T	O	H	T	O
3	6	0	0	8	7

Multiply each digit by the value of its position.

- The value of the digit 7 is 7.
  The digit 7 is in the ones place, so multiply 7 by 1.
  $7 \times 1 = 7$

- The value of the digit 8 is 80.
  The digit 8 is in the tens place, so multiply 8 by 10.
  $8 \times 10 = 80$

- The value of the digit 6 is 60 000.
  The digit 6 is in the ten thousands position, so multiply 6 by 10 000.
  $6 \times 10\ 000 = 60\ 000$

- The value of the digit 3 is 300 000.
  The digit 3 is in the hundred thousands position, so multiply 3 by 100 000.
  $3 \times 100\ 000 = 300\ 000$

Remember: The zeros in the hundreds position and the thousands position have no values. They are placeholders.

NOTES

 Time to Try 1

Show the number 902 030 in a place value chart. Explain the value of each digit.

Thousands			Ones		
H	T	O	H	T	O

56

PRACTICE EXERCISES

Use the following information to answer the next question.

The number 808 080 is represented in this place value chart.

Thousands			Ones		
H	T	O	H	T	O
8	0	8	0	8	0

1. Which digit 8 has a value of 800 000? Explain your answer.

Use the following information to answer the next question.

The number 781 703 is represented in this place value chart.

Thousands			Ones		
H	T	O	H	T	O
5	8	1	5	0	3

2. Use the place value chart to help you determine the values of each digit 5. Explain your answer.

Use the following information to answer the next question.

The number 205 340 is represented in this place value chart.

Thousands			Ones		
H	T	O	H	T	O
2	0	5	3	4	0

3. Use the place value chart to help you determine the values of each digit. Show your work.

Lesson 3   USING EXPANDED NOTATION

REPRESENTING NUMERALS AS EXPANDED NOTATION

Numbers can be written in expanded notation or form.
Expanded form takes a number and shows it expanded (or stretched out) into an expression based on the place value of each digit.
The values of all the digits are added.

To write expanded notation:
1. Start with the digit in the largest place value position. Replace the digits to the right with zeros.
2. Place a plus sign (+) between the sets of values.
3. The zeros in the number are not included in expanded notation, as they are placeholders in the number.

 Example

Write the expanded notation for the number 805 210.

Solution

Step 1

Start at the left (the largest place value), and write the value of each digit in the number.

- 8 has a value of 800 000. $(8 \times 100\ 000)$
- 0 indicates that there are no ten thousands.
- 5 has a value of 5 000. $(5 \times 1\ 000)$
- 2 has a value of 200. (2×100)
- 1 has a value of 10. (1×10)
- 0 indicates that there are no ones.

Step 2

Start at the left, and write the values horizontally with a + sign between each pair of values.

Expanded notation can be written two ways:
- $800\ 000 + 5\ 000 + 200 + 10$
- $(8 \times 100\ 000) + (5 \times 1\ 000) + (2 \times 100) + (1 \times 10)$

 Time to Try 1

Write the expanded form of the number 107 063.

58

REPRESENTING EXPANDED NOTATION AS NUMERALS

When you represent an expanded notation as a numeral, it is
important to remember to have a digit for each place value.
Zeros will act as placeholders.

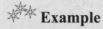 **Example**

Write the numeral that represents the expanded notation
$300\ 000 + 50\ 000 + 400 + 8$.

Solution

Step 1

Place the values shown in the expanded notation in a place
value chart.

Thousands			Ones		
H	**T**	**O**	**H**	**T**	**O**
3	5		4		8

Step 2

Place zeros as placeholders in the tens and thousands positions.

Thousands			Ones		
H	**T**	**O**	**H**	**T**	**O**
3	5	0	4	0	8

The expanded notation $300\ 000 + 50\ 000 + 400 + 8$ represents the
numeral 350 408.

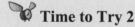 **Time to Try 2**

Karina writes a particular number in expanded notation.
$900\ 000 + 50\ 000 + 4\ 000 + 300 + 1$

What number is represented by the expanded notation Karina wrote?

PRACTICE EXERCISES

1. Write the expanded notation for the number 45 687 in two ways.

2. Write the expanded notation for the number 702 009 in two ways.

3. Write the numeral that represents the expanded notation $400\,000 + 50\,000 + 4\,000 + 800$.
   Use the place value chart to help you.

Thousands			Ones		
H	T	O	H	T	O

4. Write the numeral that represents the expanded notation
   $(3 \times 100\,000) + (7 \times 10\,000) + (4 \times 100) + (8 \times 1)$. Use the place value chart to help you.

Thousands			Ones		
H	T	O	H	T	O

Lesson 4   READING AND WRITING NUMBERS TO ONE MILLION

To read and write whole numbers up to one million (1 000 000), it is important to know the place value of each digit.

Place values for large numbers are arranged in groups of three. Each group of three is called a period. Each period shows the number of ones, tens, and hundreds in a particular number.

EXPRESSING NUMERALS IN WORD FORM

When you write whole numbers in words, write each period from left to right.

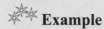 **Example**

The population of Niagara Falls in 2006 was 82 184. Read the number 82 184, and then write it using words.

Solution

Step 1
Put the numbers into a place value chart so you can easily see the place value positions of each digit.

Thousands Period			Ones Period		
H	T	O	H	T	O
	8	2	1	8	4

- H = Hundreds
- T = Tens
- O = Ones

Step 2
Read the number.

To read the number 82 184, start at the left, and say the words for the digits in the thousands period (82) followed by the word thousand: eighty-two thousand.

Then, say the words for the digits in the ones period (184): one hundred eighty-four.

Do not say the word *and*. Altogether, you would say "eighty-two thousand one hundred eighty-four."

NOTES

Step 3
Write the number in words.

Start at the left, and write the thousands period first:
eighty-two thousand.

Follow the thousands period with the ones period:
one hundred eighty-four.

Putting the two periods together, you would write 82 184 in words as eighty-two thousand one hundred eighty-four.

 Time to Try 1

Read the number 120 945, and then write it using words.

EXPRESSING WORD FORMS AS NUMERALS
When writing a numeral represented in written form, leave a space between the periods (millions and thousands; thousands and ones).

If there are no digits to the left of the thousands position, the space between the thousands period and ones period is often omitted. For example, the number one thousand three hundred twelve can be written as 1 312 (with a space between the thousands and ones periods) or as 1312 (with the space omitted).
• When writing in numeric form, remember to use a digit for each place value. A zero will act as a placeholder.
• The words that represent the part of the number in the thousands period are located to the left of the word *thousand*.
• The words that represent the part of the number in the ones period are located to the right of the word *thousand*.

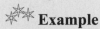 **Example**

For an election campaign, one party printed seven hundred fourteen thousand five hundred pamphlets.

Written as a numeral, how many pamphlets were printed?

Solution

Step 1

Start with the thousands period.

Enter the digits that represent the words *seven hundred fourteen* into the chart.

Thousands Period			Ones Period		
H	T	O	H	T	O
7	1	4			

Step 2

Move to the ones period.

Enter the digits that represent the words *five hundred* into the chart.

Thousands Period			Ones Period		
H	T	O	H	T	O
7	1	4	5	0	0

There were 714 500 pamphlets printed.

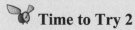 **Time to Try 2**

Write the number three hundred twenty-six thousand eight hundred three as a numeral.

PRACTICE EXERCISES

1. Write the number 872 835 in words.

Thousands Period			Ones Period		
H	T	O	H	T	O
8	7	2	8	3	5

2. Write the number 507 080 in words.

Thousands Period			Ones Period		
H	T	O	H	T	O
5	0	7	0	8	0

3. Write the numeral form of the number two hundred ninety-six thousand twelve.
   Use the place value chart to help you.

Thousands			Ones		
H	T	O	H	T	O

4. Write the numeral form of the number two hundred two thousand six hundred fifty.
   Use the place value chart to help you.

Thousands			Ones		
H	T	O	H	T	O

Lesson 5   COMPARING AND ORDERING NUMBERS UP TO ONE MILLION

When comparing and ordering numbers, start by organizing the numbers being compared.

One way to do this is to write the digits of each number being compared in their correct positions in a place value chart.

Another way to organize the numbers you are comparing is to write the numbers one below the other, lining up the same place values.

Regardless of which method you choose to organize the numbers, comparing and ordering numbers is easier to do when the same place values are lined up.

COMPARING NUMBERS

Here are some tips to help you compare numbers:
- Start with the greatest place value.
- Work from left to right, and compare the digits in each position.
- Compare only the digits in the same place value position.
- When two or more numbers have the same value in the same place value position, move to the right (the next position) for those numbers, and compare the digits in that position.
- Use the greater than (>) symbol, the less than (<) symbol, or the equal to (=) symbol to express comparisons.

✳ Example

When the numbers 233 590, 233 905, and 243 950 are compared, which number has the **least** value?

Solution

Step 1
Write the numbers one below the other, lining up the place values.
233 590
233 905
243 950

Step 2
Compare the digits in the greatest place value.

Since there is a 2 in each number in the hundred thousands position, move right to the next position (ten thousands).

NOTES

Step 3
Compare the digits in the ten thousands position.

Since $3 < 4$, you know that the number 243 950 has the greatest value.

Step 4
Compare the digits in the thousands position of 23<u>3</u> 590 and 23<u>3</u> 905.

Since both numbers have a 3 in the thousands position, move right to the next position (hundreds).

Step 5
Compare the digits in the hundreds position.

Since $5 < 9$, you know that the number 233 590 has the least value.

 Time to Try 1

When the numbers 448 201, 438 200, and 338 020 are compared, which number has the **greatest** value?

ORDERING NUMBERS

When ordering numbers, follow the same steps as when comparing numbers.

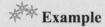 **Example**

Write the numbers 593 450, 565 345, and 900 900 in order from least to greatest (ascending order).

Solution

Step 1

Make a place value chart.

Enter the digits of each number in their correct place value positions.

Thousands			Ones		
H	**T**	**O**	**H**	**T**	**O**
5	9	3	4	5	0
5	6	5	3	4	5
9	0	0	9	0	0

Step 2

Compare the digits in the hundred thousands position.

Since $9 > 5$, the greatest number is 900 900.

Step 3

Compare the digits in the ten thousands position for 593 450 and 565 345.

Since $9 > 6$, the number 593 450 is greater than 565 345.
565 345 < 593 450 < 900 900

Written in order from least to greatest, the numbers are 565 345, 593 450, 900 900.

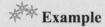 **Time to Try 2**

Write the numbers 707 990, 770 909, and 907 709 from greatest to least (descending order).

PRACTICE EXERCISES

1. Which of the numbers 418 134, 398 432, and 389 413 has the **least** value?
    Explain your answer.

2. Which of the numbers 322 432, 322 567, and 323 764 has the **greatest** value?
    Explain your answer.

3. Order the numbers 435 923, 445 234, and 234 534 from least to greatest (ascending order).
    You can use the place value chart to help you organize the numbers.

Thousands			Ones		
H	T	O	H	T	O

4. Order the numbers 141 141, 114 411, and 144 114 from greatest to least (descending order).
    You can use the place value chart to help you organize the numbers.

Thousands			Ones		
H	T	O	H	T	O

Lesson 6   *UNDERSTANDING THE MAGNITUDE OF NUMBERS UP TO ONE MILLION*

Here are some tips for solving problems that involve the number 1 000 000:

- When you are working with a large number like 1 000 000, you may find it more practical to use a calculator.
- If you do not need an exact calculation, round numbers to make them easier to handle. Use whatever estimation strategy works best for you.
- You may need to use relationships between numbers to solve some problems. Use relationships that you already know.
- Solving problems involving large numbers is easier when you break the problem into smaller parts and work through the problem step-by-step.

✳ Example

Daria read in *Challenge* magazine that if it took an average of one second to count one number out loud, it would take a little less than 12 days to count from 1 to 1 000 000. She used her calculator to determine if that was a reasonable estimation.

Use your calculator to determine about how many days it would take to count out loud from 1 to 1 000 000. Explain your work.

Solution

Step 1
Determine approximately how many numbers you would be able to count out loud in one hour.

Since there are 60 seconds in one minute and 60 minutes in one hour, multiply 60 by 60.
$60 \times 60 = 3\ 600$

You might be able to count 3 600 numbers out loud in one hour.

Step 2

Estimate how many numbers you might be able to count in one day.

Since there are 24 hours in one day, multiply 3 600 by 24.
$3\ 600 \times 24 = 86\ 400$

You might be able to count 86 400 numbers in 24 hours (one day).

Round this number to the nearest hundred thousand.

Since $8 > 5$, you might be able to count close to 100 000 numbers out loud in one day.

Step 3

Determine the estimated number of days it would take to count 1 000 000 numbers.

Since 1 000 000 is 10 times greater than 100 000, it would take more than 10 days to count out loud to one million (that is, counting continuously, without any breaks).

🦋 Time to Try 1

Jesse read on the Internet that the oldest person in a particular country was 1 000 000 hours old.

Using a calculator, estimate about how many years old the person was.

PRACTICE EXERCISES

Use the following information to answer the next question.

> A pen manufacturing company places eight pens into each package. Twenty-five packages of pens are then placed into each box.

1. How many boxes are needed to package 1 000 000 pens?

2. A particular bus can accommodate 52 passengers. How many of the same kind of buses would be needed to accommodate 1 000 000 passengers? Using a calculator, estimate about how many buses will be needed.

Use the following information to answer the next question.

> A thousands cube is made up of 1 000 units.
>
>

3. How many of these thousands cubes are needed to represent the number 1 000 000?

4. The fastest laser printer can print 100 pages per minute. Printing at this same rate, about how many days would it take the printer to print 1 000 000 pages?

REVIEW SUMMARY

- When working with numbers, it is important to know the place value of each digit. Place value is the value of each digit based on its position in a number.
- Each number has a place value position. From right to left, they are ones, tens, hundreds, thousands, ten thousands, hundred thousands, and millions.
- Moving from the ones to the millions (right to left), each place value is 10 times greater than the place value on the immediate right.
- Large numbers are grouped in sets of three. The sets are called periods; the thousands period and ones period.
- When numbers are written in expanded notation, the numbers are stretched out into an expression based on the place value of each digit. The values of the digit are added.
- Read numbers from left to right. Say the word *thousand* after the digits in the thousands period. Do not say the word *and*.
- Write numbers from left to right. Write the word *thousand* after the words that represent the digits in the thousands period. Do not write the word *and*.
- When comparing or ordering numbers, start with the largest place value, and compare the digits in the same place value positions. Work from left to right.
- When solving problems involving the number 1 000 000, you may need to use a calculator, use estimation strategies that work for you, and use relationships you already know.

PRACTICE TEST

Use the following information to answer the next question.

The number 401 071 is represented in the table of values.

Thousands			Ones		
H	T	O	H	T	O
4	0	1	0	7	1

1. How many times does the value of the digit 1 in the ones period need to be multiplied by 10 to equal the value of the digit 1 in the thousands period?

Use the following information to answer the next question.

The number 510 903 is represented in the table of values.

Thousands Period			Ones Period		
H	T	O	H	T	O
5	1	0	9	0	3

2. Write the number 510 903 in words.

3. Which of the numbers 462 362, 461 192, and 461 155 has the **least** value? Use the place value chart to help you organize the numbers.

Thousands			Ones		
H	T	O	H	T	O

4. Write the numeral that represents the expanded notation $(8\times100\ 000)+(5\times10\ 000)+(5\times100)+(2\times10)$. Use the place value chart to help you.

Thousands			Ones		
H	T	O	H	T	O

5. Write the expanded notation for the number 777 070 in two ways.

6. Order the numbers 535 983, 545 264, and 434 574 from least to greatest (ascending order). Use the place value chart to organize the numbers.

Thousands			Ones		
H	T	O	H	T	O

7. Write the numeral form of the number three hundred twenty-six thousand fifteen. Use the place value chart to help you.

Thousands			Ones		
H	T	O	H	T	O

8. Write the numeral that represents the expanded notation 80 000 + 2 000 + 20 + 7. Use the place value chart to help you.

Thousands			Ones		
H	T	O	H	T	O

Use the following information to answer the next question.

A pen manufacturing company places 12 pens into each package. Twenty packages of pens are then placed into each box.

9. How many boxes are needed to package 1 000 000 pens?

Use the following information to answer the next question.

The number 679 601 is represented in this place value chart.

Thousands			Ones		
H	T	O	H	T	O
7	6	9	6	0	1

10. Use the place value chart to help you determine the values of each digit 6. Explain your answer.

Use the following information to answer the next question.

The number 444 400 is represented in this place value chart.

Thousands			Ones		
H	T	O	H	T	O
4	4	4	4	0	0

11. Which digit 4 has a value of 400 000? Explain your answer.

ESTIMATION STRATEGIES

When you are finished this unit, you will be able to...
- understand the uses of estimation
- estimate a solution to a problem using front-end estimation
- use comparative language to describe estimated sums, differences, products, and quotients
- estimate a sum or product using compatible numbers
- estimate a solution to a problem using compensation
- estimate a solution to a problem using the rounding rule

PREREQUISITE SKILLS AND KNOWLEDGE

Prior to starting this unit, you should be able to...
- understand when and why you would estimate
- estimate sums with answers to ten thousand
- estimate the corresponding differences from ten thousand
- add and subtract three- and four-digit numerals

Lesson 1   UNDERSTANDING ESTIMATION

Estimation is a strategy used to calculate an approximate amount. Estimation involves using numbers that are close to the original numbers in the problem so they can be worked with easily.

WHEN ESTIMATION IS USEFUL

Being able to estimate is useful when solving problems. You can use estimation in the following situations:

• When an exact answer is not needed
• When you are judging whether or not a solution is reasonable
• When you are predicting what a solution should be close to

When working with large numbers, it is always best to start with an estimation of the calculation. The estimation is a prediction of what the calculations should be close to.

When you compare the estimate to the actual calculation and the two are close, you know that the actual answer is most likely reasonable and that you made a reasonable estimation.

For example, when Jake multiplied 42×18, he got an answer of 378. When he rounded the numbers of the multiplication problem (40×20) to get an estimate, he got an answer of 800. Since his estimate and his solution were so far apart, he knew that 378 was not a reasonable answer. Jake then checked his multiplication to see where he had made an error.

UNDERESTIMATING AND OVERESTIMATING

An underestimate results in a total that is less than the exact or actual amount. An overestimate results in a total larger than the exact amount. Usually it does not matter if you underestimate or overestimate, as long as the estimate is close to the actual amount.

However, sometimes, an estimate that is lower than the actual amount is not helpful. Following are some situations where it would be best to overestimate.

- When estimating the amount of food needed for a party, most hosts and hostesses want to have more food than needed. Running out of food could ruin the party.
- When estimating the amount of ingredients needed to bake a particular recipe, you must have the exact or greater amount of ingredients needed. Having less than what the recipe asks for could ruin the baking.
- When estimating the amount of money needed to buy something, and paying in cash, you must have the exact or greater amount of cash to pay with. A store will not sell you the items if you do not have the money to pay for them.
- When estimating the amount of cars or buses needed to transport a specific number of people, you need to be sure that each of the given people have transportation and are not left behind.

PRACTICE EXERCISES

Use the following information to answer the next question.

A group of students used 314 yellow cubes and 250 red cubes to build a figure. Their teacher wanted to know about how many cubes were used.

1. Explain why the students should estimate the number of cubes used instead of calculating the exact sum.

Use the following information to answer the next question.

Nelson multiplied 37 by 43 and got a product of 591. Mr. Dawson told Nelson to estimate the product and then compare the two products.

2. Explain why Nelson should estimate the product and then compare it to the actual product.

Use the following information to answer the next question.

Lynette wants to buy a sweater that costs $23.98 and a pair of jeans that cost $52.45. When she asks her dad for some money, her dad asks her about how much money she needs.

3. Explain why it would be best for Lynette to overestimate the amount of money needed.

Lesson 2   USING FRONT-END ESTIMATION

When you use front-end estimation, you keep the front or first digits (the numbers with the greatest place values) and replace all the digits to the right with zeros. You then add, subtract, multiply, or divide the estimated numbers as needed.

Front-end estimates are always lower than the actual calculations.

 Example

A school bought 25 boxes of markers for the art room. Each box contained 24 markers.

Use the strategy of front-end estimation to determine approximately how many markers the school bought.

Solution

Step 1
Determine the operation needed to solve the problem.

Since you need to determine the total number of markers, you need to multiply.

Step 2
Use front-end estimation for the number of boxes and number of markers in each box.
$25 \rightarrow 20$
$24 \rightarrow 20$

Step 3
Multiply the two estimated amounts.
$20 \times 20 = 400$

The school bought approximately 400 markers for the art room.

 Time to Try 1

Abraham collected 93 packages of hockey cards. Each package contained 25 cards.

Use the strategy of front-end estimation to determine about how many hockey cards Abraham has.

PRACTICE EXERCISES

Use the strategy of front-end estimation to answer the following questions.

Use the following information to answer the next question.

Don, Shawn, and Bill all collect autographs. Don has 142 autographs, Shawn has 167 autographs, and Bill has 201 autographs.

1. About how many autographs did the three boys have in total?

Use the following information to answer the next question.

Anna has a total of 1 742 stamps in her collection. Tim is just starting to collect stamps, so Anna gave him 345 of her duplicate stamps to start his collection.

2. About how many stamps did Anna have left in her collection?

Use the following information to answer the next question.

Kevin works for a small company that sells packages of balls to pet stores. One of his jobs is to place 12 balls into each package. On Monday, Kevin placed 492 balls into packages.

3. About how packages did Kevin make on Monday?

82

Lesson 3 USING COMPARATIVE LANGUAGE

One way to estimate is to first apply front-end estimation to the numbers of the given calculation. The next step is to describe the solution to the calculation in terms of the estimated solution, using comparative language.

The following descriptions are examples of comparative language:
- Less than
- More than
- Greater than
- Close to
- Almost the same as

The words you use will depend on how close or how far away the estimated numbers are from the actual numbers. For example, you can estimate the product of 22×21 as being close to or almost the same as $20 \times 20 = 400$ because the numbers 22 and 21 are close to the estimated numbers of 20 and 20.

USING COMPARATIVE LANGUAGE TO ESTIMATE SUMS

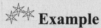 **Example**

After applying front-end estimation, use comparative language to describe the sum of $948 + 327$.

Solution

Step 1
Use front-end estimation for the two numbers (addends).
$948 \rightarrow 900$
$327 \rightarrow 300$

Step 2
Use comparative language to describe the sum of $948 + 327$. Since both addends were rounded down, the actual sum will be more than the estimated sum.

You can describe the sum of $948 + 327$ as being **greater than** the sum of $900 + 300 = 1\ 200$.

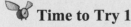 **Time to Try 1**

After applying front-end estimation, use comparative language to describe the sum of $105 + 610$.

USING COMPARATIVE LANGUAGE TO ESTIMATE DIFFERENCES

 Example

After applying front-end estimation, use comparative language to describe the difference of 905 – 403.

Solution

Step 1
Use front-end estimation for the two numbers.
$905 \rightarrow 900$
$403 \rightarrow 400$

Step 2
Use comparative language to describe the difference of
905 – 403.

Since both numbers were rounded down but both numbers were very close to the rounded amounts, the actual difference will also be very close to the estimated difference.

You can describe the difference of 905 – 403 as being **very close** to the difference of 900 – 400 = 500.

 Time to Try 2

After applying front-end estimation, use comparative language to estimate the difference of 699 – 208.

USING COMPARATIVE LANGUAGE TO ESTIMATE PRODUCTS

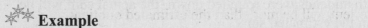 **Example**

After applying front-end estimation, use comparative language to describe the product of 42 × 68.

Solution

Step 1
Use front-end estimation for the two factors.
$42 \rightarrow 40$
$68 \rightarrow 60$

Step 2
Use comparative language to describe the product of 42 × 68.

Since both factors were rounded down, the actual product will be greater than 40 × 60.

You can describe the product of 42 × 68 as being **greater than** the product of 40 × 60 = 2 400.

 Time to Try 3

After applying front-end estimation, use comparative language to describe the product of 11 × 81.

USING COMPARATIVE LANGUAGE TO ESTIMATE QUOTIENTS

 Example

After applying front-end estimation, use comparative language to describe the quotient of 457 ÷ 5.

Solution
Step 1
Use front-end estimation for the dividend.
457 → 400

Since the divisor is a one-digit number, it will stay as 5.

Step 2
Use comparative language to describe the quotient of 457 ÷ 5.

Since the actual dividend is rounded down (457 → 400), the actual quotient will be more than the estimated quotient.

You can describe the quotient of 457 ÷ 5 as being **more than** the quotient of 400 ÷ 5 = 80.

 Time to Try 4

After applying front-end estimation, use comparative language to estimate the quotient of 707 ÷ 4.

PRACTICE EXERCISES

1. After applying front-end estimation, use comparative language to describe the sum of 301 + 409 + 502.

2. After applying front-end estimation, use comparative language to describe the difference of 6 984 – 1 127.

3. After applying front-end estimation, use comparative language to describe the product of 51 × 61.

4. After applying front-end estimation, use comparative language to describe the quotient of 753 ÷ 2.

Lesson 4—Using Compensation

Lesson 4   USING COMPENSATION

Compensation is a strategy that is very similar to front-end estimation. It is mainly used when estimating the sum of at least three numbers. When adding three numbers, compensation requires that you use the front digits for the first two numbers but use the front digit +1 for the last number.

Compensation will usually give a more accurate estimation than front-end estimation.

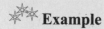 **Example**

Evan uses compensation to estimate the sum of 532 + 910 + 647 before he calculates the actual sum.

Compare the estimated sum to the actual sum.

Solution
Step 1
Use front-end estimation for the first two numbers.
532 → 500
910 → 900

Use front-end estimation +1 for the third number.
647 → 700 (6+1)

Step 2
Add the three estimations.
500 + 900 + 700 = 2 100

Step 3
Determine the actual sum.
532 + 910 + 647 = 2 089

Step 4
Compare the estimated sum to the actual sum.

The estimated sum of 2 100 is very close to the actual sum of 2 089. There is only a difference of 11 between the two sums.

Compensation was a very good strategy for Evan to use because it gave him quite an accurate estimation.

NOTES

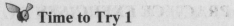 **Time to Try 1**

Mrs. Marsh has a pail of coloured counting chips in her classroom. There are 654 blue chips, 509 green chips, and 753 yellow chips in the pail.

Using the strategy of compensation, estimate the number of coloured chips in the pail.

PRACTICE EXERCISES

1. Use the strategy of compensation to estimate the sum of $920 + 449 + 738$. Compare the estimated sum to the actual sum.

Use the following information to answer the next question.

Mrs. Bentley works in a kiosk that sells magazines and snacks.
- In January, she sold 258 magazines.
- In February, she sold 325 magazines.
- In March, she sold 238 magazines.

2. Using the strategy of compensation, estimate the total number of magazines sold over the three-month period. Show your work.

Use the following information to answer the next question.

At Karim's school, 317 children, 156 women, and 144 men bought tickets to watch the spring concert.

3. Using the strategy of compensation, estimate the total number of people who bought tickets for the concert.

Lesson 5   USING COMPATIBLE NUMBERS

When you estimate using compatible numbers, you are looking for numbers that are easy to work with mentally. Compatible numbers are often related to each other in some way.

For example, when adding 78 and 19, you can think of numbers like 75 and 25 which are close to 78 and 19, but are easier to add in your head. You can think of numbers like 80 and 20 which are even closer to 78 and 18, and are also easy to add in your head.

You can estimate using compatible numbers with any operation, but this strategy works especially well when multiplying or dividing, as the compatible numbers could be factors or multiples.

The number 10 and its multiples are compatible with all factors.

USING COMPATIBLE NUMBERS FOR MULTIPLICATION
✷✷ **Example**

Mr. Williams makes personalized skateboards as a hobby. He can make up to 76 skateboards in one month.

Using the strategy of compatible numbers, estimate about how many skateboards Mr. Williams can make in one year. Explain your work.

Solution
Step 1
Determine the compatible numbers.

Since 10 is close to 12 (the number of months in one year), you can use 10 to represent 12 months.
Since 10 is compatible with all factors, you do not need to represent the number 76 with any other number.

The compatible numbers are 10 and 76.

Step 2
Multiply the compatible numbers.
$76 \times 10 = 760$

Mr. Williams can make about 760 skateboards in one year.

Time to Try 1

Using the strategy of compatible numbers, estimate the product of 42 × 26. Explain your work.

USING COMPATIBLE NUMBERS FOR DIVISION

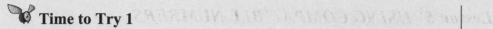 Example

Shaylah is making up treat bags to give out to trick-or-treaters on Halloween. She has 395 candies to put into the treat bags. She plans to put five candies into each bag. The packages of treat bags come in groups of 25. Shaylah estimates the number of bags she will need and then buys four packages of bags.

Use the estimation strategy of compatible numbers to judge the reasonableness of Shaylah's decision to buy four packages of bags.

Solution

Step 1
Determine the operation needed to solve this problem.
Since you need to determine the number of groups (bags needed), you need to divide.

Step 2
Think of a number close to 395 that can be easily divided by 5.
395 → 400

Since 40 can be easily divided by 5, 400 and 5 are compatible numbers.

Step 3
Divide 400 by 5.
400 ÷ 5 = 80

Shaylah will need about 80 bags.

Step 4
Determine the number of packages of bags needed.
Since there are 25 bags in a package, Shaylah will need four packages:
25, 50, 75, 100

Shaylah made a reasonable estimate when she decided to buy four packages of treat bags for the 395 candies.

NOTES

 Time to Try 2

A particular school has a total of 356 students in grades 1 through 6. Each grade has about the same number of students.

Use the estimation strategy of compatible numbers to determine about how many students are in each grade.

PRACTICE EXERCISES

1. Using the strategy of compatible numbers, estimate the product of 39 × 21.
    Explain your work.

2. A theatre has 24 rows of seats with 18 seats in each row. Using the strategy of
    compatible numbers, estimate the total number of seats in the theatre.

3. Using the strategy of compatible numbers, estimate the sum of 458 + 837
    Explain your work.

Use the following information to answer the next question.

Henri saved $197 over a period of five months. He saved about the same amount of money
each month.

4. Use the estimation strategy of compatible numbers to determine about how much money
    Henri saved each month.

Lesson 6   USING THE ROUNDING RULE

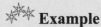

NOTES

Rounding is one of the most commonly used strategies when estimating sums, differences, products, and quotients. The reason it is so widely used is that the estimations are usually very accurate.

Usually, you round factors to their largest place value. However, you can round to other place values as well, such as multiples of 10, 100, 1 000, or 10 000.

Sometimes, you will round both numbers in a problem, and other times, you will only round one number.

The same rounding rules are followed regardless of the place value that you are rounding to:

1.   Look at the number to the right of the number you are rounding to.
2.   If the digit to the right is 5 or greater, round up.
3.   If the digit to the right is less than 5, round down.
4.   After rounding, replace the digits to the right of the number you rounded to with zeros.

Here are some examples of rounding:
- Rounding to the nearest ten: $8\underline{4} \rightarrow 80$ because $4 < 5$
- Rounding to the nearest hundred: $4\underline{2}3 \rightarrow 400$ because $2 < 5$
- Rounding to the nearest thousand: $2\ \underline{6}35 \rightarrow 3\ 000$ because $6 > 5$
- Rounding to the nearest ten thousand: $1\underline{8}\ 620 \rightarrow 20\ 000$ because $8 > 5$
- Rounding to the nearest hundred thousand: $3\underline{1}2\ 647 \rightarrow 300\ 000$ because $1 < 5$

⁂ Example
Using the rounding rule, estimate the difference of the subtraction problem $54\ 593 - 1\ 987$.

Solution
Step 1
Round both numbers to the nearest thousand.

Since one of the numbers (1 978) only goes to thousands, round both numbers the same way.
$54\ \underline{5}93 \rightarrow 55\ 000$ because $5 = 5$
$1\ \underline{9}87 \rightarrow 2\ 000$ because $9 > 5$

Step 2
Subtract the rounded numbers to determine the estimated difference.
55 000 – 2 000 = 53 000

 Time to Try 1

At a craft centre, there was a basket containing a total of 6 198 buttons. Of these, 2 702 were black buttons. The rest of the buttons were white.

Trina calculated that there were 4 496 white buttons in the basket.

Use the rounding strategy to judge whether Trina's calculation was reasonable or not. Explain your answer.

PRACTICE EXERCISES

1. There were 408 trucks, 512 cars, and 165 vans parked in a mall parking lot. Use the rounding rule to determine the total number of vehicles in the parking lot.

2. The attendance at one school fair was 691 children and 522 adults. Using the rounding rule, estimate how many more children than adults were at the fair

3. A bakery sells dinner buns in packages of 12. Use the rounding rule to determine the approximate number of dinner buns in 17 packages.

Use the following information to answer the next question.

A flower shop just received a shipment of 108 roses that need to be placed into vases of water. The florist plans to use five big vases and put approximately the same number of roses into each vase.

4. Using the rounding rule, estimate about how many roses will be placed into each vase.

REVIEW SUMMARY

- Estimation is a strategy used to calculate an approximate amount.

- Estimation can be used to predict a solution, determine an approximate answer, or check the reasonableness of an answer.

- In front-end estimation, keep the front digits (greatest places values), and replace all the digits to the right with zeros. Front-end estimates are always lower than the actual calculations.

- Front-end estimates can be expressed using comparative language, such as *less than*, *more than*, and *close to*.

- In compensation, use front-end estimation for the first two numbers and the front digit +1 for the third number. Compensation gives a more accurate estimate than front-end estimation.

- To use compatible numbers, choose numbers that are easy to work with, numbers that are related to each other in some way, like factors or multiples.

- The number 10 and its multiples are compatible with all factors.

- The rounding rule tells you to look at the digit to the right of the number you are rounding to. If it is 5 or greater, round up. If it is less than 5, round down. Replace all digits to the right with zeros.

- For contexts involving money, recipes, groups of people, it is sometimes best to overestimate.

PRACTICE TEST

Use the following information to answer the next question.

Patrice has 839 hockey cards, and his friend Matt has 459 hockey cards.

1. Use the strategy of front-end estimation to estimate about how many hockey cards the two boys have in total. Show your work.

2. Using compatible numbers, estimate the sum of 279 + 123. Explain your work.

Use the following information to answer the next question.

On the first day of spring, Nikki's flower shop set out 28 baskets of tulips. There were about 53 tulips in each basket.

3. Using the strategy of compatible numbers, estimate the total number of tulips in the baskets. Show your work.

Use the following information to answer the next question.

Camille used 1 341 connecting cubes to build a bridge. Sandra used 798 connecting cubes to build a tower.

4. Using the strategy of front-end estimation, estimate about how many more connecting cubes Camille used than Sandra used. Show your work.

5. After applying front-end estimation, use comparative language to describe the quotient of 279 ÷ 5.

Use the following information to answer the next question.

Josie saved $217 over a period of seven months. She saved about the same amount of money each month.

6. Use the estimation strategy of compatible numbers to determine about how much money Josie saved each month. Explain your work.

Use the following information to answer the next question.

There were 538 silver vehicles, 312 white vehicles, and 495 blue vehicles parked in a theatre's parking lot.

7. Use the strategy of compensation to estimate the total number of vehicles in the parking lot.

Use the following information to answer the next question.

Molly was helping the grade 2 teacher place some guided reading books on some tables for the children to read. There were 53 books, and each book had 32 pages.

8. Using the strategy of front-end estimation, estimate about how many pages the books had in all. Show your work.

Use the following information to answer the next question.

Mrs. Rabou travelled 476 metres from her house to the post office, where she mailed some letters. She then travelled 228 metres from the post office to the town library, where she dropped off some books. She continued to travel another 215 metres to reach the school where she teaches.

9. Using the strategy of compensation, estimate how many metres in total Mrs. Rabou travelled. Explain why compensation is a good strategy to use for this estimation.

MENTAL STRATEGIES

When you are finished this unit, you will be able to...

- apply mental strategies to help you determine answers for basic multiplication and related division facts
- understand the relationship between multiplication and division
- use the strategy of counting up or down from a known fact
- use the strategy of doubling or repeated doubling
- use the strategy of halving or repeated halving
- use patterns in the nines facts
- use the strategy of annexing, then adding 0
- use the strategy of halving and doubling
- use the distributive property

PREREQUISITE SKILLS AND KNOWLEDGE

Prior to starting this unit, you should be able to...

- skip count
- double numbers
- halve numbers
- add or subtract one group
- identify patterns in numbers, like 5s and 10s
- apply the 1 property for multiplication and division
- apply the 0 property for multiplication

Lesson 1 RELATING DIVISION FACTS TO MULTIPLICATION FACTS

When you multiply two numbers, it does not matter what order you place the numbers in. The answer will be the same. For every fact that you learn, you can reverse the numbers and know two facts.

For example, if you know that $7 \times 5 = 35$, then you also know that $5 \times 7 = 35$.

Since multiplication and division are opposite or inverse operations, you can use the same numbers and learn two related division facts.

For example, if you know that $5 \times 7 = 35$, then you also know that $35 \div 7 = 5$.

If you know that $7 \times 5 = 35$ then you also know that $35 \div 5 = 7$.

Two related multiplication facts and their two related division facts are often referred to as a **fact family**. If you know one of the facts, you actually know four facts: two multiplication facts and two division facts.

To solve a division fact, think of its related multiplication fact. For example, to solve $45 \div 9$, think of $9 \times 5 = 45$. If $9 \times 5 = 45$, then $45 \div 9 = 5$.

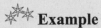 **Example**

This grouping of cookies can be represented by the multiplication facts $6 \times 4 = 24$ and $4 \times 6 = 24$.

What two related division facts can also represent the given grouping of cookies? Explain how the multiplication and division facts are related.

Solution

Step 1
Determine the related division facts.

If $6 \times 4 = 24$, then $24 \div 4 = 6$.
If $4 \times 6 = 24$, then $24 \div 6 = 4$.

Step 2

Explain how the facts are related.

All four facts represent four groups of cookies with six cookies in each group and a total of 24 cookies.

In the multiplication facts, you are putting the four groups of six cookies each together for a total of 24 cookies.

In the division facts, you are sorting the total number of 24 cookies into four groups, placing six cookies in each group.

 Time to Try 1

One multiplication fact that can represent the given grouping of circles is $4 \times 7 = 28$.

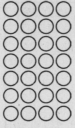

Write the two related division facts that can represent the same grouping of circles.

PRACTICE EXERCISES

Use the following information to answer the next question.

Two facts that can represent this grouping of books is $6 \times 2 = 12$ and $2 \times 6 = 12$

1. Write two related division facts that can represent the grouping of books.

Use the following information to answer the next question.

This grouping of basketballs can be represented by the facts $4 \times 5 = 20$ and $20 \div 5 = 4$.

2. Explain what the two facts represent and how they are related.

Use the following information to answer the next question.

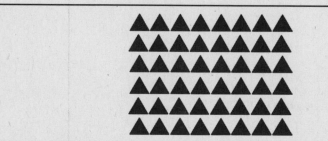

3. Write a fact family to represent the array of triangles. Write two multiplication facts and their related division facts.

Lesson 2   RELATING THE ZERO PROPERTY TO MULTIPLICATION AND DIVISION FACTS

The **zero property of multiplication** states that any number multiplied by 0 always equals 0.

For example, three groups of zero is always zero because there is nothing in the groups.
$3 \times 0 = 0$

Zero groups of three is always zero because there are no groups, so you cannot have anything in the groups.
$0 \times 3 = 0$

The **zero property of division** states that division by zero is an operation for which there is no answer. To understand this, it is important to understand the relationship between division and multiplication.

Multiplication and division are opposite operations.
If $24 \div 6 = 4$, then $4 \times 6 = 24$.

However, if you say that $24 \div 0 = 0$, then 0×0 would have to equal 24. This is not possible because any number multiplied by 0 equals 0.

Therefore, division by zero is undefined. It is not possible.

PRACTICE EXERCISES

1. Explain why $6 \times 0 = 0$. Draw a diagram to help you explain.

2. Explain why $0 \times 5 = 0$.

3. Explain why it is impossible to have an answer for the division problem $6 \div 0$.

Lesson 3   SKIP COUNTING UP FROM A KNOWN FACT

If you know a certain fact, you can skip count up (forward) from that fact to solve a different fact, as long as both groups (both facts) have the same number of items.

NOTES

SKIP COUNTING UP BY ONE GROUP

When you skip count up by one group, you are adding one group.

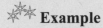 **Example**

Amanda used the fact $5 \times 7 = 35$ to help her solve the expression 6×7.

Explain the skip-counting strategy that Amanda could use to solve the expression 6×7.

Solution

Step 1
Compare the two facts.

In 5×7, there are five groups with seven items in each group.
In 6×7, there is one more group of seven than there is in 5×7.

Step 2
Skip count up by one group.

Since $5 \times 7 = 35$, then 6×7 is equal to $35 + 7$ (one more group of 7).
Since $5 \times 7 = 35$, then $6 \times 7 = 42$.

Time to Try 1

Kenton used the fact $6 \times 8 = 48$ to help him solve the expression 7×8. Explain the skip-counting strategy that Kenton could use to solve the expression 7×8.

NOTES

SKIP COUNTING UP BY TWO GROUPS

You can also skip count up from a known fact by more than one group to solve another fact. Remember that for this strategy to work, both groups must have the same number in each group.

 Example

Donald uses the fact $3 \times 9 = 27$ to help him solve the expression 5×9.

Explain the skip-counting pattern that Donald can use to help him solve the expression 5×9.

Solution

Step 1
Compare the two facts.

In 3×9, there are three groups with nine items in each group. In 5×9, there are two more groups of nine than there are in 3×9.

Step 2
Skip count up for two groups.

Since $3 \times 9 = 27$, then 5×9 is equal to $27 + 9 + 9$ (two more groups of 9).
Since $3 \times 9 = 27$, then $5 \times 9 = 45$.

 Time to Try 2

Kim starts with the fact $4 \times 6 = 24$ to help her solve the multiplication problem 6×6. Explain the skip-counting pattern that Kim could use to solve the expression 6×6.

PRACTICE EXERCISES

1. Olivia used the fact 8 × 7 = 56 to help her solve the expression 9 × 7. Explain the skip-counting strategy that Olivia could use to solve the expression 9 × 7.

2. Jack used the fact 7 × 6 = 42 to help him solve the expression 8 × 6. Explain the skip-counting strategy that Jack could use to solve the expression 8 × 6.

3. Daniel used the fact 4 × 8 = 32 to help him solve the expression 6 × 8. Explain the skip-counting pattern that Daniel could use to help him solve the expression 6 × 8.

4. Rosalie used the fact 7 × 6 = 42 to help her solve the expression 9 × 6. Explain the skip-counting pattern that Rosalie could use to help her solve the expression 9 × 6.

Lesson 4 SKIP COUNTING DOWN FROM A KNOWN FACT

If you know a certain fact, you can skip count down (backward) from that fact to solve a different fact, as long as there are the same number of items in both groups.

SKIP COUNTING DOWN BY ONE GROUP

When you skip count down by one group, you are subtracting one group.

 Example

Nicole used the fact $7 \times 8 = 56$ to help her solve the expression 6×8.

Explain the skip-counting strategy that Nicole could use to solve the expression 6×8.

> *Solution*
> **Step 1**
> Compare the two facts.
>
> In 7×8, there are seven groups with eight items in each group. In 6×8, there is one less group of eight than there is in 7×8.
>
> **Step 2**
> Skip count down by one group.
>
> Since $7 \times 8 = 56$, then 6×8 is equal to $56 - 8$ (one less group of 8).
> Since $7 \times 8 = 56$, then $6 \times 8 = 48$.

 Time to Try 1

Darian used the fact $9 \times 7 = 63$ to help him solve the expression 8×7.

Explain the skip-counting strategy that Darian could use to solve the expression 8×7.

SKIP COUNTING DOWN BY TWO GROUPS

You can also skip count down from a known fact by more than one group to solve another fact. Remember that for this strategy to work, both groups must have the same number in each group.

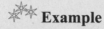 **Example**

Shabir used the fact $5 \times 8 = 40$ to solve the problem 3×8.

Explain the skip-counting strategy that Shabir could use to solve the problem 3×8.

Solution

Step 1
Compare the two facts.

In 5×8, there are five groups with eight items in each group. In 3×8, there are two fewer groups of eight than there are in 5×8.

Step 2
Skip count down by two groups.

Since $5 \times 8 = 40$, then 3×8 is equal to $40 - 8 - 8$ (two fewer groups of eight).
Since $5 \times 8 = 40$, then $3 \times 8 = 24$

 Time to Try 2

Jaymeson used the fact $8 \times 8 = 64$ to solve the problem 6×8.

Explain the skip-counting strategy that Jaymeson could use to solve the problem 6×8.

PRACTICE EXERCISES

1. Cody used the fact $9 \times 9 = 81$ to help him solve the expression 8×9. Explain the skip-counting strategy that Cody could use to solve the expression 8×9.

2. Tyler used the fact $8 \times 7 = 56$ to help him solve the expression 7×7. Explain the skip-counting strategy that Tyler could use to solve the expression 7×7.

3. Parker used the fact $8 \times 9 = 72$ to solve the problem 6×9. Explain the skip-counting strategy that Parker could use to solve the problem 6×9.

4. Alicia used the fact $9 \times 4 = 36$ to solve the problem 7×4. Explain the skip-counting strategy that Alicia could use to solve the problem 7×4.

Lesson 5   USING DOUBLING AND REPEATED DOUBLING

A double is the same number added to itself. For example, $4 + 4$ is a double. A double can also be expressed as a number times 2. For example, the double $4 + 4$ can be expressed as 4×2.

DOUBLING

You can use doubling to help you solve more difficult multiplication facts, as long as there are the same number of items in each group for both facts.

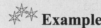 **Example**

Ben solved the expression 4×9 in his head by applying the mental math strategy of doubling.

Explain how Ben could have solved the problem by applying the strategy of doubling.

> *Solution*
> Since 4 is a double of 2, Ben could have started with the easier fact of $2 \times 9 = 18$.
> Since $2 \times 9 = 18$, then $4 \times 9 = 18 + 18$.
> Since $2 \times 9 = 18$, then $4 \times 9 = 36$.

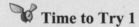 **Time to Try 1**

Explain how the fact 3×4 can be used to solve the expression 6×4.

REPEATED DOUBLING

Repeated doubling is a strategy that works well when you are multiplying larger numbers in your head. When you use repeated doubling, you are starting with a simpler fact and then doubling the answer more than once. Remember, the number in each group must be the same for this strategy to work.

NOTES

 **Example**

Jason used the fact 2×3 to help him solve the problem 8×3.

Explain how Jason could have used the strategy of repeated doubling to solve the problem.

Solution
Step 1
Double $2 \times 3 = 6$.

When 2 is doubled, it becomes 4. $(2 + 2 = 4)$
Since $2 \times 3 = 6$, then $4 \times 3 = 6 + 6$.
Since $2 \times 3 = 6$, then $4 \times 3 = 12$.

Step 2
Double 4×3.

When 4 is doubled, it becomes 8. $(4 + 4 = 8)$
Since $4 \times 3 = 12$, then $8 \times 3 = 12 + 12$.
Since $4 \times 3 = 12$, then $8 \times 3 = 24$.

 Time to Try 2

Explain how you can use the strategy of repeated doubling to solve the problem 8×4.

114

PRACTICE EXERCISES

1. Susan solved the problem 4×7 in her head by applying the mental math strategy of doubling. She started with the simpler fact of 2×7. Explain how Susan solved the problem.

2. Kevin solved the problem 6×9 in his head by applying the mental math strategy of doubling. Explain how Kevin could have solved the problem.

3. To solve the problem 8×2, Jack used the strategy of repeated doubling. He started with the simpler fact of 2×2. Explain how Jack solved the problem.

4. To solve the problem 8×7, William used the strategy of repeated doubling. He started with 2×7. Explain how William could have solved the problem.

Lesson 6   USING HALVING AND REPEATED HALVING

NOTES

When halving, you are dividing a larger group into two smaller but equal groups. For example, 8×3 can be divided evenly into 4×3 and 4×3.

The sum of the products of the two smaller groups $(12 + 12)$ will equal the product of the larger group (24).

For this strategy to work, one of the factors of the multiplication problem must be an even number so that it can be divided into two equal groups.

✳ Example

Use the strategy of halving to solve the expression 5×4.
Show your work.

Solution

Step 1

Divide the larger group into two smaller but equal groups.

Half of 4 is 2, so half of 5×4 is 5×2.

Step 2

Solve the problem.

Multiply 5 by 2.
$5 \times 2 = 10$

Double the product.
$10 + 10 = 20$

Therefore, $5 \times 4 = 20$.

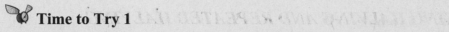

NOTES

Time to Try 1

Apply the strategy of halving to solve the expression 6 × 7.
Show your work.

6 × 7

REPEATED HALVING

Repeated halving works well when you are multiplying larger
numbers. When you use repeated halving, you divide the larger
group into two smaller but equal groups. You then divide each of
the two smaller groups into two smaller but equal groups.

Remember that one of the factors of the multiplication problem must
be an even number.

NOTES

✳✳✳ Example

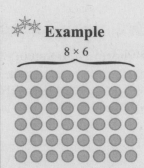

8×6

Apply the strategy of repeated halving to solve the expression 8×6. Show your work.

Solution

Step 1

Divide the larger group into two smaller and equal groups.

Half of 8 is 4, so half of 8×6 is 4×6.

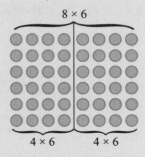

Step 2

Divide each smaller group into two smaller and equal groups.

Half of 4 is 2, so half of 4×6 is 2×6.

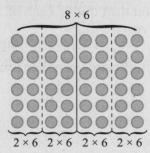

Step 3
Solve the problem.

Multiply 2 by 6.
$2 \times 6 = 12$

Double the product.
$12 + 12 = 24$

Double the new product.
$24 + 24 = 48$

Therefore, $8 \times 6 = 48$.

Time to Try 2

Apply the strategy of repeated halving to solve the expression 8×5.
Show your work.

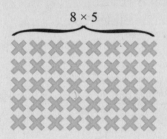

PRACTICE EXERCISES

Use the following information to answer the next question.

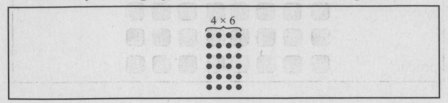

1. Use the strategy of halving to solve the expression 4 × 6. Show your work.

Use the following information to answer the next question.

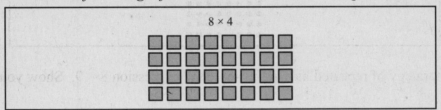

2. Use the strategy of halving to solve the expression 8 × 4. Show your work.

Use the following information to answer the next question.

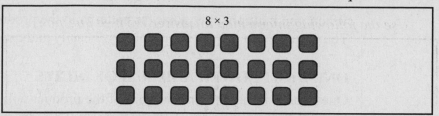

3. Apply the strategy of repeated halving to solve the expression 8 × 3. Show your work.

Use the following information to answer the next question.

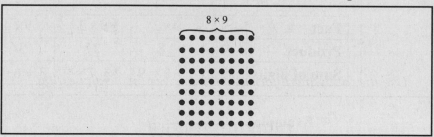

4. Apply the strategy of repeated halving to solve the expression 8 × 9. Show your work.

Lesson 7   *USING PATTERNS IN THE NINES FACTS*

When you multiply by 9, look for patterns in the products. The patterns can help you multiply by 9 easily and quickly.

ONE DIGIT LOWER AND SUM OF DIGITS

One pattern is that the first number of the product will be one digit lower than the multiplier. For example, in 9 × 3, the multiplier is 3, so the product will start with 2 (27).

Another pattern is that the sum of the digits in the product will always equal 9.

These two patterns work hand-in-hand to help you determine the products of 9 facts.

The following chart will help you see how the two patterns work together.

Fact	9×1	9×2	9×3	9×4	9×5
Product	9	18	27	36	45
Sum of digits	9	1 + 8 = 9	2 + 7 = 9	3 + 6 = 9	4 + 5 = 9

 Example

Explain how you can determine the product of 9 × 3 by using the nines pattern that the first number of the product will be one digit lower than the multiplier and the sum of the digits will equal 9.

Solution

Step 1
Determine the multiplier.

In the problem 9 × 3, the multiplier is 3.

Therefore, the answer will start with 2, one less than 3.

Step 2
Determine the next digit in the product.

Since the digits of the product must add up to 9, the next digit will be 7. (2 + 7 = 9)
9 × 3 = 27

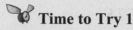 **Time to Try 1**

Julie says that $9 \times 4 = 36$, and Robbie says that $9 \times 4 = 32$.

Who is correct? Justify your answer by referring to the sum of the digits.

TENS FACT MINUS ONE GROUP

There is another pattern in the nines facts that can help you multiply in your head. The product of the nines fact is equal to the product of the corresponding tens fact minus one group of the other factor.

For example, in 9×4, the other factor is 4. Since $10 \times 4 = 40$, according to this pattern, $9 \times 4 = 40 - 4 = 36$.

It does not matter whether 9 is the first factor (9×3) or the second factor (3×9). You can solve the problem the same way.

$$3 \times 9 = ?$$
$$3 \times 10 = 30$$
$$30 - 3 = 27$$
$$3 \times 9 = 27$$

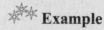 **Example**

Use a tens fact to solve the expression 6×9.

Solution

Since 9 is one less than 10, the nines fact 6×9 will be one group of six less than the tens fact of 6×10.

$$6 \times 9 = ?$$
$$6 \times 10 = 60$$
$$60 - 6 = 54$$
$$6 \times 9 = 54$$

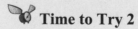 **Time to Try 2**

Explain how a tens fact can be used to solve the problem 9×7.

PRACTICE EXERCISES

1. Explain how you can determine the answer to 9×5 by using the nines patterns of one digit lower and sum of digits.

2. Explain how you can determine the answer to 9×8 by using the nines patterns of one digit lower and sum of digits.

3. Use a tens fact to solve the expression 4×9. Show your work.

4. Use a tens fact to solve the expression 9×9. Show your work.

Lesson 8 ANNEXING, THEN ADDING ZERO

When one of the factors in a multiplication problem is a multiple that ends in a zero or zeros, you can annex (drop) the zero or zeros, multiply the remaining fact, and then add the dropped zero or zeros to the end of the product.

MULTIPLES OF 10

When one factor ends in a multiple of 10, drop the zero, multiply the basic fact, and then add the zero to the end of the product.

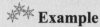 **Example**

Apply the strategy of annexing, then adding zero to solve the problem 6 × 80. Explain your work.

Solution

Drop the zero from 80.
80 → 8

Multiply the remaining fact.
6 × 8 = 48

Add the dropped zero to the end of the product.
48 → 48<u>0</u>

Therefore, 6 × 80 = 480.

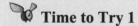 **Time to Try 1**

Apply the strategy of annexing, then adding zero to solve 70 × 9. Explain your work.

MULTIPLES OF 100

When one of the factors is a multiple of 100, drop the two zeros, multiply the remaining fact, then add the two zeros to the end of the product.

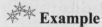 **Example**

Apply the strategy of annexing, then adding zero to solve the problem 900 × 9. Explain your work.

Solution

Drop the two zeros from 900.
900 → 9

NOTES

Multiply the remaining fact.
$9 \times 9 = 81$

Add the two dropped zeros to the end of the product.
$81 \rightarrow 8\ 1\underline{00}$

Therefore, $900 \times 9 = 8\ 100$.

 Time to Try 2

Apply the strategy of annexing, then adding zero to solve the problem 5×200. Explain your work.

MULTIPLES OF 1 000

When one of the factors is a multiple of 1 000, drop the three zeros, multiply the remaining fact, then add the three dropped zeros to the end of the product.

 Example

Apply the strategy of annexing, then adding zero to solve $4 \times 2\ 000$. Explain your work.

Solution
Drop the three zeros from 2 000.
$2\ 000 \rightarrow 2$

Multiply the remaining fact.
$4 \times 2 = 8$

Add the three dropped zeros to the end of the product.
$8 \rightarrow 8\ \underline{000}$

Therefore, $4 \times 2\ 000 = 8\ 000$.

 Time to Try 3

Apply the strategy of annexing, then adding zero to solve the problem $5\ 000 \times 7$. Explain your work.

PRACTICE EXERCISES

Apply the strategy of annexing, then adding zero to solve the following three expressions.

1. 8×60

2. 9×500

3. $7\,000 \times 7$

Lesson 9 HALVING ONE FACTOR AND DOUBLING THE OTHER FACTOR

NOTES

The mental strategy of halving and doubling is when you double one factor and use half of the other factor to make numbers that are easier to work with. For example, it is easier to multiply in your head if one of the factors is a multiple of 10.

When you double one factor and halve the other factor, the relationship between the numbers will stay the same. For example, 36×5 has the same value as 18×10.

 Example

Use the strategy of halving and doubling to solve the expression 64×5. Explain your work.

Solution

Double the 5.
$5 \times 2 = 10$
Multiplying by 10 is easier than multiplying by 5.

Halve the 64.
$64 \div 2 = 32$

The expression 32×10 has the same value as 64×5.
Since $32 \times 10 = 320$, then $64 \times 5 = 320$.

 Time to Try 1

Use the strategy of halving and doubling to solve the expression 15×6. Explain your work.

PRACTICE EXERCISES

Use the strategy of halving and doubling to solve the following expressions.

1. 5×46

2. 15×4

3. 25×6

4. 8×45

Lesson 10 USING THE DISTRIBUTIVE PROPERTY

The distributive property can be used to multiply numbers. The distributive property can be used in two ways: with addition or with subtraction.

USING ADDITION

The **distributive property** states that multiplying a sum by a number is the same as multiplying each addend by the number and then adding the products. This property is helpful when you multiply large numbers in your head.

Follow these steps to apply the distributive property using addition:
- Think of the larger number in expanded notation.
- Multiply each place value by the multiplier.
- Add the products.

Distributive Property
Multiplication: 8×22
$22 = 20 + 2$ $8 \times 22 = (8 \times 20) + (8 \times 2)$ $8 \times 22 = 160 + 16$ $8 \times 22 = 176$

 Example

Use the distributive property with addition to solve the problem 8×58. Show your work.

Solution

Step 1
Think of the number 58 in expanded notation.
$58 = 50 + 8$

Step 2
Multiply each place value by the factor 8.
$(8 \times 50) + (8 \times 8)$

Step 3
Perform the calculations.
$(8 \times 50) + (8 \times 8)$
$= 400 + 64$
$= 464$

$8 \times 58 = 464$

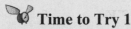 **Time to Try 1**

Using the distributive property, solve the problem 6 × 34.
Show your work.

USING SUBTRACTION

You can apply the distributive property in a different way, a way that
involves subtraction instead of addition. This strategy works best
when the factors you are multiplying are close to multiples of 10.

To apply the distributive property using subtraction, follow
these steps:

- Think of the larger number as a subtraction fact using a multiple
  of 10.
- Multiply each place value by the multiplier.
- Perform the calculations.

Distributive Property
Multiplication: 98 × 6
$98 = 100 - 2$ $98 \times 6 = (100 \times 6) - (2 \times 6)$ $98 \times 6 = 600 - 12$ $98 \times 6 = 588$

NOTES

 Example

Use the distributive property with subtraction to determine the value of 8×58.

Solution

Step 1
Think of the number 58 as a subtraction fact using a multiple of 10.
$58 = 60 - 2$

Step 2
Multiply each place value by the factor 8.
$(8 \times 60) - (8 \times 2)$

Step 3
Perform the calculations.
$(8 \times 60) - (8 \times 2)$
$= 480 - 16$
$= 464$

$8 \times 58 = 464$

Time to Try 2

Use the distributive property with subtraction to determine the value of 9×37.

PRACTICE EXERCISES

Use the distributive property with addition to solve the following two problems.
Show your work.

1. 2×54

2. 6×38

Use the distributive property with subtraction to solve the following two problems.
Show your work.

3. 8×29

4. 7×27

REVIEW SUMMARY

- Mental strategies are plans to help you calculate in your head.
- Since multiplication and division are inverse operations, you can learn a division fact by thinking of its related multiplication fact.
- The zero property of multiplication tells you that any number multiplied by zero always equals zero.
- It is not possible to divide by zero.
- Skip counting up (forward) from a known fact involves adding one or more than one group.
- Skip counting down (backward) from a known fact involves subtracting one or more than one group.
- Doubling involves thinking of an easier fact (half the number of groups) and then adding the product to itself.
- Repeated doubling involves adding the product to itself more than once.
- Halving involves dividing a larger group into two smaller but equal groups, then adding the products of the two smaller groups.
- Repeated halving involves dividing the two smaller groups into two smaller but equal groups, then adding the products of the four small groups.
- One nines pattern is that the product starts with one digit lower than the multiplier, and the sum of the digits always equals 9.
- The product of a nines fact is equal to the product of the corresponding tens fact minus one group of the other factor.
- When one of the factors is a multiple of 10, 100, or 1 000, drop the zeros, multiply the fact, and then add the same number of zeros that you dropped to the end of the product.
- Double one factor and halve the other factor to make easier numbers to work with, like multiples of 10.
- To use the distributive property with addition, write the larger number in expanded notation. Multiply each place value by the multiplier, and add the products.
- To use the distributive property with subtraction, write the larger number as a subtraction fact using a multiple of 10. Multiply each place value by the multiplier, and subtract the products.

PRACTICE TEST

1. Apply the strategy of annexing, then adding zero to solve the expression 7×20. Explain your work.

2. Kyla solved the expression 6×8 in her head by applying the mental math strategy of doubling. Explain how Kyla solved the problem.

3. To solve the problem 8×4, Mali used the strategy of repeated doubling. She started with $2 \times 4 = 8$. Explain how Mali solved the problem.

4. Use the strategy of halving and doubling to solve the expression 32×5. Explain your work.

5. Dayton used the fact $6 \times 6 = 36$ to solve the problem 4×6. Explain the skip-counting strategy that Dayton could use to solve 4×6.

6. Apply the strategy of annexing, then adding zero to solve the expression 7×700. Explain your work.

7. Explain how a tens fact can be used to solve the problem 9×7.

8. Apply the strategy of annexing, then adding zero to solve the expression $4 \times 5\ 000$. Explain your work.

9. Use the distributive property with addition to solve the problem 6×32. Show your work.

10. Explain how you can determine the answer to the expression 9×6 by using the nines patterns of one digit lower and sum of digits.

Use the following information to answer the next question.

One multiplication fact that represents the array of soccer balls is 3 × 6 = 18.

11. Write the related multiplication fact and two related division facts that also represent the array of soccer balls.

12. Use the distributive property with subtraction to determine the value of the expression 4 × 29.

13. Ray used the fact 7 × 7 = 47 to help him solve the expression 9 × 7. Explain the skip-counting strategy that Ray could use to solve the expression 9 × 7.

Use the following information to answer the next question.

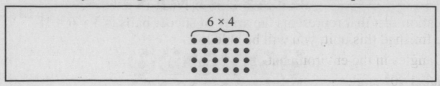

14. Use the strategy of halving to solve the expression 6 × 4. Show your work.

Use the following information to answer the next question.

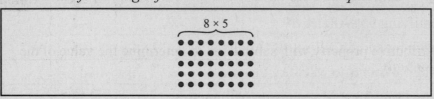

15. Apply the strategy of repeated halving to solve the expression 8 × 5. Show your work.

MEASUREMENT

When you are finished this unit, you will be able to…

- identify 90° angles in the environment
- sketch and label 90° angles
- use referents to measure millimetre, centimetre, and metre lengths
- understand equivalent measures for millimetres and centimetres and for millimetres and metres
- use millimetres as the unit of measure
- understand the relationship between perimeter and area
- construct rectangles for a given area
- construct rectangles for a given perimeter
- construct rectangles for a given area and perimeter
- describe the shapes of the rectangles that have the greatest and least areas for a given perimeter

PREREQUISITE SKILLS AND KNOWLEDGE

Prior to starting this unit, you should be able to...
- estimate length using referents for centimetres and metres
- measure length using centimetres and metres
- understand the relationship between centimetres and metres
- determine the perimeter of a rectangle by adding the two lengths and two widths
- understand that different rectangles can have the same perimeter
- recognize that area is measured in square units
- determine the area of a rectangle by multiplying the length by the width
- understand that different rectangles can have the same area

Lesson 1 IDENTIFYING 90° ANGLES

An **angle** forms when two rays or lines meet at a vertex. The space between the two rays or lines at the vertex is the angle.

An angle that forms a square corner, like the corner on a sheet of paper, is called a **right angle**.

Think about a square or a rectangle. All of the corners in a square and a rectangle are right angles. The right angles are shaded in the following diagrams to help you see how they make square corners.

Angles are measured in units called **degrees** (°). The number of degrees tells how far one ray of the angle is from the other ray of the angle. Whenever you write the measure of an angle, you must also write the degree symbol after the number.

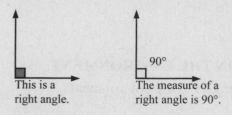

This is a
right angle.

90°

The measure of a
right angle is 90°.

The lengths of the rays do not affect the measure of the angle.

✳ **Example**

As a class assignment, Ravi was to take a pipe cleaner and bend it in such a way that a 90° angle was formed. This is the angle that Ravi made.

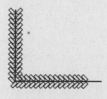

Did Ravi make a 90° angle? Justify your answer.

Solution

Yes, Ravi made a 90° angle.

The angle forms a square corner where the two sides of the pipe cleaner meet; therefore, it is a right angle. The measure of a right angle is 90°.

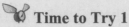 **Time to Try 1**

Manuel's homework assignment was to sort these angles into two groups:
Group 1 has 90° angles.
Group 2 has no 90° angles.

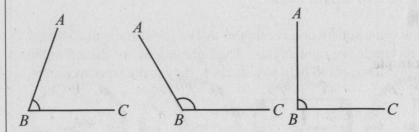

How should Manuel sort the angles? Justify your answer.

EXAMPLES OF 90° ANGLES IN THE ENVIRONMENT

There are many examples of 90° angles in the environment.

Walls have 90° angles.

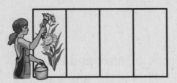

A tool like a carpenter's square has a right angle.

A lamp post meets the ground at a 90° angle.

✳✳ Example

The hands on a clock form an angle where they intersect (cross). Which clocks show 90° angles? Justify your answer.

Solution

Of the four given clocks, the only clock that shows a 90° angle is the clock that shows the time of 9:00. A square corner is formed where the two hands intersect.

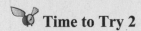

🦋 Time to Try 2

Walking home from school one day, Carla saw these four traffic signs. Looking at the shapes of the signs, she saw that two of the signs had 90° angles.

Which two signs have 90° angles? Justify your answer.

PRACTICE EXERCISES

Use the following information to answer the next question.

Jake's homework assignment was to write down as many examples
as possible of 90° angles found at home. This staircase is one of
Jake's examples.

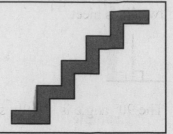

1. Is the staircase a good example of 90° angles? Justify your answer.

Use the following information to answer the next question.

Carlton drew four shapes to show different kinds of angles.

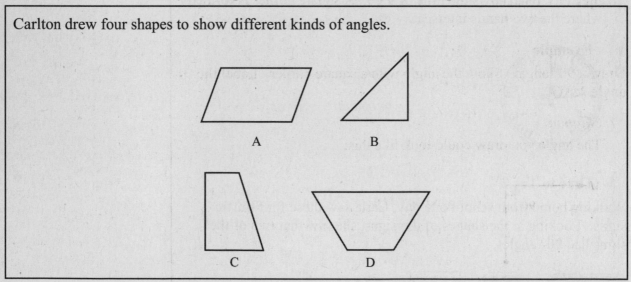

2. In which of the shapes did Carlton make 90° angles? Justify your answer by drawing square
    corners where the 90° angles are located.

Lesson 2   SKETCHING AND LABELLING 90° ANGLES

You can sketch a 90° angle by drawing a vertical (↑) line that meets a horizontal (→) line, making a square corner where the two lines meet.

The 90° angle is usually shown by a square or arc.

Sometimes, angles are labelled with three letters.
• One letter is placed at the end of one ray (line).
• The middle letter is placed by the angle.
• The last letter is placed at the end of the other ray (line).

For example, this diagram shows a 90° angle labelled *ABC*.
The angle can also be read as angle *CBA*.

✳ Example

Draw a 90° angle. Show the angle with a square corner. Label the angle *MNO*.

Solution

The angle you draw could look like this:

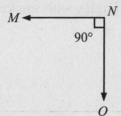

🦋 Time to Try 1

Draw a 90° angle. Show the angle with a square or an arc.
Label the angle with three letters.

PRACTICE EXERCISES

Use the following information to answer the next question.

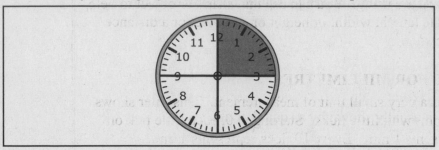

1. The clock shows four right angles. Draw the 90° angle shown by the shaded part. Show the angle with a square corner. Label the angle *UVW*.

Use the following information to answer the next question.

The circle shows four 90° angles.

2. Draw the 90° angles shown by the shaded parts of the circle. Show the angles with square corners. Label one angle *ABC* and the other angle *ZXY*.

Lesson 3 USING REFERENTS TO MEASURE LENGTH

A **referent** is a shape or object that has about the same size as the measure that you are using. You can use that shape or object to help you estimate the length, width, or height or an object or a distance between objects.

REFERENTS FOR MILLIMETRES

A millimetre is a very small unit of measurement. This ruler shows millimetres (mm) with little ticks. Starting at 0, each little tick on the ruler represents 1 mm. Every 10 ticks represents 1 cm.

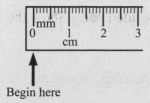

Begin here

Following are some common referents that are about the size of 1 mm:

• The thickness of a dime
• The thickness of a fingernail
• The thickness of a paperclip

You can use these benchmarks or referents when you estimate the length of an object in millimetres. Only small objects are measured in millimetres.

Example

Estimate the length (height) of the crayon using the thickness of a dime as a referent for 1 mm.

Thickness of a dime

Solution

You could stack about 23 dimes to measure the length (height) of the crayon.

23 dimes

The crayon is about 23 mm in length (height).

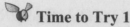 **Time to Try 1**

Estimate the width of the paperclip using a dime as a referent for 1 mm.

Thickness of a dime

REFERENTS FOR CENTIMETRES (CM)

A centimetre is a larger unit than a millimetre, but it is still considered to be a small unit of measure.

This ruler shows numbered centimetres. Each number represents one more centimetre.

Following are some common referents that are about the size of 1 cm:
• The width of a pointer finger
• The length or width of a number cube
• The length or width of a sugar cube

You can use these benchmarks or referents to help you estimate the length of a small object like a glue stick.

✳ **Example**

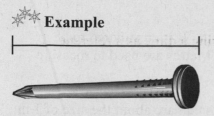

Estimate the length of the nail using the width of your pointer finger as a referent for 1 cm.

Pointer finger

Solution

Make a tick on the line for each width of your pointer finger. Try to make each space the same width.

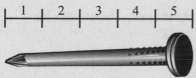

It would take about five finger widths to measure the length of the nail.

The nail is about 5 cm long.

🐝 **Time to Try 2**

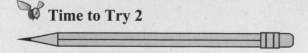

Estimate the length of the pencil using the width of your pointer finger as a referent for 1 cm.

REFERENTS FOR METRES (M)

A metre is a larger unit of measurement. It is considered to be a standard unit and is commonly used. Metres are used to measure longer distances or heights.

Following are some common referents that are about the size of 1 m:
• The height from the floor to the doorknob on a door
• The distance from fingertip to fingertip when your arms are spread wide
• The distance of one giant step
• The height of an object that is about 1 m in height, like a large dog, a small child, or a desk

You can use these benchmarks or referents to help you estimate the distance or height of an object in metres.

✳✳ Example

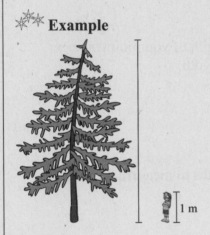

1 m

Estimate the height of the tree using the child's height as a referent for 1 m.

Solution

Since the child's height is 1 m, make a tick on the line for each metre. Count the number of equal sized spaces on the line.

The height of the tree is about 6 m.

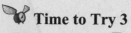

Time to Try 3

1 m

Estimate the height of the giraffe using the dog's height as a referent for 1 m.

PRACTICE EXERCISES

Use the following information to answer the next question.

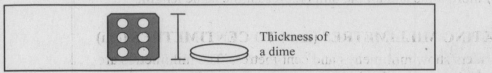

Thickness of a dime

1. Estimate the height of the die using the thickness of a dime as a referent for 1 mm.

Use the following information to answer the next question.

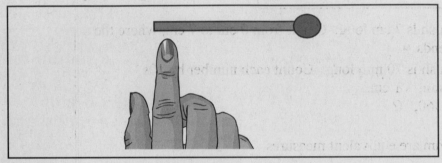

2. Estimate the length of the spoon using the width of a pointer finger as a referent for 1 cm.

Use the following information to answer the next question.

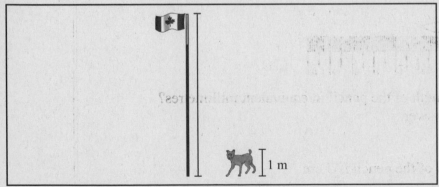

1 m

3. Estimate the height of the flagpole, using the height of the dog as a referent for 1 m.

Lesson 4   USING EQUIVALENT MEASURES FOR MILLIMETRES

Equivalent measures are when a particular length can be recorded in two or more units and all the units represent the same length.

RELATING MILLIMETRES (mm) TO CENTIMETRES (cm)

Most rulers show millimetres and centimetres. The millimetres are shown by little ticks. Each tick represents 1 mm. Centimetres are shown by lines that are slightly longer than the millimetre ticks.

For example, this ruler shows the length of a paintbrush in two ways.

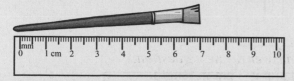

- The paintbrush is 7 cm long: Count from 0 cm to 7 cm, where the paintbrush ends.
- The paintbrush is 70 mm long: Count each number by 10s because 10 mm = 1 cm.
  10, 20, 30… 60, 70

7 cm and 70 mm are equivalent measures.

Since 1 cm = 10 mm, multiply the given number of centimetres by 10 to determine the equivalent number of millimetres.
7 cm × 10 = 70 mm

✳✳ Example

Michael uses a centimetre (cm) ruler to measure the length of one of his pencils.

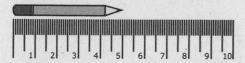

What is the length of the pencil in equivalent millimetres?
Justify your answer.

Solution

The length of the pencil is 5 cm.

Since 1 cm = 10 mm, you need to multiply 5 cm by 10 to determine the equivalent number of millimetres.
5 × 10 = 50

The equivalent length of the pencil is 50 mm.

🦋 Time to Try 1

Johanna collects stamps from every country she visits. This stamp is her favourite:

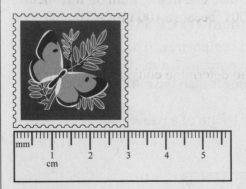

Each side of the square stamp is 3 cm in length.

What is the length of each side of the stamp in equivalent millimetres? Justify you answer.

RELATING MILLIMETRES TO METRES

Since there are 10 mm in 1 cm and 100 cm in 1 m, there are 1 000 mm in 1 m.
$10 \times 100 = 1\ 000$

For example, this metre stick shows the height of a fence in three ways.

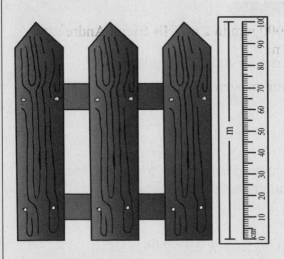

- The fence is 1 m high.
- The fence is 100 cm high: Count by 10s to 100 since each multiple of 10 represents 10 cm on this metre stick.
- The fence is 1 000 mm high: Since one tick = 1 cm on this metre stick, count each number by 100s (because 100 mm = 10 cm). 100, 200… 900, 1 000

The following chart shows how to determine equivalent measures for millimetres and metres.

1 m = 1 000 mm
2 m = 2 000 mm (2×1 000)
3 m = 3 000 mm (3×1 000)

Multiply the number of metres by 1 000 mm.

 Example

How many millimetres are there in 5 m? Explain your work.

Solution

Since there are 1 000 mm in 1 m, multiply the number of metres (5) by 1 000 to determine the number of millimetres in 5 m.
1 m = 1 000 mm
5 m = 5×1 000 = 5 000 mm

A quick way to multiply by 1 000 is to add three zeros to the end of the other number.
5×1 000 = 5 <u>000</u>

There are 5 000 mm in 5 m.

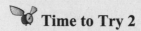 **Time to Try 2**

Marc says that there are 2 000 mm in 2 m. His friend Andre says that there are 200 mm in 2 m.

Who is correct? Justify your answer.

PRACTICE EXERCISES

Use the following information to answer the next question

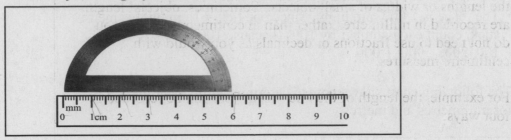

1. Rita measures the length of a protractor she sees in her math text. It is 6 cm long. How long is the protractor in millimetres?

2. Martha has a book that is 15 cm long. She wants to know if the book will fit a paper cover that is 250 mm long. Will the book fit into the cover? Justify your answer.

3. The height of a flagpole is 8 m. What is the height of the flagpole in millimetres?

4. John is 1.2 m tall and Peter is 1 300 mm tall. Who is taller? Justify your answer.

Lesson 5   *USING MILLIMETRES AS THE UNIT OF MEASURE*

Millimetres are small units of measure that are used to measure the lengths or widths of small objects. Sometimes, objects' lengths are recorded in millimetres rather than in centimetres so that you do not need to use fractions or decimals as you would with centimetre measures.

For example, the length of the line shown here can be recorded in four ways:

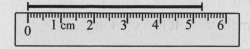

- As a combination of centimetres and millimetres (5 cm and 3 mm)
- As a fraction ($5\frac{3}{10}$ cm)
- As a decimal (5.3 cm)
- In millimetres only (53 mm)

It may be more practical to record the length of the line as 53 mm.

You can measure with millimetres in two ways:

1. Count each little tick that represents 1 mm. For example, 1, 2, 3, 4, 5.

    This method is impractical unless the object being measured is less than 1 cm.

2. Count by 10s as you pass each numbered centimetre.
    Count by 5s as you get to the midpoint between the last two centimetre measurements (if needed).
    Count by 1s after the last count.
    For example, 10, 20, 25, 26, 27.

    This method is more practical for longer lengths.

NOTES

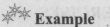 **Example**

John measures the length of his pencil sharpener.

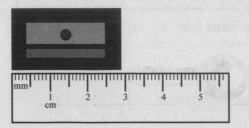

How long is the pencil sharpener in millimetres? Explain how you determined the measurement.

Solution

Step 1
Since 10 mm = 1 cm, count by 10s as you pass each numbered centimetre.
10, 20

Step 2
Count by 5s as you get to the mid-tick.
10, 20, 25

Step 3
Count each tick after 25 by 1s.
… 25, 26, 27, 28, 29

The pencil sharpener has a length of 29 mm.

 Time to Try 1

John measures the width of his pencil sharpener.

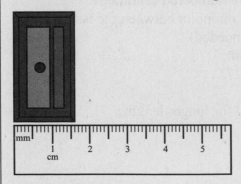

How wide is the pencil sharpener? Explain how you determined the measurement.

PRACTICE EXERCISES

Use the following information to answer the next question.

Chad measures the length of his house key.

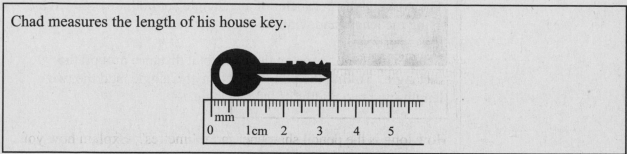

1. What is the length of the key in millimetres? Justify your answer.

Use the following information to answer the next question.

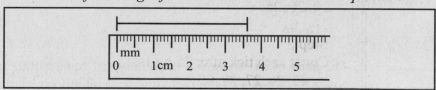

2. What is the length of the line in millimetres? Justify your answer.

Lesson 6 *UNDERSTANDING THE RELATIONSHIP BETWEEN AREA AND PERIMETER*

The area and the perimeter of a rectangle are both determined by using the length and width of the rectangle.

The **perimeter** of a rectangle is the total distance around the rectangle. To find the perimeter of any rectangle, add the two lengths and two widths of the rectangle.

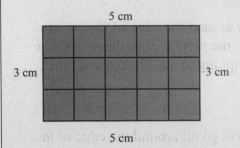

To determine the distance all around the rectangle shown, you can use the following formula.

$P = l + w + l + w$
$ = 5 + 3 + 5 + 3$
$ = 16$ cm

The **area** of a rectangle is the number of square units needed to cover the surface of the rectangle without any overlapping or spaces left. Area is measured in square units.

To determine the area of the rectangle shown, multiply the length by the width. When you multiply the length by the width, it is the same as counting all the square units that cover the surface.

$A = l \times w$
$ = 5 \times 3$
$ = 15$ cm^2

You need to know the difference between these two kinds of measurements in order to solve everyday problems.

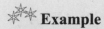 **Example**

Mrs. Martin wants to put a border around the edge of the bulletin board. Does she need to calculate the perimeter or the area of the bulletin board before she goes shopping to buy the material she needs? Explain your reasoning.

Solution

Since a border is a strip that will go all around the edge of the bulletin board, Mrs. Martin needs to know the perimeter.

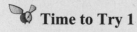 **Time to Try 1**

Sarah wants her dad to paint one wall in her bedroom dark blue. Does her dad need to know the area or the perimeter of the wall before he shops for some paint? Explain your reasoning.

PRACTICE EXERCISES

1. Mrs. Mullen made a patchwork quilt. She wants to put a border around the quilt. Does she need to calculate the perimeter or the area of the quilt? Justify your answer.

2. Jane's family moved into a new house. Her dad ordered enough sod to cover the backyard with grass. Did Jane's dad need to know the area or the perimeter of the backyard when he ordered the sod? Justify your answer

3. Shawn is going to help his dad build a fence for a dog pen. Would it be more useful for Shawn and his dad to know the area or the perimeter of the dog pen before they buy the supplies they need? Justify your answer.

Lesson 7   CONSTRUCTING RECTANGLES FOR A GIVEN AREA

Rectangles with different lengths and widths can have the same area. For example, three rectangles are shaded on this grid. Each rectangle has an area of 24 units^2.

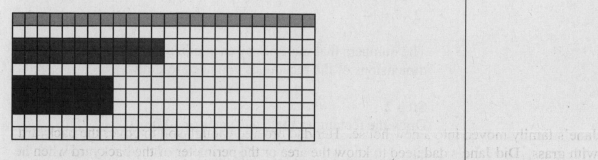

$$A = l \times w$$
$$24 \text{ cm}^2 = 24 \times 1$$
$$24 \text{ cm}^2 = 12 \times 2$$
$$24 \text{ cm}^2 = 8 \times 3$$

When you draw rectangles to represent a given area, remember that the product of the length and the width must be the same for each rectangle.

When you draw rectangles, be sure to draw distinct rectangles. Distinct rectangles have different dimensions.

For example, if one rectangle has a length of 8 cm and a width of 3 cm, and another rectangle has a width of 8 cm and a length of 3 cm, these rectangles would not be considered distinct rectangles.

✳ Example

On the grid shown, draw two distinct rectangles that each have an area of 14 square units (units^2). Label the lengths and widths of the rectangles.

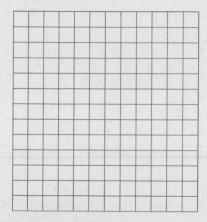

NOTES

Solution

Step 1

Determine all the factors that equal 14 when multiplied by each other.

$1 \times 14 = 14$
$2 \times 7 = 14$

The numbers that multiply by each other to equal 14 are the dimensions of the rectangles you need to draw.

Step 2

Draw the rectangles that have areas of 14 units^2.

The rectangles could look like this:

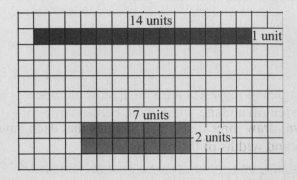

 Time to Try 1

On the grid shown, draw two distinct rectangles that both have an area of 6 units^2.

Use only whole numbers for the lengths and widths of the rectangles. Label the lengths and widths of the rectangles.

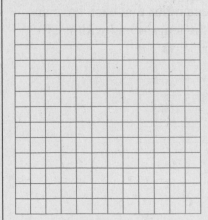

PRACTICE EXERCISES

1. On the grid shown, draw two distinct rectangles that each have an area of 15 units².
    Label the lengths and widths of the rectangles.

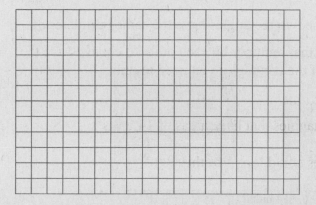

2. On the grid shown, draw three distinct rectangles that each have an area of 18 units².
    Label the lengths and widths of the rectangles.

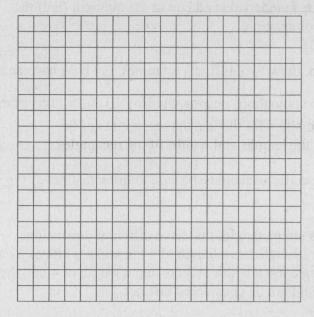

Lesson 8   CONSTRUCTING RECTANGLES FOR A GIVEN PERIMETER

NOTES

Rectangles with different lengths and widths can have the same perimeter. Although their perimeters are the same, their different lengths and widths mean their shapes will be different.

For example, these two rectangles have the same perimeter of 14 units.

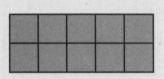
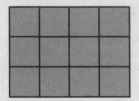

$$P = l + w + l + w$$
$$14 = 5 + 2 + 5 + 2$$
$$14 = 4 + 3 + 4 + 3$$

Follow these three steps to help you determine the possible lengths and widths for a given perimeter:

1.   Divide the given perimeter by 2. For example, $14 \div 2 = 7$.
2.   Think of all the numbers that add up to the quotient (half the perimeter). For example,
$$1 + 6 = 7$$
$$2 + 5 = 7$$
$$3 + 4 = 7$$
3.   The number combinations become the lengths and widths of the rectangles that you can draw.

When you draw specific rectangles, be sure to draw distinct rectangles.

Distinct rectangles are rectangles that have different dimensions. For example, if a rectangle has a length of 4 cm and a width of 3 cm and another rectangle has a width of 3 cm and a length of 4 cm, the two rectangles would not be considered distinct.

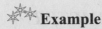 **Example**

Draw two distinct rectangles that each have a perimeter of 10 units. Label the side lengths of each rectangle.

Solution

Step 1
Determine all the possible lengths and widths.

Divide the perimeter by 2.
$10 \div 2 = 5$

Think of all the numbers that add up to 5.
$1 + 4 = 5$
$2 + 3 = 5$

The number combinations become the lengths and widths of the rectangles.

Step 2
Draw the rectangles.

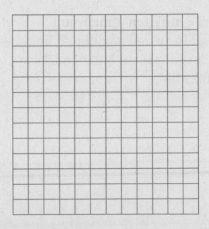

 Time to Try 1

On the grid shown, draw three different rectangles that each have a perimeter of 12 units. Label the side lengths of each rectangle.

PRACTICE EXERCISES

1. On the grid shown, draw two different rectangles that each have a perimeter of 8 units. Label the side lengths of each rectangle.

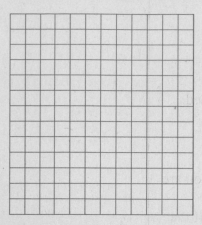

2. On the grid shown, draw four distinct rectangles that each have a perimeter of 18 units. Label the side lengths of each rectangle.

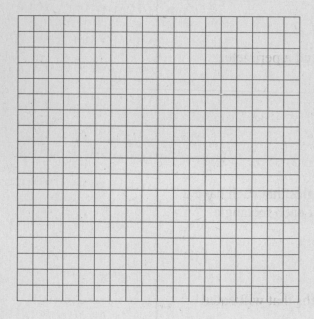

Lesson 9 CONSTRUCTING RECTANGLES WHEN AREA AND PERIMETER ARE GIVEN

When you are given the area and perimeter of a rectangle and need to construct that rectangle, you need to look at the relationship between the numbers that will represent the length and width.

- For area, the length is multiplied by the width.
  $A = l \times w$
- For perimeter, the length and width are added and then doubled (multiplied by 2).
  $P = 2(l \times w)$

Follow these steps to determine the dimensions needed when you are drawing a rectangle for a given area and perimeter:

1. Determine all the possible dimensions for the given area.
2. Identify which of the possible dimensions, when added, will equal half the perimeter.
3. Select the length and width that equal the given area when multiplied together and the perimeter when added together.
4. Draw the rectangle and label the dimensions.

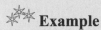 **Example**

Draw a rectangle that has an area of 20 units^2 and a perimeter of 24 units.

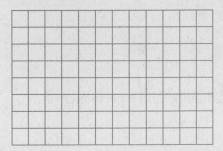

Solution

Step 1
Determine all the possible lengths and widths that will equal 20 units^2 when multiplied by each other.
$1 \times 20 = 20$
$2 \times 10 = 20$
$4 \times 5 = 20$

NOTES

Step 2
Identify which length and width will equal 12 (half of the perimeter, which is 24 units) when added to each other.
$$1 + 20 = 21$$
$$2 + 10 = 12$$
$$4 + 5 = 9$$

Step 3
Select the length and width that equal 20 when multiplied by each other, and that equal 12 when added together.

The dimensions for the rectangle you need to draw are 2 units by 10 units.

$$A = l \times w \qquad\qquad P = 2 \times (l + w)$$
$$= 2 \times 10 \qquad\qquad\quad = 2 \times (2 + 10)$$
$$= 20 \text{ units}^2 \qquad\qquad = 24 \text{ units}$$

Step 4
Draw and label the rectangle.
The rectangle you draw could look like this:

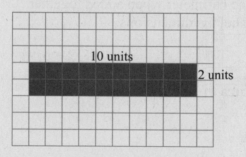

 Time to Try 1

Draw a rectangle that has an area of 28 units^2 and a perimeter of 22 units.

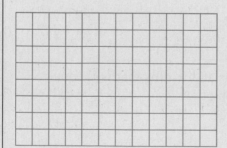

PRACTICE EXERCISES

1. Draw and label a rectangle that has an area of 24 units^2 and a perimeter of 22 units.

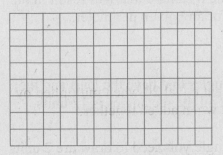

2. Draw and label a rectangle that has an area of 12 units^2 and a perimeter of 14 units.

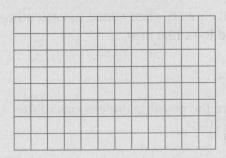

3. Draw and label a rectangle that has an area of 18 units^2 and a perimeter of 18 units.

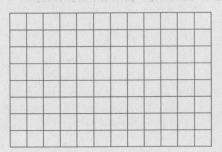

Lesson 10 DESCRIBING SHAPES THAT RESULT IN THE GREATEST AND LEAST AREAS FOR A GIVEN PERIMETER

NOTES

You can describe the shape of the rectangle that will result in the least area and the greatest area for any given perimeter.

 Example

Describe the shapes of the rectangles that have the least and the greatest areas if the perimeter of all the rectangles is 12 units.

Solution

Step 1

Determine all the possible dimensions for a rectangle with a perimeter of 12 units.

Divide the perimeter by 2.
$12 \div 2 = 6$

Think of all the numbers that equal 6 when added to each other.
$1 + 5 = 6$
$2 + 4 = 6$
$3 + 3 = 6$

The number combinations are the possible dimensions of the rectangles.

Step 2

Draw the rectangles.

This is what your rectangles could look like:

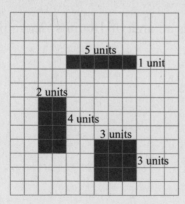

Step 3
Determine the areas of the three rectangles:

$A = l \times w$

$A = 1 \times 5 = 5 \text{ units}^2$

$A = 2 \times 4 = 8 \text{ units}^2$

$A = 3 \times 3 = 9 \text{ units}^2$

Step 4
Describe the shapes.

The least area is 5 units^2. The rectangle with the least area has a long and narrow shape.

The greatest area is 9 units^2. The rectangle with the greatest area has a square shape.

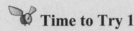 Time to Try 1

Describe the shapes of the rectangles that have the least and the greatest areas if all the rectangles have a perimeter of 14 units.

Draw the rectangles on this grid so that you can see the shapes.

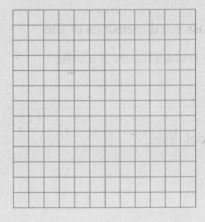

PRACTICE EXERCISES

1. Describe the shapes of the rectangles that have the least and greatest areas if all the rectangles have a perimeter of 16 units.

   Draw the rectangles on this grid so you can see the shapes.

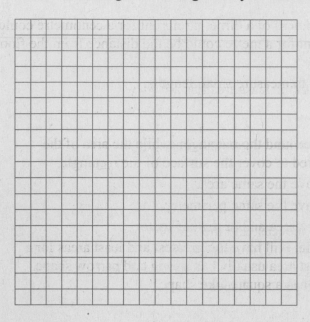

2. Describe the shapes of the rectangles that have the least and the greatest areas if all the rectangles have a perimeter of 18 units.

   Draw the rectangles on this grid so you can see their shapes.

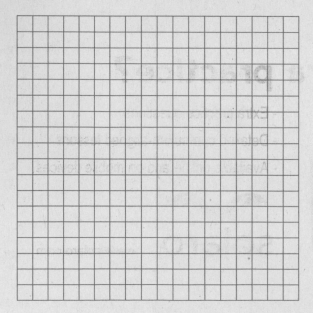

REVIEW SUMMARY

- A 90° angle, often called a right angle, forms a square corner where the two rays of the angle meet.
- You can draw a 90° angle by drawing a vertical line that meets a horizontal line.
- A referent is a shape or object that is about the size of a standard unit. You can use referents to estimate lengths.
- A referent for a millimetre could be the thickness of a dime; a referent for a centimetre could be the width of your pointer finger; a referent for a metre could be the distance from the floor to a doorknob.
- Millimetres are small units of measure used to measure small lengths.
- An equivalent measure to 10 mm is 1 cm.
  An equivalent measure to 1 000 mm is 1 m.
- The perimeter of a rectangle is the distance around the rectangle, while the area of the rectangle is the number of square units needed to cover the surface of the rectangle.
- Rectangles with different dimensions can have the same area.
- Rectangles with different dimensions can have the same perimeter.
- You can construct rectangles if you know the area and/or the perimeter.
- You can describe the shapes of rectangles that will have the greatest and least areas for a given perimeter. The rectangle with the least area usually has a long and narrow shape. The rectangle with the greatest area usually has a square-like shape.

PRACTICE TEST

Use the following information to answer the next question.

Jeff draws these angles.

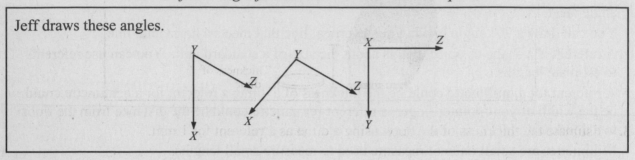

1. Which angle is an example of a 90° angle? Justify your answer.

Use the following information to answer the next question.

Matt makes a spinner with four colours. Each coloured part on the spinner forms a 90° angle.

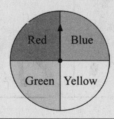

2. Draw the 90° angle shown by the red-coloured part of the spinner. Show the angle with a square corner. Label the angle *XYZ*.

Use the following information to answer the next question.

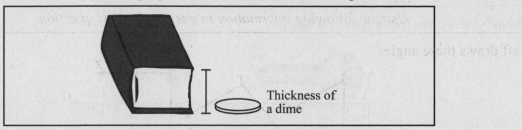

Thickness of
a dime

3. Estimate the thickness of the book using a dime as a referent for 1 mm.

Use the following information to answer the next question.

1 m

4. Estimate the height of the ladder using the height of the dog as a referent for 1 m.

5. Jaimie is 1 490 mm tall and Lee is 1.54 m tall. Who is shorter? Justify your answer.

Use the following information to answer the next question.

Mandy measures the length of a key.

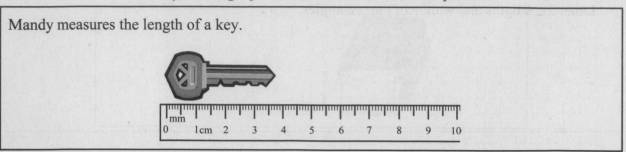

6. What is the length of the key in millimetres? Justify your answer.

Use the following information to answer the next question.

Bill estimates the width of his sunglasses by using a die to represent 1 cm.

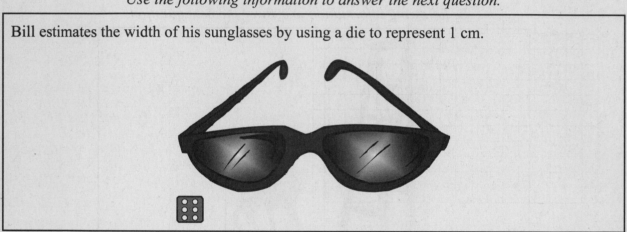

7. About how wide are the sunglasses? Show your work.

8. Mrs. Hailes wants to cover the bulletin board in her classroom with coloured paper. To decide how much paper she needs, should Mrs. Hailes calculate the area or the perimeter of the bulletin board? Justify your answer.

9. On the grid shown, draw three distinct rectangles that each have an area of 16 units^2. Label the lengths and widths of the rectangles.

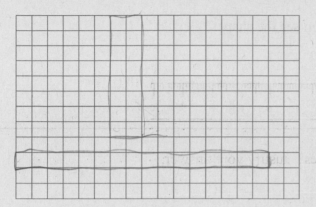

10. On the grid shown, draw three distinct rectangles that each have a perimeter of 14 units. Label the side lengths of each rectangle.

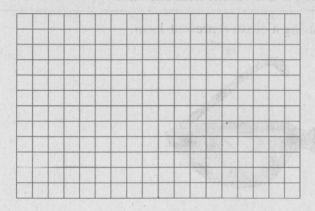

11. Draw a rectangle that has an area of 8 units^2 and a perimeter of 12 units.

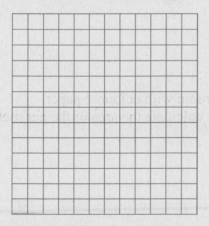

12. If the perimeter of a rectangle is 22 units, what is the least and greatest areas it can have? Describe the shapes of the rectangles.

Draw the rectangles on this grid so you can see the shapes.

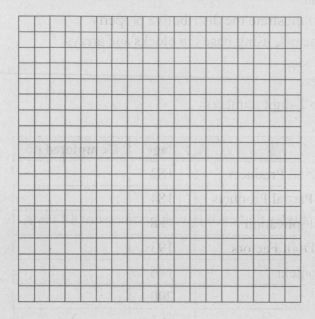

MULTIPLICATION OF TWO 2-DIGIT FACTORS

When you are finished this unit, you will be able to…
- illustrate partial products in expanded notation
- represent both factors in expanded notation to illustrate the distributive property
- model the steps for multiplying two 2-digit factors, using base ten blocks and arrays
- use an algorithm to multiply two 2-digit numbers
- solve problems involving two 2-digit numbers
- create and then solve problems involving two 2-digit numbers

PREREQUISITE SKILLS AND KNOWLEDGE

Prior to starting this unit, you should be able to…
- know basic multiplication facts to 9×9
- demonstrate an understanding of the process of multiplication using arrays or base ten blocks
- regroup ones, tens, or hundreds when multiplying
- understand that the number carried to the next place value is added to the next product
- multiply 2-digit numbers by 1-digit numbers
- multiply 3-digit numbers by 1-digit numbers

Lesson 1   USING EXPANDED NOTATION TO SHOW PARTIAL PRODUCTS

NOTES

When multiplying two 2-digit numbers, you can use expanded notation to determine partial products.

The partial products show you what operations you will need to do to determine the actual product.

You can determine the partial product by following these steps:
1. Write each factor in expanded notation.
2. Place a multiplication sign between the two expanded notations.

 Example

Use expanded notation to illustrate the partial product of 38 × 24.

> *Solution*
> **Step 1**
> Write each factor in expanded notation.
> $38 \rightarrow (30+8)$
> $24 \rightarrow (20+4)$
>
> **Step 2**
> Place a multiplication sign between the two expanded notations.
> $(30+8)\times(20+4)$
>
> The partial product of 38 × 24 is $(30+8)\times(20+4)$.

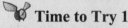 **Time to Try 1**

Use expanded notation to illustrate the partial product of 77 × 39.

PRACTICE EXERCISES

1. Ben says that the partial product of 66×37 is $(60+6)+(30+7)$. Is Ben correct? Justify your answer.

2. Ryder wrote the partial product for 85×57 as $(8+5) \times (5+7)$. Is Ryder correct? Justify your answer.

3. To solve the expression 69×33, Caleb starts by writing the problem as a partial product. How should Caleb write the partial product of 69×33?

Lesson 2 *APPLYING THE DISTRIBUTIVE PROPERTY TO PARTIAL PRODUCTS*

The **distributive property** tells you that you can multiply each addend separately and then add the products.

To apply the distributive property, follow these steps:

1. Determine the partial product using expanded notation.
2. Apply the distributive property to the partial product.
   - Multiply each addend in the first bracket by each addend in the second bracket.
   - Place a + sign between the two sets of brackets.
   - Place a + sign between the two sets of partial products from steps 1 and 2.
3. Complete the multiplication. Then, add the products.

✳ Example

To solve the expression 25×13, use the strategy of applying the distributive property to its partial product. Show your work.

Solution

Step 1
Determine the partial product using expanded notation.
$25 \rightarrow (20+5)$
$13 \rightarrow (10+3)$

The partial product of 25×13 is $(20+5) \times (10+3)$.

Step 2
Apply the distributive property to the partial product.

- Multiply 20 by 10 and 20 by 3, placing a + sign between the partial products.
  $(20 \times 10) + (20 \times 3)$

- Multiply 5 by 10 and 5 by 3, placing a + sign between the partial products.
  $(5 \times 10) + (5 \times 3)$

- Place a + sign between the two sets of partial products.
  $(20 \times 10) + (20 \times 3) + (5 \times 10) + (5 \times 3)$

Step 3

Complete the multiplication. Then, add the products.

$$(20\times10)+(20\times3)+(5\times10)+(5\times3)$$
$$=200+60+50+15$$

$$\begin{array}{r} 200 \\ 60 \\ 50 \\ +15 \\ \hline 325 \end{array}$$

$$25 \times 13 = 325$$

 Time to Try 1

To solve the expression 18 × 42, use the strategy of applying the distributive property to its partial product. Show your work.

APPLYING THE ORDER OF OPERATIONS

Sometimes, you may see step 3 (complete the multiplication, then add the products) expressed without the brackets, like in the following example:
20 × 10 + 20 × 2 + 6 × 10 + 6 × 2

Remember to solve the multiplication facts first, and then add the products.
200 + 40 + 60 + 12

To help you remember the order of operations, you may want to rewrite the expanded notation, placing brackets around the multiplication facts. Doing this may simplify the expression for you.
$(20\times10)+(20\times2)+(6\times10)+(6\times2)$

NOTES

 Example

To solve the expression 43×52, Kalen applied the distributive property to its partial product. This is as far as Kalen got in the multiplication process:
$40 \times 50 + 40 \times 2 + 3 \times 50 + 3 \times 2$

Complete the multiplication process to determine the product of 43×52. Show your work.

Solution

Step 1
Simplify the expression by placing brackets around the multiplication facts.
$(40 \times 50) + (40 \times 2) + (3 \times 50) + (3 \times 2)$

Step 2
Complete the multiplication. Then, add the products.
$(40 \times 50) + (40 \times 2) + (3 \times 50) + (3 \times 2)$
$= 2\ 000 + 80 + 150 + 6$

$$
\begin{array}{r}
2\ 000 \\
80 \\
150 \\
+\quad 6 \\
\hline
2\ 236
\end{array}
$$

$43 \times 52 = 2\ 236$.

 Time to Try 2

Alana was solving the problem 63×36 by applying the distributive property to its partial product. This is as far as Alana got in the multiplication process before the recess bell rang:
$60 \times 30 + 60 \times 6 + 3 \times 30 + 3 \times 6$

Complete the multiplication process to determine the product of 63×36. Show your work.

186

PRACTICE EXERCISES

Solve the following two problems by using the strategy of applying the distributive property to the partial product. Show your work.

1. 24×19

2. 36×14

3. Marnie uses the distributive property to multiply 41×57. This is the expression she wrote to solve the problem: $40 \times 50 + 40 \times 7 + 1 \times 50 + 1 \times 7$. Complete the multiplication process to determine the product of 41×57.

Lesson 3   USING MODELS TO ILLUSTRATE 2-DIGIT MULTIPLICATION

One way to illustrate the process of multiplying 2-digit factors is to use base ten blocks.

BASE TEN BLOCKS

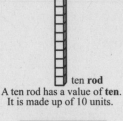

□ **unit**
A unit has a value of **one**.

ten **rod**
A ten rod has a value of **ten**.
It is made up of 10 units.

hundred **flat**
A hundred flat has a value of **one hundred**.
It is made up of 10 ten rods or 100 units.

To model the steps for multiplying two 2-digit factors using base ten blocks, follow these steps:

1. Write the factors as partial products (expanded notation)
2. Apply the distributive property.
3. Use base ten blocks to illustrate each of the four products (from the distributive property).
4. Add the four sets of base ten blocks to determine the product.

Example

Using base ten blocks, model the steps for multiplying 13×11.

Solution

Step 1
Write the multiplication fact as partial products using expanded notation.
$(10+3) \times (10+1)$

Step 2
Apply the distributive property to the partial products.
$(10 \times 10) + (10 \times 1) + (3 \times 10) + (3 \times 1)$

Step 3
Use base ten blocks to illustrate each product.

$10 \times 10 = 100$

$10 \times 1 = 10$

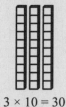

$3 \times 10 = 30$

$3 \times 1 = 3$

Step 4
Add the four sets of base ten blocks to show the product of 13×11.

One hundred flat plus four ten rods plus three units equals 143.

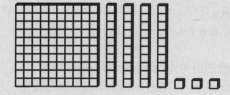

$13 \times 11 = 143$

Time to Try 1

Using base ten blocks, model the steps for multiplying 15×21.

USING GRIDS

Another way to illustrate the process of multiplying two 2-digit factors is to use an array. One type of array that is easy to use is a grid. A grid is a pattern of horizontal and vertical lines that form rectangles and squares. Each square on the grid represents the number 1. A grid is sometimes referred to as an area model.

To illustrate products, it is best to use grids based on tens wherever possible. For example, this grid of 6 squares by 10 squares can represent $6 \times 10 = 60$.

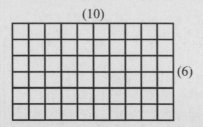

To model the steps for multiplying two 2-digit factors using grids, follow these steps:

1. Write the factors as partial products (expanded notation).
2. Apply the distributive property.
3. Use grids to illustrate each of the four products (from the distributive property).
4. Add the four sets of grids together to form a rectangle that has the same dimensions as the factors of the multiplication fact.

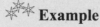 Example

Using grids, model the steps for multiplying 15×12.

Solution

Step 1
Write the multiplication fact as partial products using expanded notation.
$(10+5) \times (10+2)$

Step 2
Apply the distributive property to the partial products.
$(10 \times 10) + (10 \times 2) + (5 \times 10) + (5 \times 2)$

Step 3
Use grids to illustrate each product.

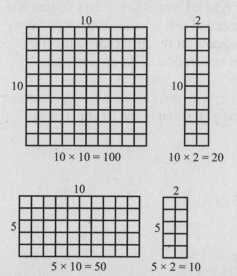

$10 \times 10 = 100$ $10 \times 2 = 20$

$5 \times 10 = 50$ $5 \times 2 = 10$

Step 4
Add the four sets of grids together to form a rectangle.

The rectangle formed will be 15 squares by 12 squares (15×12).

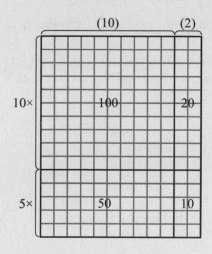

$100 + 50 + 20 + 10 = 180$
$15 \times 12 = 180$

Time to Try 2
Using grids, model the steps for multiplying 19×12.

PRACTICE EXERCISES

1. Using base ten blocks, model the steps for multiplying 12×11.

2. Using base ten blocks, model the steps for multiplying 15×13.

3. Using grids, model the steps for multiplying 17×11.

4. Using grids, model the steps for multiplying 16×13.

Lesson 4   USING ALGORITHMS TO MULTIPLY TWO 2-DIGIT FACTORS

An **algorithm** is an organized step-by-step plan to help you calculate.

When multiplying by a 2-digit number, follow this plan.
• Think of the multiplier in expanded notation.
• Multiply the ones.
• Multiply the tens.
• Add the products of the ones and tens.

 Example

Using an algorithm, calculate the product of 21 × 14.

Solution

Step 1
Following the algorithm plan.

Think of the multiplier (14) as the expanded notation 10 + 4.

Multiply 21 by the 4 ones.
21 × 4

Multiply 21 by the 10.
21 × 10.

Add the products.

Step 2
Show your work
```
   21
 × 14
   84  ← Multiply by the 4 ones:  21 × 4 = 84
  210  ← Multiply by the 1 ten:  21 × 10 = 210
  294  ← Add the products:  84 × 210 = 294
```

21 × 14 = 294

 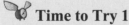 **Time to Try 1**

Using an algorithm, calculate the product of 81 × 18.
Show your work.

NOTES

WITH REGROUPING

Sometimes, you need to regroup the ones when you multiply. When you regroup the ones, you can write the number that you carry above the tens. Remember that after you multiply the basic fact, you need to add the number that you carried.

 Example

Using an algorithm, calculate the product of 67×44.
Show your work.

Solution

Step 1
Follow the algorithm plan.

Think of the multiplier (44) in expanded notation. (40 + 4)

Multiply 67 by the 4 ones, regrouping where necessary.
67×4

Multiply 67 by the 4 tens, regrouping where necessary.
67×40

Add the products of the ones and tens.

Step 2
Show your work.

$$
\begin{array}{r}
{\scriptstyle 2} \\
{\scriptstyle 2} \\
67 \\
\times\ \ 44 \\
\hline
268 \\
2\,680 \\
\hline
2\,948
\end{array}
$$

$67 \times 44 = 2\,948$

 Time to Try 2

Using an algorithm, calculate the product of 62×27.
Show your work.

PRACTICE EXERCISES

Use algorithms to solve the following expressions. Show your work.

1. 24×31

2. 64×23

3. 82×28

4. 85×16

Lesson 5 SOLVING MULTIPLICATION PROBLEMS IN CONTEXT

When solving multiplication problems, there is no one correct way of determining the product. You can use any strategy that works for you.

Depending on the problem, some strategies may work better than others. You may even need to use several strategies.

Here are some suggestions that may help you decide which strategy to use:

- If both factors end in 0, like in the expression 50×70, you might want to use the strategy of annexing and then adding 0.
- If the factors are low, like in the expression 11×11, you might want to use base ten blocks or draw grids.
- If the factors are large, like in the expression 93×87, you might want to use algorithms.
- If the factors are in the mid range, like 25×32, you might want to apply the distributive property.

Remember, a personal strategy is one that gives you the greatest success when solving problems.

 Example

Su-Ling bought 25 boxes of chocolates. In each box, there were 12 chocolates.

How many chocolates did Su-Ling buy in total? Show your work.

Solution

Step 1
Decide which multiplication strategy you will use to solve this problem.

Step 2
One example of a strategy you can use is to apply the distributive property.

Write the multiplication fact in expanded notation.
$(20+5) \times (10+2)$

Apply the distributive property.
$(20 \times 10) + (20 \times 2) + (5 \times 10) + (5 \times 2)$

196

Add the products.
$$200 + 40 + 50 + 10 = 300$$

$$25 \times 12 = 300$$

Su-Ling bought a total of 300 chocolates.

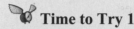 **Time to Try 1**

In an auditorium, there are 50 rows of chairs. There are 12 chairs in each row.

What is the total number of chairs in the auditorium?
Show your work.

WRITING A PROBLEM AND THEN SOLVING IT

You can also solve multiplication problems that you create.
Remember to have equal-sized groups in the problems you create.

Choose any strategy that works for you to solve the problem
you created.

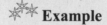 **Example**

There are a total of 14 groups. There are 11 items in each group.

Write a problem for the given information. Solve the problem you
wrote, showing your work.

Solution
Step 1
Write a problem using the given information.
Here is an example of a problem that uses the given information:

Marnie has a stamp book that has 14 pages. She pasted
11 stamps on each page. How many stamps did she paste
in total?

NOTES

Step 2

Solve the problem, using a strategy that works for you.

Here is an example of solving the problem with base ten blocks:

Write the multiplication fact 14×11 in expanded notation.
$(10+4) \times (10+1)$

Apply the distributive property.
$(10 \times 10) + (10 \times 1) + (4 \times 10) + (4 \times 1)$

Represent each product with base ten blocks.

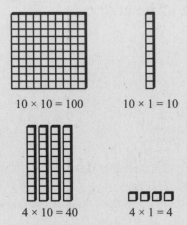

$10 \times 10 = 100$ $10 \times 1 = 10$

$4 \times 10 = 40$ $4 \times 1 = 4$

The product 14×11 is one hundred plus five tens plus four ones.

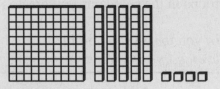

$14 \times 11 = 154$

Marnie pasted a total of 154 stamps in her stamp book.

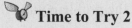 **Time to Try 2**

There are 25 groups with 75 items in each group.

Write a problem for the given information. Solve the problem you wrote, showing your work.

PRACTICE EXERCISES

Solve the following three problems using the strategies that work best for you.

1. If one book costs $35, how much would 15 of the same book cost?

2. Helena made 11 beaded bracelets for her friends. Each bracelet was made out of 22 beads. How many beads did Helena use altogether?

3. Katelyn spends 45 minutes in dance class per day. How many hours does she spend in dance class in 13 days?

Use the following information to answer the next question.

There are a total of 13 colours. There are 11 items in each colour

4. Write a problem for the given information. Solve the problem you wrote, showing your work.

REVIEW SUMMARY

- Partial products are the two 2-digit factors shown in expanded notation.
- Partial products show the operations you need to do in order to determine the actual product.
- The distributive property tells you that you can multiply a sum by multiplying each addend separately and then adding the products.
- You can apply the distributive property to partial products to calculate the actual product.
- You can illustrate the process of multiplication using base ten blocks or grids to represent the products after the distributive property is applied.
- An algorithm is an organized step-by-step plan to help you calculate products.
- When a problem involves equal groups, you can multiply to determine the total number.
- There is no one correct way to solve a multiplication problem. Any multiplication strategy can be used to determine the product. You should use the strategy that works best for you.

PRACTICE TEST

1. Use expanded notation to illustrate the partial product of 86×28.

2. To solve 28×13, use the strategy of applying the distributive property to its partial product. Show your work.

3. Using base ten blocks, model the steps for multiplying 13×21.

Use the following information to answer the next question.

Emma was solving the problem 74×47 by applying the distributive property to its partial product. This is as far as Emma got in the multiplication process when the recess bell rang: $70 \times 40 + 70 \times 7 + 4 \times 40 + 4 \times 7$.

4. Complete the multiplication process to determine the product of 74×47. Show your work.

5. Using an algorithm, calculate the product of 46×13. Show your work.

6. Using grids, model the steps for multiplying 18×15.

Solve the following two problems using the strategies that work best for you.

7. Mrs. Star sold 45 boxes of cupcakes at the school's bake sale. In each box, there were 15 cupcakes. How many cupcakes did Mrs. Star sell in total?

8. Peter and his dad picked 60 bags of apples from the apple trees in their orchard. They placed 18 apples into each bag. How many apples did Peter and his dad pick?

DATA MANAGEMENT

When you are finished this unit, you will be able to…
- explain the difference between first-hand and second-hand data
- ask appropriate questions to collect first-hand and second-hand data
- identify attributes of double bar graphs
- interpret data presented in a double bar graph
- draw conclusions from the data presented in a double bar graph
- represent a given set of data by creating a double bar graph

PREREQUISITE SKILLS AND KNOWLEDGE

Prior to starting this unit, you should be able to…
- collect first-hand data by using tally marks, line plots, charts, or lists
- understand many-to-one correspondence
- identify attributes of a bar graph
- interpret data presented in a bar graph

Lesson 1   DIFFERENTIATING BETWEEN FIRST-HAND AND SECOND-HAND DATA

NOTES

The data you collect for the question that you are investigating can be either first-hand data or second-hand data.

FIRST-HAND DATA

First-hand data is information that you collect on your own by counting, collecting, or conducting experiments or surveys. First-hand data is information given directly to you by a primary source.

For example, if you ask a runner how a marathon went, you are getting information from a primary source, someone who actually ran the race. Another name for first-hand data is **primary data.**

SECOND-HAND DATA

Second-hand data is information that you collect from secondary sources such as books, newspapers, television, the media, databases, and the Internet. The data has already been collected and recorded by another person and then made available to you. Another name for second-hand data is **secondary data**.

 Example

Emma wanted to know how many students in her school were wearing red shirts on Valentine's Day. To collect the data she wanted, this is what she did:

- She visited the classrooms of the students in grades 1, 2, and 3 and counted the number of students wearing red.
- She asked her friend to visit the classrooms of the students in grades 4, 5, and 6 and to count the number of students wearing red.
- She asked the kindergarten teacher to tell her how many of her students were wearing red.

Was Emma collecting first-hand or second-hand data?
Justify your answer.

> *Solution*
> **Step 1**
> Identify the data.
>
> Emma was collecting first- and second-hand data.

Step 2
Justify your answer.

When Emma collected data from the students in grades 1, 2, and 3, she did the actual collecting and recording of the data herself. Therefore, she was collecting first-hand data.

However, when Emma had someone else collect the information (her friend and the teacher), she was collecting second-hand data. Someone else collected and recorded the data and then gave the data to Emma.

Time to Try 1

Jared used a survey to collect data from the students in grades 5 and 6 at his school. This is how he conducted the survey:
- He asked a specific question: "What is your favourite weekend activity?"
- He offered options: playing sports, watching television, playing video games, spending time with friends.
- He used tallies to record the answers given.

Was Jared collecting first-hand or second-hand data?
Justify your answer.

PRACTICE EXERCISES

Use the following information to answer the next question.

Miss Martin wanted to know the reasons why students came late to school. To collect the data, this is what she did:

• She pasted a two-column sheet on the door for one month.

• When students were late, they had to write their names in one column and the reason they were late in the other column.

1. Was Miss Martin collecting first-hand or second-hand data? Justify your answer.

Use the following information to answer the next question.

Mila wants to know the highest temperature recorded in Edmonton between July 4 and July 11. She keeps track of the daily temperatures by watching the evening weather report on one of the local TV stations.

2. Was Mila collecting first-hand or second-hand data? Justify your answer.

Lesson 2   ASKING APPROPRIATE QUESTIONS TO COLLECT DATA

When collecting data, it is very important to ask questions that will promote the best and most relevant responses.

QUESTIONS FOR COLLECTING FIRST-HAND DATA

Some questions can be best answered by collecting first-hand data. These questions are usually aimed at smaller groups and involve personal opinions.

When collecting first-hand data, the question asked should be specific to the kind of data you want to collect. If you give choices, you will collect more meaningful responses. Without choices, your data may be very general and might be difficult to organize.

It is also very important that you make sure that your questions do not mislead or influence the answers that may be given.

✸✸ Example

Trisha conducts a survey of students in her class by asking them each a question. She makes this graph to show the results of the first-hand data she collected.

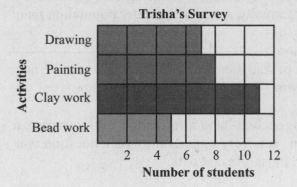

To get the results shown on the graph, what kind of question could Trisha have asked the students?

Solution

To find out what question Trisha could have asked, look at the information given on the graph.

The graph lists four different art activities. It also gives a number of students for each activity.

Therefore, the question had to be about the four activities. The number could mean how many students chose each activity.

NOTES

Here are some examples of a survey question that Trisha could have asked:
- Which of the following art activities do you like the most?
- Which of the following activities have you done in art class?
- Which of the following activities have you taken lessons for?

 Time to Try 1

Nathan wants to collect data about the kinds of things that the students in his class have learned from the TV show "It's Your World." To collect the data, he will ask the students a question.

What kind of question could Nathan ask to give him the widest range of information about the data he plans to collect?

QUESTIONS FOR COLLECTING SECOND-HAND DATA

Some questions can best be answered by collecting second-hand data. These questions are usually aimed at a greater population than just the people you know.
The issues for investigation m
ay involve the collection of statistics or information that you are not able to collect on your own.

The first step in collecting second-hand information is to formulate a question for investigation. It is very important to ask a question that will result in the best and most relevant data.

- Your question should be direct and specific.
- It should be clearly stated.
- It should be able to be answered through research.
- It should be relevant to the type of data you want to collect.

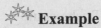 **Example**

Amy lives in Alberta where the winters get quite cold. She notices that all the butterflies leave before the cold temperatures arrive. She wants to learn where the butterflies go for the winter.

When Amy plans her research, what kinds of questions could she ask to find the data she wants?

Solution

Amy needs to ask questions that are relevant to what she wants to learn. Since she wants to know where butterflies go for the winter, she could ask questions like these:

- Where do butterflies migrate for the winter?
- What happens to butterflies when the weather gets too cold in Canada?
- Do butterflies migrate to the United States or Mexico?
- How far away do butterflies fly when they migrate?

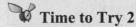 **Time to Try 2**

Jordyn is writing a report about North American animals who only eat plants. She plans to do some online research to obtain some secondary data.

To collect the data that she needs for her report, what kind of questions could she ask to start her investigation?

PRACTICE EXERCISES

Use the following information to answer the next question.

Some Grade 6 students are conducting a survey in their school to find out which Canadian city is most popular.

1. In order to get meaningful and relevant first-hand data, what kinds of questions could the students ask? Explain your answer.

Use the following information to answer the next question.

Katrina wants to research the life span of zebras in zoos. She plans to collect some first-hand data by interviewing people who work with zebras at the zoo in a neighbouring city.

2. When Katrina interviews the workers, what kind of questions could she ask to collect the information she wants? Explain your answer.

Use the following information to answer the next question.

Sam sees that many of the birds that live near Moose Lake migrate to warmer climates when the weather gets cold. He wants to learn more about birds that migrate to warmer climates.

3. When Sam does his research on the Internet, what kinds of questions could he ask to find the data he wants? Explain your answer.

Lesson 3   IDENTIFYING ATTRIBUTES OF DOUBLE BAR GRAPHS

Double bar graphs show two sets of similar data. A double bar graph has two bars side by side on an axis. The two bars represent two sets of similar data. The two sets of data are usually shown using two different colours. This helps you see the differences or similarities more easily. The double bars can be horizontal or vertical.

NOTES

ATTRIBUTES OF DOUBLE BAR GRAPHS

This double bar graph shows the number of students who drank white or chocolate milk over a period of three months.

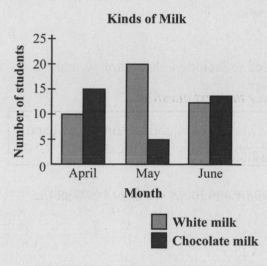

- The **legend** or key explains which coloured bar represents the two sets of similar data. The grey bar represents white milk, and the black bar represents chocolate milk.

- The **title** tells you what the graph is about. The title lets you know that the graph is about the kinds of milk the students drank.

- The **x-axis** is labelled to show what information is presented on the horizontal axis. The x-axis shows the months that were included in the survey (April, May, and June).

- The **y-axis** is labelled to show what information is presented on the vertical axis. The y-axis shows the number of students who drank white or chocolate milk during the three-month period.

- The **interval** shows you what number is represented by each line. An equal interval of 5 is used. The numbers count up by 5s from 0 to 25.

NOTES

✳✳✳ **Example**

Blake started making this double bar graph but did not complete it.

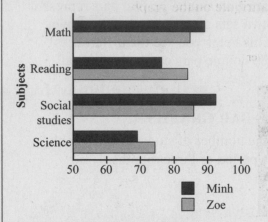

What attributes does Blake need to include in his graph to make it complete? Explain your answer.

Solution

Step 1
Determine the missing attributes.

Blake needs to label the *x*-axis and make a title to complete his graph.

Step 2
Explain your answer.

The numbers on the *x*-axis are not labelled, so you do not know for sure what they represent.

They could be the number of questions completed, the number of minutes taken to complete a test, percentages on a particular test, or a final mark in the class. Without a label, you do not know.

The title is missing, so you do not know for sure what the graph is trying to show. You can only assume that it has something to do with marks in subjects and with two people named Minh and Zoe.

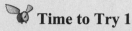 **Time to Try 1**

What attribute is missing from this double bar graph? Explain why it is important to include that attribute on the graph.

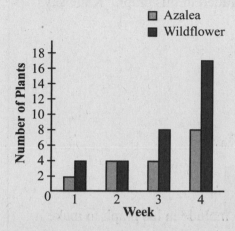

PRACTICE EXERCISES

Use the following information to answer the next question.

Daria says that all the attributes of a double bar graph are included in this graph. Katie says that one attribute is missing.

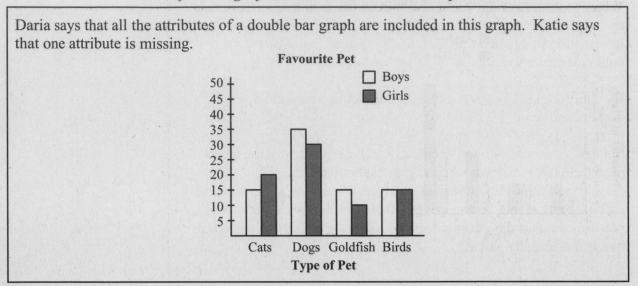

1. Who is correct? Justify your answer.

Use the following information to answer the next question.

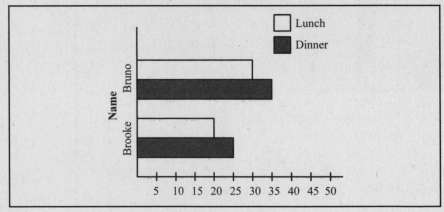

2. Identify the missing attributes in the double bar graph. Explain why it is important to include those attributes on the graph.

Lesson 4 INTERPRETING DOUBLE BAR GRAPHS TO DRAW CONCLUSIONS

When you interpret the data presented on a graph, you are figuring out what the information means. You may need to compare information that is presented, or you may need to perform a mathematical operation on some of the data.

By interpreting the data presented, you should be able to answer questions about it.

Being able to read a graph accurately and interpret what the data means enables you to draw conclusions about the data. In order to draw conclusions about the data presented, you need to consider all the information that you are given. When you draw a conclusion, you are using all the information to make a statement about the data that is not actually stated.

Example

A teacher counted the number of times she heard her students use the word *because* when they were talking to each other over a period of two hours (120 minutes).

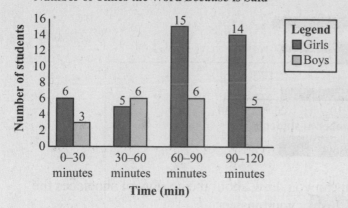

Number of Times the Word *Because* is Said

What conclusion can you draw about the number of times the boys and girls said the word *because*. Justify your answer.

Solution

Step 1
Draw a conclusion from the data presented.

One conclusion you can draw from the data presented is that the girls said the word *because* more often than the boys said it.

NOTES

Step 2

Justify your conclusion.

When you compare the two bars for the four time periods, you can see that the girls used the word *because* more than the boys did for three of those time periods.

Adding up the total number of times the word *because* was used shows that the girls used the word 40 times and the boys only used the word 20 times, half as many times as the girls did.

 Time to Try 1

One school planned to purchase a number of coloured shoelaces to use as small rewards for reading a certain number of pages of books for the school's reading program.

The principal surveyed a number of students to see which of four colours they wanted. The results are shown on the following double bar graph.

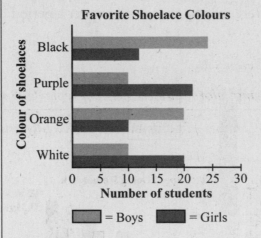

What conclusion can you draw about the colours of shoelaces the students chose? Justify your answer.

PRACTICE EXERCISES

Use the following information to answer the next two questions.

This graph shows the number of gold, silver, and bronze medals won by girls and boys who competed in a school's winter games competition.

1. What conclusion can you draw about the kinds of medals the boys and girls won? Justify your answer.

Use the following information to answer the next two questions.

This graph shows the average number of hours in a week that boys and girls in grades 1 to 6 spend doing homework.

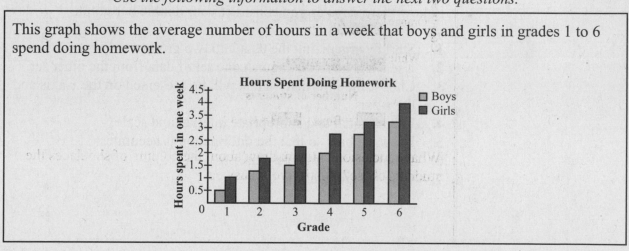

2. What two conclusions can you draw about the amount of homework students do? Justify your answers.

Lesson 5 CONSTRUCTING A DOUBLE BAR GRAPH

When you are displaying data in graphs, you need to be sure to label the *x*-axis and the *y*-axis and give the graph a title. Here is an example of the location of these labels on a graph.

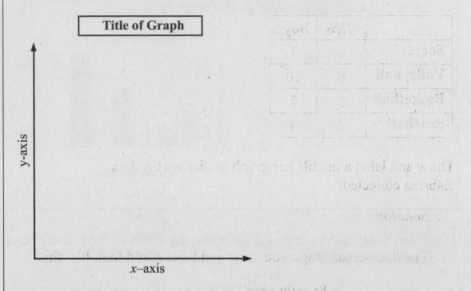

Having these labels will ensure that anyone trying to interpret your observations and data will be able to read the graph. People need to know what the numbers on the graph represent, so you must ensure that appropriate and equal intervals, are used and labelled properly.

Follow these steps as you construct your double bar graph:

1. Start by organizing the data into two groups.
2. Use a legend to distinguish one set of data from the other set.
3. Choose the information that will be presented on the *x*-axis and the *y*-axis.
4. Use an equal and appropriate interval and scale.
5. Draw the bars so that the information is accurate.
6. Label the *x*-axis and *y*-axis.
7. Give the graph a title.

✸✸✸ Example

Sabrina collected data about the favourite sports of students in her school. To display the data in a double bar graph, she first organized the data into two groups.

	Girls	Boys
Soccer	6	3
Volleyball	8	10
Basketball	5	7
Baseball	4	4

Draw and label a double bar graph to display the data Sabrina collected.

Solution

The double bar graph you draw and label could look like this:

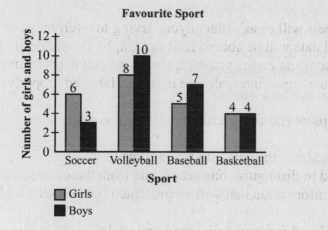

On this graph, the numbers are placed above the bars so that you can easily check to see if you drew the bars accurately.

NOTES

Clarkson surveyed students in Grade 5 to see what type of movie they would like to see at their end-of-school party. He organized his data as follows:

Type of Movie	Girls	Boys
Comedy	8	4
Drama	8	8
Action	6	12
Thriller	4	8
Romance	10	4

Draw and label a double bar graph to display the data Clarkson collected.

Ask yourself these questions as you make your graph:
- Did I make a legend?
- Did I make the two types of bars distinct?
- Did I join the two distinct bars?
- Did I draw the bars accurately?
- Did I use an appropriate interval?
- Did I label the *x*-axis and *y*-axis?
- Did I make a title?

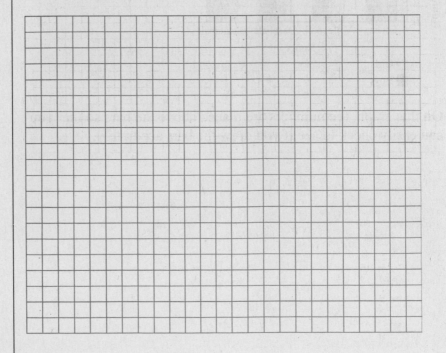

PRACTICE EXERCISES

Use the following information to answer the next question.

Ben and his family have a cottage at a lake. For four years, Ben kept a record of the number of coyotes and rabbits he saw near the cottage. To display the data he collected in a double bar graph, Ben first organized the data into two groups.

	Rabbits	Coyotes
2004	80	10
2005	60	20
2006	40	30
2007	20	40

1. Draw and label a double bar graph to display the data Ben collected.

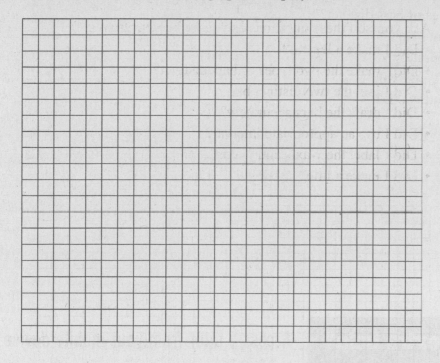

REVIEW SUMMARY

- First-hand data (primary data) is data you collect on your own by counting, collecting, or conducting experiments or surveys.
- Second-hand data (secondary data) is information you collect from sources such as books, television, databases, or the Internet. You are getting the information from someone or something else.
- When collecting data, the question asked should be specific to the kind of data you want to collect.
- Attributes of double bar graphs include a legend, a title, axes that are labelled, and an equal and appropriate interval.
- In order to draw a conclusion from a double bar graph, you need to look at all the information presented and figure out what it means.
- When constructing a double bar graph, be sure that all the attributes are presented.
- After constructing a double bar graph, ask yourself these questions:
  - Did I make a legend?
  - Did I make the two types of bars distinct?
  - Did I join the two distinct bars?
  - Did I draw the bars accurately?
  - Did I use an appropriate interval?
  - Did I label the x-axis and y-axis?
  - Did I make a title?

PRACTICE TEST

Use the following information to answer the next question.

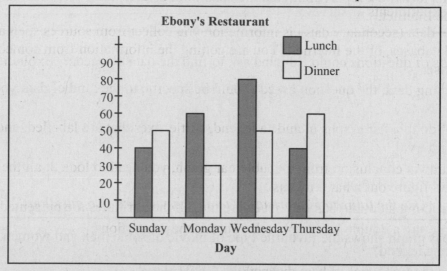

1. What attribute is missing from the double bar graph? Explain why it is important to include that attribute on the graph.

Use the following information to answer the next question.

Elena wanted to know how many students at her school took swimming lessons. To collect the data she wanted, this is what she did:

• She visited the classrooms of the students in grades 1, 2, and 3 and counted the number of students who took swimming lessons.

• She asked friends to visit all the classrooms of students in grades 4, 5, and 6 and count the number of students who took swimming lessons.

2. Was Elena collecting first-hand or second-hand data? Justify your answer.

Use the following information to answer the next question.

Edmund wants to write a report about the life span of dogs. He plans to collect the data from sources on the Internet.

3. What kinds of questions could Edmund ask to find the data he needs? Explain your answer.

Use the following information to answer the next two questions.

The double bar graph shows the favourite type of movie of some men and women.

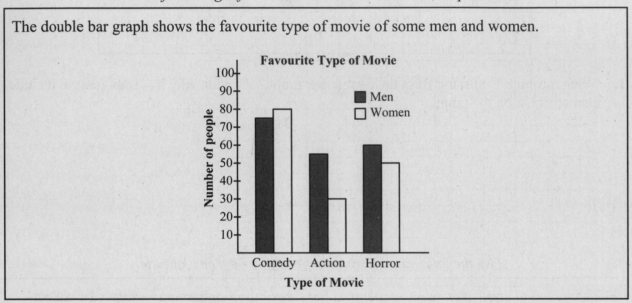

4. Draw two conclusions about the kinds of movies men and women prefer. Justify your answers.

Use the following information to answer the next question.

The following chart shows the number of people who visited a particular park on the first Monday, Tuesday, Wednesday, and Thursday in March and April.

Day	March	April
Monday	120	150
Tuesday	180	120
Wednesday	200	160
Thursday	170	150

5. Draw and label a double bar graph to show the data in the chart.

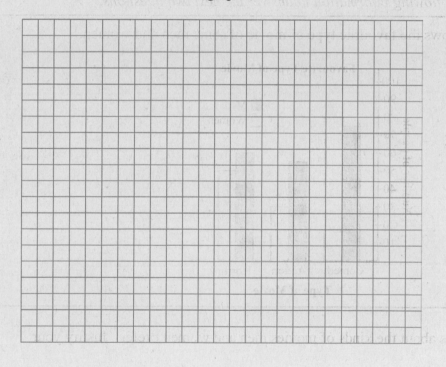

NOTES

DIVISION OF 3-DIGIT BY 1-DIGIT NUMBERS

When you are finished this unit, you will be able to…
- model the division process as equal sharing using base ten blocks
- use an algorithm to divide 3-digit numbers by 1-digit numbers
- interpret a remainder by rounding up the quotient or by ignoring the remainder
- express a remainder as a fraction and as a decimal
- solve problems involving 3-digit by 1-digit division
- create and solve problems involving 3-digit by 1-digit division

PREREQUISITE SKILLS AND KNOWLEDGE

Prior to starting this unit, you should be able to…
- relate division to multiplication
- know basic multiplication and related division facts to 9×9
- divide 2-digit numbers by a 1-digit divisor
- solve division problems involving 2-digit by 1-digit division
- estimate quotients

Lesson 1   USING MODELS TO ILLUSTRATE THE PROCESS OF EQUAL SHARING

NOTES

You can model the division process as equal sharing using base ten blocks.

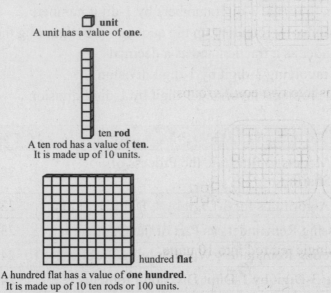

unit
A unit has a value of **one**.

ten **rod**
A ten rod has a value of **ten**.
It is made up of 10 units.

hundred **flat**
A hundred flat has a value of **one hundred**.
It is made up of 10 ten rods or 100 units.

To show equal sharing with base ten blocks, follow these steps:

1. Represent the dividend with base ten blocks.
2. Divide the hundreds into equal groups, regrouping if necessary.
3. Divide the tens into equal groups, regrouping if necessary.
4. Divide the ones into equal groups.
5. The number of hundreds, tens, and ones in each group will be the quotient.

 Example

To show the division process of equal sharing, solve $234 \div 2$ using base ten blocks.

Solution

Step 1
Represent the dividend 234 with base ten blocks.

In 234, there are 2 hundreds, 3 tens, and 4 ones.

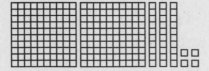

Step 2
Divide the hundreds into two equal groups (by the divisor 2).

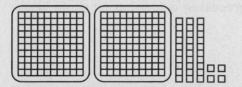

Step 3
Divide the tens into two equal groups.

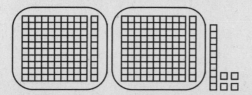

Step 4
Regroup the single ten rod into 10 units.

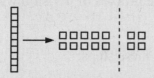

Step 5
Divide the ones (units) into two equal groups.

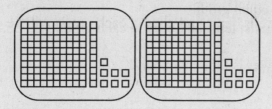

Step 6
Determine the quotient.

Each group has 1 hundred flat (100), 1 ten rod (10), and 7 units (7).
100 + 10 + 7 = 117

234 ÷ 2 = 117

NOTES

 Time to Try 1

To show the division process of equal sharing, solve $312 \div 3$ using base ten blocks.

WITH A REMAINDER

If parts are left over after the process of equal sharing, the parts are the remainder.

You can use base ten blocks to illustrate the process of division with a remainder.

To show division with a remainder, follow these steps:

1. Represent the dividend with base ten blocks.
2. Divide the hundreds into equal groups, regrouping if necessary.
3. Divide the tens into equal groups, regrouping if necessary.
4. Divide the ones into equal groups.
5. The number of hundreds, tens, and ones in each group will be the quotient.
6. The part that is left over is the remainder.

 Example

To show the process of equal sharing, solve $124 \div 3$ using base ten blocks.

Solution

Step 1
Represent the dividend 124 with base ten blocks.

In 124, there is 1 hundred, 2 tens, and 4 ones.

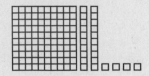

Step 2

Regroup the hundred flat into 10 ten rods.

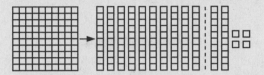

Step 3

Divide the tens into three equal groups (by the divisor 3).

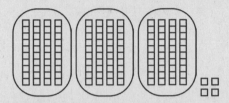

Step 4

Divide the units into three equal groups.

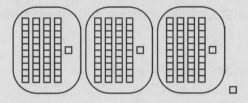

Step 5

Determine the quotient.

Each group has 4 ten rods (40) and 1 unit (1).
40 + 1 = 41

There is one unit that is left over; therefore, $124 \div 3 = 41$ with a remainder of 1.
$124 \div 3 = 41$ R1

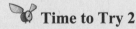 **Time to Try 2**

To show the process of equal sharing, solve $227 \div 2$ using base ten blocks.

PRACTICE EXERCISES

Show the division process of equal sharing using base ten blocks.

1. $236 \div 2$

2. $203 \div 2$

3. $331 \div 3$

Lesson 2   USING ALGORITHMS FOR 3-DIGIT BY 1-DIGIT DIVISION

When dividing, the **dividend** is the number that is being divided, the **divisor** is the number by which the dividend is being divided, and the **quotient** is the result of the division process (the answer).

$$\text{divisor} \longrightarrow 4\overline{)8} \longleftarrow \text{dividend} \qquad 8 \div 4 = 2$$

quotient above the 2, dividend above the 8, quotient above the 2, divisor below the 4

An algorithm is a step-by-step plan to help you calculate.

AN ALGORITHM THAT USES PLACE VALUE

First, look at the divisor to see if it greater than (>) or less than (<) the first digit of the dividend.

• If the divisor is **equal to** or **less than** the first digit of the dividend, the first digit of the quotient (answer) will be placed above the digit in the hundreds place.

• If the divisor is **greater than** the first digit of the dividend, the first digit of the quotient (answer) will be placed above the digit in the tens place.

✳✳ Example

Divide 235 by 5.

$5\overline{)235}$

Solution

In the dividend 235, the 2 is in the hundreds place, the 3 is in the tens place, and the 5 is in the ones place.

Follow these steps to see the division process.

Step 1

There are 23 tens in the dividend 235. How many groups of 5 can you make out of 23 tens?

$4 \times 5 = 20$

You can make four groups of 5 tens.
Put the 4 above the 3 of 23. Put the 20 below the 23.

$$5\overline{)235} \\ \underline{20}$$

with 4 above the 3

Step 2

Subtract 20 from 23 (23 − 20 = 3). Bring down the 5 ones from 235. Put the 5 to the right of the 3 tens. You now have 35 ones.

```
      4
  5)235
    20
    ‾‾
    35
```

Step 3

How many groups of five can you make out of 35 ones?
$7 \times 5 = 35$

You can make seven groups of 5 ones.

Put the 7 above the 5 of 235 (to the right of the 4). Put the 35 below the 35.

```
     47
  5)235
    20
    ‾‾
    35
    35
    ‾‾
```

Step 4

Subtract 35 from 35. You do not have a remainder.

```
     47
  5)235
    20
    ‾‾
    35
    35
    ‾‾
     0
```

$235 \div 5 = 47$

 Time to Try 1

Use an algorithm that uses place value to calculate 538 ÷ 2.
Show your work.

AN ALGORITHM THAT USES ESTIMATION

Another way to divide is to estimate how many sets or groups you can make out of the total number. Remember that estimates will usually end in zeros. The estimates are written on the right side of the algorithm.

 Example

Divide 235 by 5.

$5\overline{)235}$

Solution

The algorithm you use could look like this:

```
5)235  | 40
  200  |
   35  | +7
   35  |
    0  | 47
```

Step 1
Round 235 to the nearest hundred.
$235 \rightarrow 200$

Make an estimate of how many groups of 5 there are in 200.

Since there are 20 groups of 5 in 100, a good estimate would be 40 groups of 5 in 200. $(40 \times 5 = 200)$

Put 40 on the right side of the line by the dividend 235.
Put 200 below 235, and subtract.
$235 - 200 = 35$

Step 2
Make an estimate of how many groups of 5 there are in 35.
$7 \times 5 = 35$

You can make 7 groups of 5 out of 35.

Put the 7 on the right side of the line by the 35.
Put the 35 below the 35, and subtract.

There is no remainder.

Step 3
Add the two estimates to find the quotient.
$40 + 7 = 47$

$235 \div 5 = 47$

 Time to Try 2

Use an algorithm that uses estimation to calculate $455 \div 7$.
Show your work.

PRACTICE EXERCISES

Use an algorithm that uses place value to solve each of the following expressions.
Show your work.

1. $624 \div 2$

2. $245 \div 5$

Use an algorithm that uses estimation to solve each of the following expressions.
Show your work.

3. $112 \div 7$

4. $594 \div 6$

Lesson 3   EXPRESSING REMAINDERS AS PART OF THE QUOTIENT

NOTES

Sometimes, you are not able to make equal groups when you divide. The part that is left over is called a **remainder**.

The remainder part of the quotient can be expressed in the following ways:
- As a whole number
- As a fraction
- As a decimal

AS A WHOLE NUMBER

When expressing a remainder as a whole number, the capital letter R is used to represent the word *remainder*.
- Write the quotient.
- Write the letter R to the right of the quotient.
- Write the remainder to the right of the letter R.

 Example

Calculate $147 \div 2$, showing your work.
Using a whole number, express the remainder as part of the quotient.

Solution

Step 1
Choose a strategy to divide 147 by 2.
The expression can be solved using an algorithm that uses place value.

$$
\begin{array}{r}
73 \\
2\overline{)147} \\
14 \\
\overline{07} \\
6 \\
\overline{1}
\end{array}
$$

Step 2
Express the remainder as part of the quotient using a whole number.
$147 \div 2 = 73$ R1

 Time to Try 1

Calculate $397 \div 6$, showing your work.
Using a whole number, express the remainder as part of the quotient.

238

AS A FRACTION

When expressing the remainder as a fraction, write the remainder above the divisor. The remainder becomes the numerator, and the divisor becomes the denominator.

$$\frac{\text{numerator}}{\text{denominator}} = \frac{\text{remainder}}{\text{divisor}}$$

 Example

Calculate $489 \div 5$, showing your work.
Using a fraction, express the remainder as part of the quotient.

Solution

Step 1
Choose a strategy to divide 489 by 5.

This expression can be solved using an algorithm that uses estimation.

```
5)489 | 90
  450
   39 | + 7
   35
    4 | 97
```

Step 2
Express the remainder as part of the quotient using a fraction.

$$489 \div 5 = 97\frac{4}{5}$$

 Time to Try 2

Calculate $853 \div 2$, showing your work.
Using a fraction, express the remainder as part of the quotient.

NOTES

AS A DECIMAL

One way to express a remainder as a decimal is to write the fraction remainder as an equivalent decimal.

 Example

Calculate $447 \div 4$, showing your work.
Using a decimal, express the remainder as part of the quotient.

Solution

Step 1

Choose a strategy to divide 447 by 4.

This expression can be solved using an algorithm that uses estimation.

$$
\begin{array}{r|l}
4\overline{)447} & 100 \\
\underline{400} & \\
47 & 10 \\
\underline{40} & \\
7 & +1 \\
\underline{4} & \\
3 & \overline{111}
\end{array}
$$

Step 2

Express the remainder as a fraction.

$$447 \div 4 = 111\frac{3}{4}$$

Step 3

Express the fraction as an equivalent decimal.

$$\frac{3}{4} = 0.75$$

$$447 \div 4 = 111.75$$

 Time to Try 3

Calculate $925 \div 2$, showing your work.
Using a decimal, express the remainder as part of the quotient.

AS A DECIMAL WITH WHOLE NUMBER MONEY AMOUNTS

When dividing whole number money amounts, like $3, you can rewrite the amount as a dollar and cents value.
$3 → $3.00

When you divide the dollar and cents value, the remainder becomes the decimal number.

 Example

If Lexie paid $7 for 4 kg of apples, how much did 1 kg of apples cost?

Show your work, expressing the remainder as a decimal.

Solution

Step 1
Write $7 as a dollar and cents amount.
$7 → $7.00

Step 2
Divide $7.00 by 4

```
      1.75
   4)7.00
     4
     ──
     30
     28
     ──
      20
      20
      ──
       0
```

The cost of 1 kg of apples is $1.75.

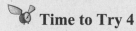 **Time to Try 4**

Kyra paid $9 for two identical T-shirts. How much did each T-shirt cost?

Show your work, expressing the remainder as a decimal.

PRACTICE EXERCISES

1. Calculate $158 \div 3$, showing your work. Using a whole number, express the remainder as part of the quotient.

2. Calculate $175 \div 3$, showing your work. Using a fraction, express the remainder as part of the quotient.

3. Calculate $846 \div 4$, showing your work. Using a decimal, express the remainder as part of the quotient.

4. The cost of four pens is $5. Determine the cost of one pen. Show your work, expressing the remainder as a decimal.

Lesson 4 INTERPRETING REMAINDERS WHEN SOLVING PROBLEMS

The interpretation of the remainder depends on the context of the problem. For some types of problems, you may need to:

- ignore the remainder
- round up the quotient
- keep the remainder as the answer

IGNORING THE REMAINDER

These kinds of problems usually involve practical situations in which you are making teams with equal groups or are sharing items in equal groups. It does not make sense to break up the remainder, so the remainder is ignored.

 Example

Mr. Kairns was placing every five students into a team for a relay race. If 102 students showed up, what is the **greatest** number of teams that could be made? Explain your answer.

Solution

Step 1
Divide 102 by 5.

```
      20
  5 ) 102
      10
      ---
      02
       0
      ---
       2
```

Step 2
Determine the greatest number of equal teams.

Since the quotient is 20, the greatest number of teams that can be made is 20 teams.

Step 3
Explain your answer.

There are not enough students to make another group of 5, so the 2 students left over cannot be part of a team.

The remainder cannot be part of the answer, so it needs to be ignored.

NOTES

 Time to Try 1

Seven boys want to share 278 trading cards equally.

What is the **greatest** number of cards each boy can have?
Explain your answer.

ROUNDING UP THE QUOTIENT

These kinds of problems usually involve situations where you need
to purchase items that are sold in packs, or when you are making
accommodations for a designated number of people.

Since you cannot break up the packs and need to keep the designated
number of people together, it makes sense to round up the quotient.

 Example

Mrs. Muchler wants to buy a Halloween pencil for each one of the
127 students attending Grade 1 in her school. The local store sells
Halloween pencils in packages of eight.

How many packages does Mrs. Muchler need to buy so every
Grade 1 student receives a pencil? Explain your answer.

Solution

Step 1
Divide 127 by 8.

```
      15
  8)127
      8
      47
      40
       7
```

Step 2
Determine the number of packages needed.

If Mrs. Muchler only bought 15 packages (the quotient),
7 students (the remainder) would not get pencils.

The quotient needs to be rounded up to 16 so that there will be
enough pencils for each student.

Mrs. Muchler needs to buy 16 packages of pencils.

Time to Try 2

A total of 123 children from one school are waiting to take their places in carts for a ride through the park. The attendant at the park places six children in each cart.

How many carts are needed so that all 123 children can go for their cart ride at the same time? Explain your answer.

THE REMAINDER AS THE ANSWER

These kinds of problems ask questions where the remainder, not the quotient, is the answer to the problem.

 Example

Jonathan puts 249 hockey cards into his new card binder. Each page in the binder has eight pockets.

If Jonathan starts with the first page and puts one card in each pocket, how many cards will he put on the last page that he uses? Explain your answer.

Solution

Step 1
Divide 249 by 8.

```
     31
8)249
    24
    ──
    09
     8
    ──
     1
```

Step 2
Determine the number of cards on the last page used.

There will be 31 pages (the quotient) that will have eight cards on each page.

The remainder of 1 represents the one card that will need to be placed in the 32nd page.

Jonathan will place one card on the last page he uses.

NOTES

 Time to Try 3

Miss Janier has 163 photos to place into a photo album before the end of the year. She plans to put five photos on each page.

How many photos will Miss Janier place on the last page?
Explain your answer.

PRACTICE EXERCISES

Use the following information to answer the next question.

Miss Lewis was organizing teams to run three-legged races. As the students arrived for the practice, she placed three students on each team.

1. If 100 students showed up, what is the **greatest** number of teams that could be made? Explain your answer.

2. A farmer has 135 chickens. If each cage holds six chickens, how many cages will the farmer need to hold all 135 chickens? Explain your answer.

Use the following information to answer the next question.

Miss Martin gave Kara 180 pencils to sort into seven pencil cases. Kara needs to place an equal number of pencils into the seven pencil cases.

3. How many of the 180 pencils will **not** be placed into pencil cases? Explain your answer.

Lesson 5 *SOLVING 3-DIGIT BY 1-DIGIT DIVISION PROBLEMS*

When a problem involves a total number and either the number of equal groups or the number in each group is given, you can divide to calculate the missing information.

When solving division problems, use the strategy that works best for you.

✷✷✷ Example

There were 264 people aboard a train. Two people shared each seat. How many seats were needed for all 264 people? Show your work.

Solution

Step 1

Choose a strategy to divide 264 by 2.

An example of a strategy you can use is base ten blocks. This would be a good strategy because each place value can easily be divided into two equal groups.

Step 2

Show your work.

Represent 264 with base ten blocks.

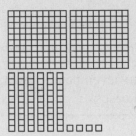

Place the hundreds into two equal groups.
Place the tens into two equal groups.
Place the ones into two equal groups

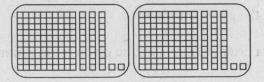

Each group has 1 hundred flat (100), 3 ten rods (30), and 2 units (2).
$100 + 30 + 2 = 132$

$264 \div 2 = 132$

A total of 132 seats were needed to seat 264 people.

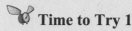 **Time to Try 1**

A total of 244 people attended a special farewell lunch for a friend. If four people sat at each table, how many tables were used?

SOLVING PROBLEMS YOU CREATE

You can also solve division problems that you create. Remember to start with a total and either the number of groups or the number in each group.

To solve the problems you create, use whatever strategy works best for you.

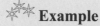 **Example**

The total is 456. There are nine in each group.

Use the given information to create a division problem. Solve the problem, showing your work.

Solution

Step 1
Write a problem using the given information.

Here is an example of a problem that uses the given information:

Molly has 456 stickers. She plans to place nine stickers on each page of her sticker book. How many pages will Molly need to use to place all of her stickers in the book?

NOTES

Step 2
Calculate $456 \div 9$ using a strategy that works for you.

Here is an example of calculating using an estimation algorithm:

$$9\overline{)456} \quad \begin{array}{r} 50 \\ \underline{450} \\ 6 \end{array} \quad \begin{array}{r} 50 \\ \underline{+0} \\ 50 \end{array}$$

Step 3
Solve the problem.

The quotient tells you that there will be 50 pages used with nine stickers on each page.

The remainder tells you that an extra page is needed because there are six stickers left over that need to be placed in the book. The quotient needs to be rounded up.

Molly will need to use 51 pages.

 Time to Try 2
There is a total of 224. There are seven groups.

Use the given information to create a division problem. Solve the problem, showing your work.

PRACTICE EXERCISES

1. A librarian places an equal number of books on each shelf of a five-tier bookshelf. If there are 350 books in total, how many books are on each shelf? Show your work.

2. James has 436 counting chips to sort equally into four groups. How many counting chips will be placed into each group? Show your work.

3. The total is 255. There are eight in each group. Use the given information to create a division problem. Solve the problem you wrote, showing your work.

REVIEW SUMMARY

- The division process involves equal sharing.
- Equal sharing can be modelled using hundred flats, ten rods, and units.
- To regroup base ten blocks, remember that 1 hundred flat is equivalent to 10 ten rods, and 1 ten rod is equivalent to 10 units.
- An algorithm is a step-by-step plan for calculating quotients.
- One type of algorithm uses estimation.
- Another type of algorithm uses place value.
- When using a place value algorithm, it is important where you put the first digit of the quotient.
  - If the divisor is equal to or less than the hundreds digit of the dividend, place the first digit of the quotient above the hundreds digit.
  - If the divisor is greater than the hundreds digit of the dividend, place the first digit of the quotient above the tens digit.
- A remainder is expressed as part of the quotient: as a whole number, as a fraction, or as a decimal.
- The interpretation of a remainder depends on the context of the problem.
- A remainder can be part of the quotient, it can be ignored, it can cause the quotient to be rounded up, or it can be the answer.
- If a problem involves a total number of items and an equal number of groups, the problem can be solved using division.
- If a problem involves a total number of items and the number of equal items in each group, the problem can be solved using division.
- There is no one correct way of dividing to solve a problem. You should use whatever strategy gives you the greatest success.

PRACTICE TEST

1. Use an algorithm that uses estimation to calculate $936 \div 9$. Explain your work.

2. Use an algorithm that uses place value to calculate $346 \div 2$. Show your work.

3. Calculate $507 \div 7$, showing your work. Using a fraction, express the remainder as part of the quotient.

4. Calculate $495 \div 4$, showing your work. Using a decimal, express the remainder as part of the quotient.

5. A coach has $136 to buy hot dogs for the team party. Each hot dog costs $3. What is the maximum number of hot dogs the coach can buy? Explain your answer.

6. Tara is packing candles in boxes. She can fit eight candles into each box. How many boxes does Tara need to pack 218 candles? Explain your answer.

7. John has 140 phone numbers written in his pocket diary. Every page but the last page has nine phone numbers written on it. How many phone numbers are written on the last page?

8. To show the division process of equal sharing, solve $235 \div 2$ using base ten blocks. Express the remainder as whole number.

2-D SHAPES AND 3-D OBJECTS

When you are finished this unit, you will be able to…

- identify parallel, intersecting, perpendicular, vertical, and horizontal line segments in the environment
- describe sides on 2-D shapes as parallel, intersecting, perpendicular, vertical, or horizontal
- describe faces on 3-D objects as parallel, intersecting, perpendicular, vertical, or horizontal
- describe edges on 3-D objects as parallel, intersecting, perpendicular, vertical, or horizontal
- draw shapes and objects to illustrate given line segments
- describe attributes of quadrilaterals
- use attributes to sort quadrilaterals
- determine the sorting rule used for a given set of sorted quadrilaterals

PREREQUISITE SKILLS AND KNOWLEDGE

Prior to starting this unit, you should be able to…

- describe 2-D shapes according to their sides
- describe 3-D objects according to the shapes of the faces
- describe 3-D objects according to the number of edges and vertices
- sort polygons (including quadrilaterals) according to the number of sides

Lesson 1 IDENTIFYING AND DESCRIBING LINE SEGMENTS IN THE ENVIRONMENT

A line is a set of points that continue in both directions. A line is usually shown with an arrow at each end.

A line segment is part of a line. It has two endpoints, so a line segment can be measured. The endpoints are sometimes shown with two points.

Lines and line segments can be described as horizontal, vertical, intersecting, perpendicular, or parallel.

HORIZONTAL LINES

A horizontal line goes straight across, like the horizon. It moves in a left-right direction.

There are many examples of horizontal line segments in the environment. For example, the layers of blankets in this picture create a set of horizontal line segments.

✳ **Example**

Shabir sees four different kinds of fences as he walks home from school.

W　　　X　　　Y　　　Z

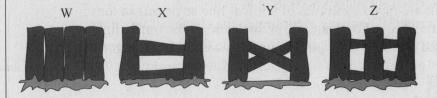

Are any of the fences examples of horizontal line segments in the environment? Justify your answer.

Solution

Step 1
Identify the horizontal line segments.

Fence X and fence Z are both examples of horizontal line segments in the environment.

Step 2
Justify your answer.

A horizontal line is one that runs straight across, like the horizon. Fence X and fence Z both have boards that run across, in the left-right direction shown by this horizontal line.

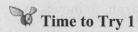

Time to Try 1

Ryder's homework assignment was to find an example of horizontal line segments in the environment. He used these pictures of tree bark as his example.

Are these pictures of tree bark an example of horizontal line segments? Justify your answer.

VERTICAL LINES

A vertical line goes straight up and down.

There are many examples of vertical line segments in the environment. For example, in this picture, the traffic lights are placed one above the other, forming a vertical line segment.

Example

As two friends walk along the lakeshore, looking for examples of line segments in the environment, they spot four large trees.

Are the trunks of the trees an example of vertical lines? Justify your answer.

Solution

Yes, the tree trunks are examples of vertical lines because they go straight up and down like the vertical line shown.

Time to Try 2

Josh watches this man parachute. Josh likes the way the parachute makes a design with its striped colours and lines.

Describe the lines of the parachute.

PARALLEL LINES

Parallel lines are lines that run side by side, always remaining the exact same distance apart. The lines will never meet or cross each other. Parallel lines do not need to be equal in length in order to be parallel.

The following diagram shows horizontal parallel lines, vertical parallel lines, and diagonal parallel lines.

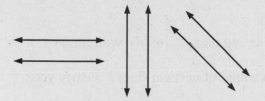

There are many examples of parallel line segments in the environment, such as the rails on a railway track. The rails must always be the same distance apart so that the wheels of a train can keep moving on them.

✳ Example

In one school, some students drew designs on boxes for the grade one students to colour. Three boxes are shown.

J   K   L

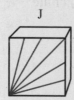 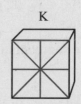 

Which box is decorated with parallel lines? Justify your answer.

Solution

Step 1
Identify the box decorated with parallel lines.

Box L is decorated with parallel lines.

Step 2
Justify your answer

The lines in box L are parallel lines because they are the same distance apart from each other at all points. Parallel line segments do not need to be the same length.

🌸 Time to Try 3

Linda takes a picture of this fence to show the class an example of parallel line segments.

Does the fence have parallel line segments? Justify your answer.

INTERSECTING LINES

Intersecting lines are lines that cross. They cross at a point, or vertex.

There are many examples of intersecting line segments in the environment.

For example, this map shows how the railroad track and the Trans-Canada Highway intersect each other. The road to Banff also intersects with the Trans-Canada highway, even though it does not actually cross it. The two roads still meet at a vertex.

A Road Map

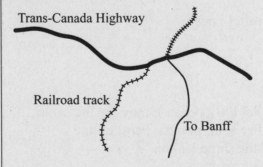

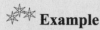 **Example**

Dayton drew a picture of a house. He highlighted two lines on the roof of the house to illustrate intersecting lines.

Are the bolded lines intersecting line segments? Justify your answer.

Solution

Yes, the bolded lines are intersecting line segments.

The bolded diagonal line segment meets the bolded horizontal line segment at a vertex, forming an angle, so the pair of line segments are examples of intersecting lines.

 **Time to Try 4**

When the phone rang, James laid down the scissors he was using and answered the phone. This is what the scissors looked like when James laid them down.

What kind of line segment do the scissors represent? Explain your answer.

PERPENDICULAR LINES

When two intersecting lines cross to form square corners at the vertex, the lines are called perpendicular lines. The square corners can also be called right angles or 90° angles.

This diagram shows a vertical line and a horizontal line crossing each other to form four square corners where they cross.

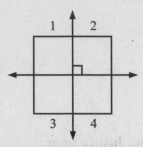

Lines do not have to be vertical and horizontal to cross at 90° angles. This diagram shows two diagonal lines crossing to form square corners at the vertex.

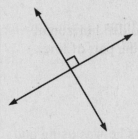

There are many examples of perpendicular line segments in the environment. For example, all rectangular boxes, like the cereal box shown, have square corners. Each square corner is made from a horizontal line and a vertical line intersecting.

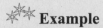 **Example**

Marc Andre sees this Railroad Crossing sign every day when his dad drives him home from school.

Identify the lines formed by the bars of the sign. Justify your answer.

Solution

The bars cross to form perpendicular lines.

The two bars of the Railroad Crossing sign form square corners (90° angles) at the vertex where they intersect.

Time to Try 5

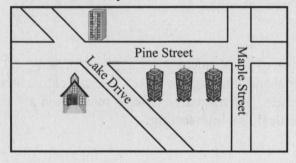

Which of the roads shown on the road map are examples of perpendicular line segments? Justify your answer.

PRACTICE EXERCISES

Identify the line segments seen in each of the following pictures. Justify your answers.

1. Pillars

2. Roads

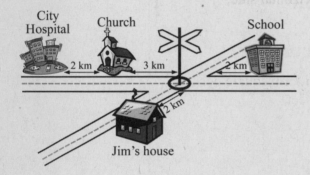

3. Railway Crossing sign

4. Crosswalk

264

Lesson 2   USING LINE SEGMENTS TO DESCRIBE SIDES OF 2-D SHAPES

All the sides of 2-D shapes are line segments.

HORIZONTAL SIDES

You can describe sides on 2-D shapes as horizontal if the sides run straight across in a left-right direction.

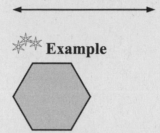

✳ **Example**

How many horizontal sides does the given hexagon have?
Verify your answer by placing an X on each horizontal side.

Solution
The given hexagon has two horizontal sides, as shown.

🐝 **Time to Try 1**

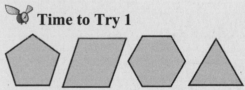

How many horizontal sides are there in total in the given 2-D shapes?
Verify your answer by placing a tick on each horizontal side.

NOTES

VERTICAL SIDES

You can describe sides on 2-D shapes as vertical if the sides run straight up and down.

 Example

How many vertical sides are there in the given octagon? Verify your answer by placing an X on each vertical side.

Solution

There are two vertical sides on the given octagon, as shown.

Time to Try 2

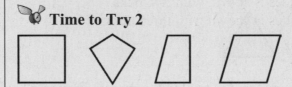

How many vertical sides are there in total in the given 2-D shapes? Verify your answer by placing an X on each vertical side.

PARALLEL SIDES

You can describe sides on 2-D shapes as parallel if the sides are opposite each other and are exactly the same distance from each other. The sides may or may not be the same length.

  Example

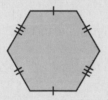

How many pairs of parallel sides are there in the given hexagon? Verify your answer by placing a different number of ticks on each pair of parallel sides.

Solution

There are three pairs of parallel sides in the given hexagon, as shown.

One pair of parallel sides is shown with one tick.
One pair of parallel sides is shown with two ticks.
One pair of parallel sides is shown with three ticks.

Time to Try 3

How many pairs of parallel sides are there in total in the given 2-D shapes? Verify your answer by marking each pair of parallel sides with a different number of ticks.

INTERSECTING SIDES

You can describe sides on 2-D shapes as intersecting if the sides meet at a vertex.

✳ Example

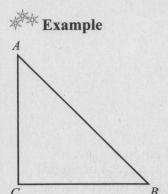

How many pairs of intersecting sides are there in the triangle? Explain your answer by describing the sides that intersect.

Solution

There are three pairs of intersecting sides.
- Sides *CA* and *AB* intersect at vertex *A*.
- Sides *AB* and *BC* intersect at vertex *B*.
- Sides *BC* and *CA* intersect at vertex *C*.

🐛 Time to Try 4

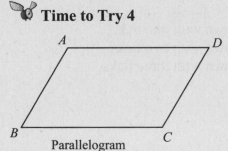

Parallelogram

How many pairs of intersecting sides are there in the parallelogram? Explain your answer by describing the sides that intersect.

PERPENDICULAR SIDES

You can describe sides on 2-D shapes as perpendicular if a horizontal side and a vertical side intersect to form a square corner or 90° angle.

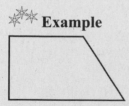 **Example**

How many pairs of perpendicular sides are there in the given trapezoid? Verify your answer by drawing square corners where the perpendicular sides meet.

Solution

There are two pairs of perpendicular sides.

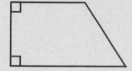

- The top horizontal side and the left vertical side meet at a square corner.
- The bottom horizontal side and the left vertical side meet at a square corner.

Time to Try 5

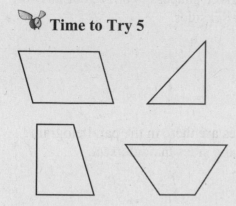

How many pairs of perpendicular sides are there in total in the given 2-D shapes? Verify your answer by drawing a square where the perpendicular sides meet.

PRACTICE EXERCISES

1. In total, how many horizontal sides are there in the given shapes? Verify your answer by placing an X on each horizontal side.

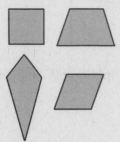

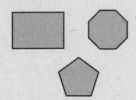

2. In total, how many vertical sides are there in the given shapes? Verify your answer by placing a tick on each vertical side.

3. In total, how many pairs of parallel sides are there in the given shapes? Verify your answer by placing a different number of ticks on each pair of parallel sides.

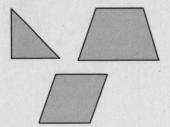

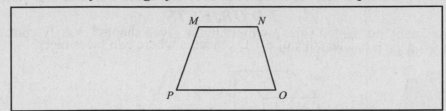

Use the following information to answer the next question.

4. How many pairs of intersecting sides are there in trapezoid *MNOP*? Explain your answer by describing the sides that intersect.

5. How many perpendicular sides does the given figure have? Verify your answer by drawing square corners where the perpendicular sides meet.

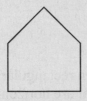

Lesson 3   USING LINE SEGMENTS TO DESCRIBE EDGES OF 3-D OBJECTS

NOTES

The edge of a 3-D object is where two faces meet.

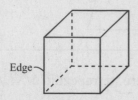

Edge

HORIZONTAL EDGES

You can describe edges on 3-D objects as horizontal if the edges run straight across in a left-right direction.

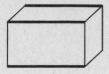

✳ **Example**

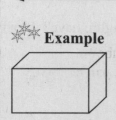

How many horizontal edges can be seen on the given rectangular prism? Verify your answer by bolding the edges that are horizontal.

Solution

Three horizontal edges can be seen, as shown by the bolded lines on this figure.

Time to Try 1

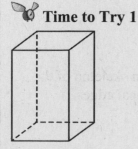

How many horizontal edges can be seen in the given skeleton of a rectangular prism? Verify your answer by bolding the edges that are horizontal.

VERTICAL EDGES

You can describe edges on 3-D objects as vertical if the edges run straight up and down.

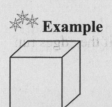 **Example**

How many vertical edges can be seen on the given cube?
Verify your answer by bolding the vertical edges that can be seen.

Solution

Three vertical edges can be seen, as shown by the bolded lines on this figure.

Time to Try 2

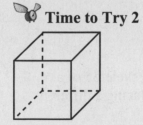

How many vertical edges can be seen on the given skeleton of the cube? Verify your answer by bolding all the vertical edges.

PARALLEL EDGES

You can describe edges on 3-D objects as parallel if the edges are exactly the same distance apart and will never meet or intersect.

✳✳ **Example**

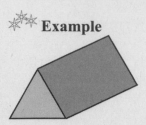

How many parallel edges can be seen in the given triangular prism? Verify your answer by placing a different number of ticks on each pair of parallel edges seen.

Solution

There are two pairs of parallel edges that can be seen. Both pairs are located on the rectangular face, as shown.

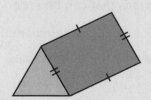

🐝 **Time to Try 3**

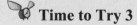
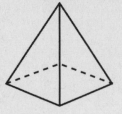

How many pairs of parallel edges are there in the skeleton of a square-based pyramid? Verify your answer by placing a different number of ticks on each pair of parallel edges.

INTERSECTING EDGES

You can describe edges on 3-D objects as intersecting if the edges meet at a vertex.

✸✸ **Example**

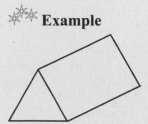

Show two pairs of intersecting edges on the triangular prism by bolding the edges. Label the vertex of one pair of intersecting edges with an *R* and the vertex of the other pair with an *S*.

Solution

Remember, any edges that meet at a vertex are intersecting edges, so there are many possibilities for you to choose from.

This diagram shows two pairs of intersecting edges bolded and labelled.

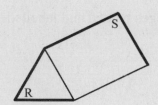
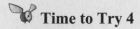

🐝 **Time to Try 4**

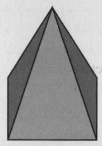

Pyramid

Show two pairs of intersecting edges on the given pyramid by bolding the edges. Label the vertex of one pair of intersecting edges with an *X* and the vertex of the other pair with a *Z*.

PERPENDICULAR EDGES

You can describe edges on 3-D objects as perpendicular if a horizontal edge meets a vertical edge to form a square corner or 90° angle.

✳ Example

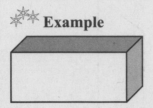

Show two pairs of perpendicular edges on the given rectangular prism by bolding the edges.

Label the vertex of one pair of perpendicular edges with an *X* and the vertex of the other pair with a *Z*.

Solution

Remember, any horizontal edge and vertical edge that meet at a vertex are perpendicular edges, so there are many possibilities for you to choose from.

This prism shows two perpendicular edges bolded and labelled.

🌿 Time to Try 5

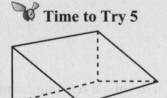

Show two pairs of perpendicular edges on the skeleton of the given triangular prism by drawing and shading squared corners at the vertices.

PRACTICE EXERCISES

Use the following information to answer the next two questions.

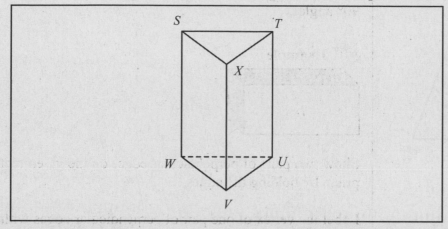

1. How many vertical edges are there in the triangular prism? Explain your answer by describing the vertical edges.

2. How many horizontal edges are there in the triangular prism? Explain your answer by describing the horizontal edges.

3. Identify any three pairs of parallel edges in the given rectangular prism. Verify your answer by placing a different number of ticks on each pair of parallel edges.

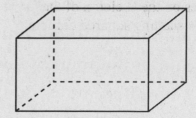

4. Show two pairs of intersecting edges on the pyramid by labelling the vertices where the edges intersect. Label the vertex of one pair of intersecting edges with an *M* and the vertex of the other pair with a *N*.

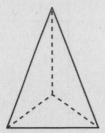

5. Show two pairs of perpendicular edges on the given trapezoidal prism by placing a square box at the vertex of the pairs of perpendicular edges.

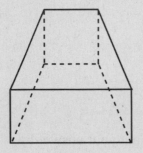

Lesson 4 USING LINE SEGMENTS TO DESCRIBE FACES OF 3-D OBJECTS

A face of a 3-D object is a flat surface of the object.

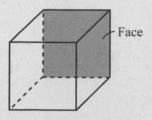

Face

HORIZONTAL FACES

You can describe faces on 3-D objects as horizontal if all the horizontal edges of the faces run straight across in a left-right direction. Horizontal faces are parallel with the flat surface of a floor.

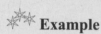

Example

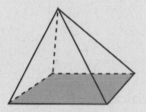

Square-based pyramid

Is the shaded face of the square-based pyramid a horizontal face? Explain your answer.

Solution

Yes, it is a horizontal face.

Since the horizontal lines of the shaded face run in a left-right direction and are parallel to the flat surface of the floor, it is a horizontal face.

NOTES

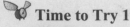

Time to Try 1

Is the shaded face of the cube a horizontal face? Explain your answer.

VERTICAL FACES

You can describe faces of 3-D objects as vertical if the faces have vertical edges that go straight up and down.

Example

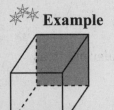

Is the shaded face of this rectangular prism a vertical face? Explain your answer.

Solution

Yes, the shaded face is a vertical face. A face can be described as vertical if the vertical edges of the face run straight up and down.

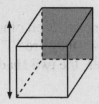

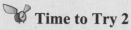

Time to Try 2

Are the shaded faces of this pentagonal prism vertical faces?
Explain your answer.

PARALLEL FACES

You can describe faces on 3-D objects as parallel if the faces
are identical and opposite each other and are exactly the same
distance apart.

Example

Ryder described the two shaded faces on the rectangular prism as
vertical parallel faces.

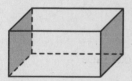

Is he correct? Justify your answer.

Solution

Yes, Ryder is correct when he describes the faces as vertical
parallel faces.

The two shaded faces are identical in shape, opposite each other,
and are exactly the same distance apart; therefore, they are
parallel faces. Since both faces are vertical faces, the two shaded
faces can be described as vertical parallel faces.

Time to Try 3

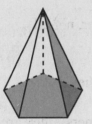

Hannah describes the two shaded faces are examples of parallel faces. Is Hannah correct? Justify your answer.

INTERSECTING FACES

You can describe faces on 3-D objects as intersecting if the faces share an edge and vertices.

Example

Explain why the two shaded faces of this pyramid can be described as intersecting faces.

Solution

The two shaded faces on the pyramid share an edge and two vertices. The faces intersect each other at the shared edge and vertices.

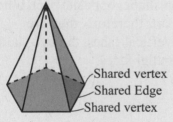

Shared vertex
Shared Edge
Shared vertex

Time to Try 4

Amber described the two shaded faces of the triangular prism as intersecting faces.

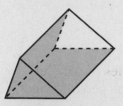

Triangular Prism

Is Amber correct? Justify your answer.

PERPENDICULAR FACES

You can describe faces on 3-D objects as perpendicular if a vertical face and a horizontal face share an edge and vertices that form 90° angles (square corners) where they intersect.

All perpendicular faces are intersecting faces. However, not all intersecting faces are perpendicular faces.

- If the faces intersect at 90° angles (square corners), they are described as perpendicular faces.
- If the faces do not intersect at 90° angles (square corners), they are described as intersecting faces.

NOTES

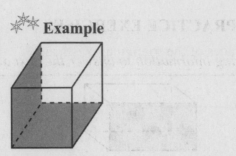

✳✳ Example

Explain why the shaded faces are better described as perpendicular faces instead of intersecting faces.

Solution

Although the shaded faces share a vertical edge and two vertices, the faces are described as perpendicular because they form square corners where they meet (intersect) each other.

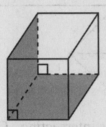

🐝 Time to Try 5

Jason describes the shaded faces on this rectangular prism as vertical perpendicular faces.

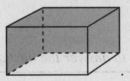

Is Jason correct? Justify your answer.

PRACTICE EXERCISES

Use the following information to answer the next question.

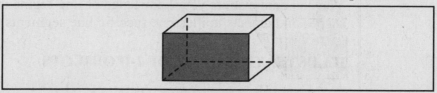

1. Is the shaded face on the rectangular prism a horizontal face or a vertical face? Justify your answer.

Use the following information to answer the next question.

Brett describes the shaded faces as intersecting. Carla describes them as perpendicular.

2. Who is correct? Justify your answer.

Use the following information to answer the next question.

Lora shaded two faces on the hexagonal prism to illustrate vertical faces.

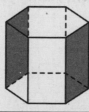

3. How else can the shaded faces be described? Justify your answer.

Lesson 5 *DRAWING SHAPES AND OBJECTS TO ILLUSTRATE LINE SEGMENTS*

NOTES

You can demonstrate your knowledge of line segments by drawing shapes and objects to illustrate specific line segments.

ILLUSTRATING SIDES OF 2-D OBJECTS

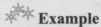 **Example**

Draw a rectangle. Bold a pair of perpendicular sides.

Solution

When a horizontal side and a vertical side intersect, forming square corners, you have a pair of perpendicular sides.

The rectangle you draw could look like this.

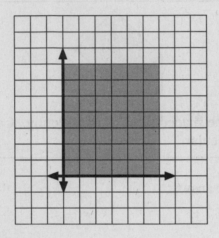

 Time to Try 1

Draw a triangle. Highlight a pair of intersecting sides.

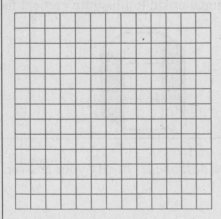

ILLUSTRATING EDGES ON 3-D OBJECTS

 Example

Draw a cube. Highlight a pair of parallel edges.

Solution

Edges that are parallel are opposite each other and are exactly the same distance apart. Your cube could look like this.

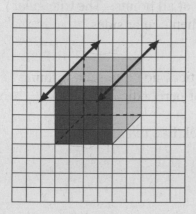

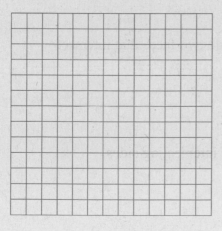 **Time to Try 2**

Draw a rectangular prism. Highlight two horizontal edges.

NOTES

ILLUSTRATING FACES ON 3-D OBJECTS

 Example

Draw a triangular prism. Shade two faces that are parallel to each other.

Solution

Parallel faces are identical faces that are opposite each other and are the exact same distance apart at all points. The triangular prism you draw could look like this.

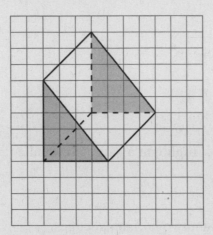

 Time to Try 3

Draw a square-based pyramid. Shade two faces that intersect each other.

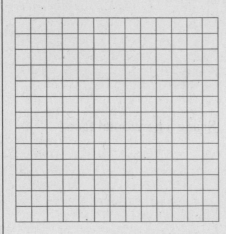

PRACTICE EXERCISES

1. Draw a parallelogram. Highlight a pair of parallel sides.

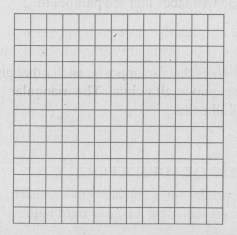

2. Draw a right triangular prism. Highlight a pair of vertical edges.

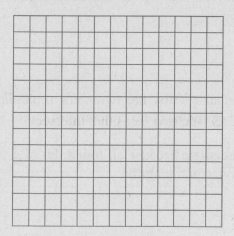

3. Draw a triangle-based pyramid. Shade a horizontal face.

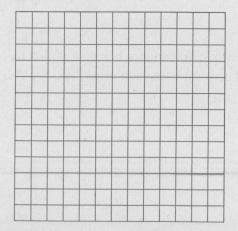

Lesson 6 ATTRIBUTES OF QUADRILATERALS

Quadrilaterals are closed, four-sided figures. All quadrilaterals have four straight sides, four vertices, and four angles.

Attributes of quadrilaterals are characteristics or properties that describe different quadrilaterals. Following are some attributes that can be used to describe quadrilaterals.
• Parallel lines
• Right angles
• Equal side lengths

DESCRIPTION OF SPECIFIC QUADRILATERALS

A **rectangle** has two pairs of parallel sides that are opposite each other, and are the same length. A rectangle has four right angles.

Rectangle

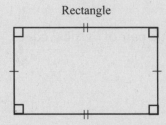

A **square** is like a rectangle because it also has two pairs of parallel sides that are opposite each other and has four right angles.

A square is a special type of rectangle because all four sides of a square are the same length (have equal length).

Square

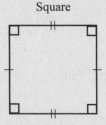

A **parallelogram** is like a rectangle and square because it also has two pairs of parallel sides that are opposite each other, and are the same length.

A parallelogram is different from a rectangle and square because it does not have any right angles.

Parallelogram

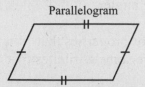

A **rhombus** is like a parallelogram, rectangle, and square because it also has two pairs of parallel sides that are opposite each other, and are the same length.

A rhombus is like a square because all four sides are equal in length.

A rhombus is different from both a rectangle and a square because a rhombus does not have any right angles.

Rhombus

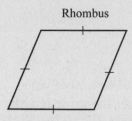

A **trapezoid** is different from a parallelogram, rectangle, rhombus, and square because a trapezoid only has one pair of parallel sides.

A trapezoid may or may not have right angles. The trapezoid shown here does not have a right angle

Trapezoid

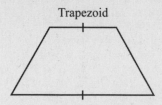

A **kite** is a quadrilateral that does not have any parallel sides, but has two pairs of equal side lengths.

A kite may or may not have a right angle. The kite shown here does not have a right angle.

NOTES

USING ATTRIBUTES TO IDENTIFY QUADRILATERALS

✳✳ **Example**

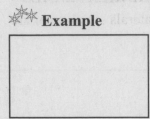

Identify the given quadrilateral by choosing the name that describes it: parallelogram, rectangle, square, rhombus, or trapezoid. Justify your answer.

Solution

Step 1
Identify the quadrilateral.

The quadrilateral shown is a rectangle.

Step 2
Justify your answer.

The quadrilateral is a rectangle because it has two pairs of sides that are opposite each other, are parallel, and are the same length. It also has four right angles (90° angles).

Rectangle

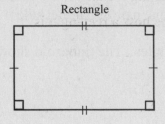

🐝 **Time to Try 1**

Identify the given quadrilateral by choosing the name that describes it: parallelogram, rectangle, square, rhombus, or trapezoid. Justify your answer.

USING ATTRIBUTES TO COMPARE QUADRILATERALS

You can use attributes to describe how quadrilaterals are alike or are different from each other.

✳ Example

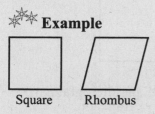

Square   Rhombus

Using attributes of quadrilaterals, describe how a square and a rhombus are alike.

Solution

A square and a rhombus share the following similarities:
- Both quadrilaterals have four sides of equal length.
- Both quadrilaterals have two pairs of parallel sides.

🐝 Time to Try 2

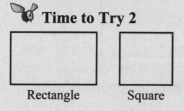

Rectangle   Square

Using attributes of quadrilaterals, describe how a rectangle is different from a square.

PRACTICE EXERCISES

Use the following information to answer the next question.

1. Identify the given quadrilateral by choosing the name that describes it: parallelogram, rectangle, square, rhombus, or trapezoid. Justify your answer.

Use the following information to answer the next question.

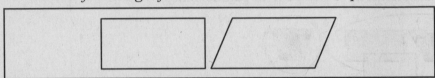

2. Using attributes of quadrilaterals, describe how a rectangle and a parallelogram are alike.

Use the following information to answer the next question.

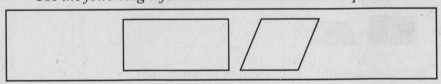

3. Using attributes of quadrilaterals, describe how a rectangle and a rhombus are alike.

Lesson 7   USING ATTRIBUTES TO SORT QUADRILATERALS

You can use specific attributes to sort quadrilaterals into groups. The attribute used becomes part of the sorting rule.

Most sorting rules are expressed in two parts. The first part of the sorting rule becomes the first group. The second part becomes the second group.

Example

Sort these quadrilaterals using the sorting rule "two pairs of parallel sides or fewer than two pairs of parallel sides".

Solution

This is how the quadrilaterals should be sorted:

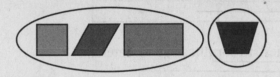

The first group has the square, rhombus, and rectangle because they all have two pairs of parallel sides.

The second group has the trapezoid because it only has one pair of parallel sides.

Time to Try 1

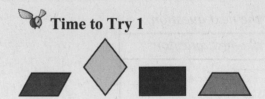

Use the sorting rule "all equal side lengths or not all equal side lengths" to sort the four quadrilaterals.

PRACTICE EXERCISES

Use the following information to answer the next question.

1. Use the sorting rule "parallel sides or no parallel sides" to sort these quadrilaterals.

Use the following information to answer the next question.

2. Use the sorting rule "right angles or no right angles" to sort these quadrilaterals.

Use the following information to answer the next question.

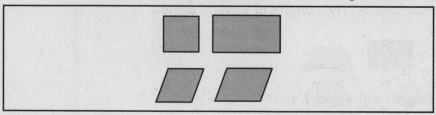

3. Use the sorting rule "two pairs of equal sides or all equal sides" to sort these quadrilaterals.

Lesson 8   DETERMINING SORTING RULES

To determine a sorting rule, examine the quadrilaterals in each group to identify which attribute was used to sort the shapes. The sorting rule is usually expressed in two parts with the word "or" between the two parts.

NOTES

✳ Example

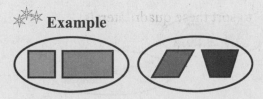

What sorting rule was used to sort these quadrilaterals?

Solution

Step 1
Compare the attributes of each group.

Group 1: Both shapes have four right angles and two pairs of parallel sides.

Group 2: Neither shape has right angles. One shape has two pairs of parallel sides. One shape has one pair of parallel sides.

Step 2
Determine the sorting rule used.

The attribute that makes the two groups different from each other is the number of right angles.

The sorting rule used is "right angles or no right angles."

🐝 Time to Try 1

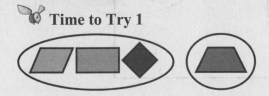

What sorting rule was used to sort these quadrilaterals?

PRACTICE EXERCISES

What sorting rule was used to sort the following quadrilaterals?

1.

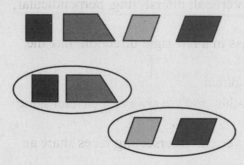

2.

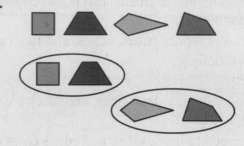

3.

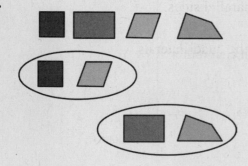

4.

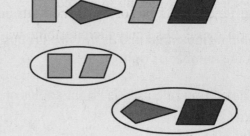

REVIEW SUMMARY

- A line is a set of points that continues in both directions.
- A line segment is part of a line.
- Lines and line segments can be described as horizontal, vertical, intersecting, perpendicular, or parallel.
- Horizontal lines, sides, edges, and faces go straight across in a left-right direction, like the horizon.
- Vertical lines, sides, edges, and faces go straight up and down.
- Parallel lines, sides, edges, and faces are opposite each other and are always the exact same distance apart.
- Intersecting lines, sides, and edges cross each other at a vertex. Intersecting faces share an edge and two vertices.
- Perpendicular lines, sides, edges, and faces cross each other at 90° angles (forming square corners).
- All quadrilaterals have four straight sides and four vertices.
- An attribute is a property or characteristic that describes a shape, such as the number of parallel sides or equal side lengths.
- A rectangle has two pairs of parallel sides and four right angles.
- A square has two pairs of parallel sides, four right angles, and four equal side lengths.
- A parallelogram has two pairs of parallel sides and no right angles.
- A rhombus has two pairs of parallel sides, four equal side lengths, and no right angles.
- A trapezoid has one pair of parallel sides and may or may not have right angles.
- A kite has two pairs of equal side lengths. It never has parallel sides.
- Quadrilaterals can be sorted by their attributes.
- A sorting rule tells you which attribute was used to sort the quadrilaterals.

PRACTICE TEST

1. How many horizontal sides does the given trapezoid have? Verify your answer by placing an X on each horizontal side.

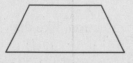

2. How many pairs of parallel sides are there in total in the three 2-D shapes? Verify your answer by marking each pair of parallel sides with a different number of ticks.

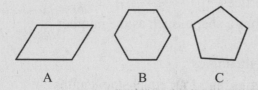

   A   B   C

3. How many pairs of perpendicular sides are there in total in the four 2-D shapes? Verify your answer by drawing squares where the perpendicular lines meet.

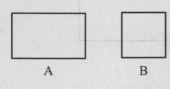

   A   B

   C   D

Use the following information to answer the next question.

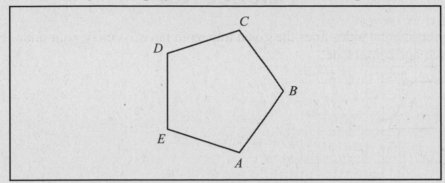

4. How many pairs of intersecting sides are there in a regular pentagon? Explain your answer by describing the sides that intersect.

Use the following information to answer the next question.

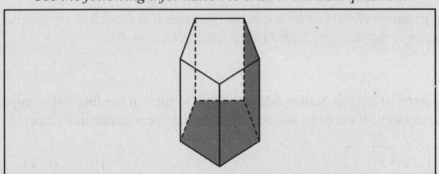

5. Describe the two shaded faces on the prism.

6. Shade a vertical face on the figure.

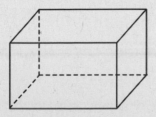

7.   Draw a cube. Highlight a pair of perpendicular edges.

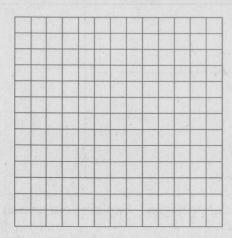

Use the following information to answer the next question.

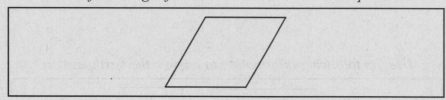

8.   Identify the given quadrilateral by choosing the name that describes it: parallelogram, rectangle, square, rhombus, or trapezoid. Justify your answer.

Use the following information to answer the next question.

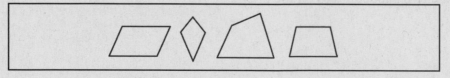

9.   Use the sorting rule "parallel sides or no parallel sides" to sort these quadrilaterals. Explain your sorting.

Use the following information to answer the next question.

Marnie sorted these quadrilaterals into two groups.

10. What sorting rule did Marnie use? Explain your answer.

Use the following information to answer the next question.

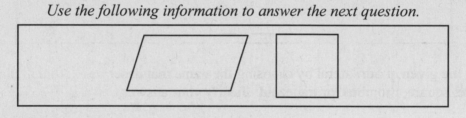

11. Using attributes of quadrilaterals, describe how a parallelogram and a square are alike.

NOTES

304

FRACTIONS AND DECIMALS

When you are finished this unit, you will be able to…
- explain why equivalent fractions represent the same quantity
- use rules for developing equivalent fractions
- create sets of equivalent fractions
- compare two fractions with unlike denominators, by creating equivalent fractions
- compare and order fractions on a number line
- represent decimals to thousandths with base ten blocks
- express decimals as equivalent decimals
- describe the value of each digit in a decimal number
- order decimals by using place value, equivalent decimals, or number line with benchmarks
- relate decimals to fractions and fractions to decimals

PREREQUISITE SKILLS AND KNOWLEDGE

Prior to starting this unit, you should be able to…
- name and record fractions for the parts of a whole or a set
- compare and order fractions
- understand that two identical fractions may not represent the same quantity
- represent and describe decimals to tenths and hundredths

Lesson 1   REPRESENTING THE SAME QUANTITY WITH EQUIVALENT FRACTIONS

NOTES

Equivalent fractions are fractions that represent the same part of a whole or the same part of a set.

 Example

The following two same size diagrams show the same amount of space shaded.

 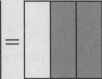

Write two equivalent fractions to represent the shaded parts of the diagrams.

Solution

The first diagram shows six out of nine parts shaded.

$\dfrac{6}{9}$

The second diagram shows two out of three parts shaded.

$\dfrac{2}{3}$

Since both diagrams represent the same shaded quantity, the fractions $\dfrac{6}{9}$ and $\dfrac{2}{3}$ are equivalent fractions.

$$\dfrac{6}{9} = \dfrac{2}{3}$$

 Time to Try 1

Kalan is asked to write two equivalent fractions that represent the shaded parts of the following set of shapes.

What two fractions could Kalan write?

USING FRACTION STRIP CHARTS

A fraction strip chart will help you see how certain fractions are equivalent. In a fraction strip chart, the segments that line up will indicate which fractions are equivalent.

✳ Example

$\frac{1}{2}$					$\frac{1}{2}$				

The fraction strip chart shows strips for $\frac{1}{2}$, $\frac{1}{4}$, $\frac{1}{6}$, $\frac{1}{8}$, and $\frac{1}{10}$.

Using the given fraction strip chart, write four fractions that are equivalent to the fraction $\frac{1}{2}$.

Solution

To determine the equivalent fractions, count the number of segments for each strip that lines up with $\frac{1}{2}$. The number of segments that line up will be the numerator, and the total number of segments for that strip will be the denominator.

The equivalent fractions are $\frac{1}{2} = \frac{2}{4} = \frac{3}{6} = \frac{4}{8} = \frac{5}{10}$.

🦋 Time to Try 2

Use the fraction chart to identify a fraction that is equivalent to $\frac{6}{8}$.

Explain how you used the fraction chart.

NOTES

DRAWING DIAGRAMS TO SHOW EQUIVALENT FRACTIONS

You can draw diagrams like fraction wheels or fraction strips to explain the relationship between equivalent fractions.

 Example

The fraction $\dfrac{4}{10}$ represents the shaded parts of this fraction wheel.

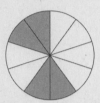

Draw another same size fraction wheel to show an equivalent fraction to $\dfrac{4}{10}$.

Solution

Draw a wheel that has five parts instead of 10 parts. Shade the same parts on the second wheel that correspond to the shaded parts on the first wheel.

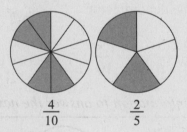

$$\frac{4}{10} \qquad \frac{2}{5}$$

The two wheels show that $\dfrac{4}{10}$ and $\dfrac{2}{5}$ are equivalent fractions because they both represent the same amount of shaded area.

 Time to Try 3

Draw two fraction strips to help you explain the relationship between the fractions $\dfrac{3}{5}$ and $\dfrac{6}{10}$.
Be sure to label the fraction strips.

PRACTICE EXERCISES

Use the following information to answer the next question.

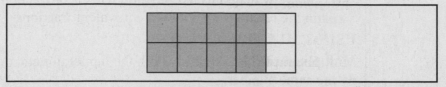

1. Write two equivalent fractions to represent the shaded area of the given figure.

Use the following information to answer the next question.

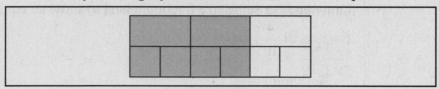

2. Identify the equivalent fractions represented by the shaded parts of the two fraction strips. Justify your answer by labelling the fraction strips.

Use the following information to answer the next question.

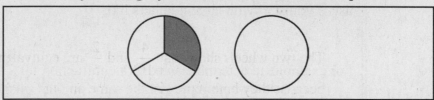

3. Write the fraction represented by the shaded part of the fraction wheel. Draw a fraction wheel to show an equivalent fraction. Write the new fraction that is equivalent to the first fraction.

Lesson 2 RULES FOR DEVELOPING EQUIVALENT FRACTIONS

NOTES

You can create equivalent fractions through multiplication or division.

USING MULTIPLICATION

Multiplication rule: Multiply both the numerator and denominator by the same number.

When multiplying the numerator and denominator by the same number, the relationship will always stay the same. Multiplication is the strategy to use when you start with small numbers like $\frac{1}{3}$.

For example, to determine an equivalent fraction for $\frac{1}{3}$, multiply the numerator (1) by 3 and the denominator (3) by 3.

$$\frac{1 \times 3 = 3}{3 \times 3 = 9}$$
$$\frac{1}{3} = \frac{3}{9}$$

USING DIVISION

Division rule: Divide both the numerator and denominator by the same number.

When dividing the numerator and denominator by the same number, the relationship will always stay the same. Division is the strategy to use if you start with large numbers like $\frac{16}{24}$.

For example, to determine an equivalent fraction for $\frac{16}{24}$, you can divide the numerator (16) by 4, and the denominator (24) by 4.

$$\frac{16 \div 4 = 4}{24 \div 4 = 6}$$
$$\frac{16}{24} = \frac{4}{6}$$

PRACTICE EXERCISES

Apply the multiplication rule to create an equivalent fraction for each of the following fractions. Show your work.

1. $\dfrac{2}{3}$

2. $\dfrac{4}{5}$

Apply the division rule to create an equivalent fraction for each of the following fractions. Show your work.

3. $\dfrac{10}{15}$

4. $\dfrac{16}{24}$

Lesson 3   CREATING SETS OF EQUIVALENT FRACTIONS

One way to create a set of equivalent fractions is to start by multiplying or dividing the numerator and denominator by the same number. Then repeat the process over and over (using the same number).

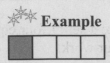 **Example**

Use the strategy of multiplying by 2 (×2) to create a set of four equivalent fractions to represent the shaded part of the figure. Show your work.

Solution

Step 1
Determine the fraction that represents the shaded part of the figure.

There is one shaded part out of a total of four parts. The fraction that represents the shaded part is $\dfrac{1}{4}$.

Step 2
Determine the equivalent fractions.

Multiply the numerator and denominator by 2. Repeat the process two more times.

$$\dfrac{1\times 2 = 2}{4\times 2 = 8} \qquad \dfrac{2\times 2 = 4}{8\times 2 = 16} \qquad \dfrac{4\times 2 = 8}{16\times 2 = 32}$$

The set of four equivalent fractions is given as follows:
$$\dfrac{1}{4} = \dfrac{2}{8} = \dfrac{4}{16} = \dfrac{8}{32}$$

Time to Try 1

Use the strategy of dividing by 2 (÷2) to create a set of three equivalent fractions to $\dfrac{8}{24}$.

312

PRACTICE EXERCISES

Use the following information to answer the next question.

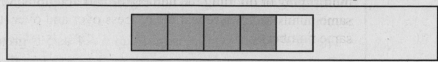

1. Use the strategy of multiplying by 3 (×3) to create a set of four equivalent fractions to represent the shaded part of the figure. Show your work.

2. Use the strategy of multiplying by 5 (×5) to create a set of four equivalent fractions for $\frac{1}{2}$. Show your work.

3. Use the strategy of dividing by 2 (÷2) to create a set of four equivalent fractions equivalent for $\frac{24}{40}$. Show your work.

Lesson 4   COMPARING FRACTIONS

When comparing two fractions, compare the fraction on the left to the fraction on the right. When comparing fractions, you can use symbols instead of words.

- The greater than symbol is >. Read $5 > 4$ as 5 is greater than 4.
- The less than symbol is <. Read $3 < 4$ as 3 is less than 4.
- The equal to symbol is =. Read $4 = 4$ as 4 is equal to 4.

FRACTIONS WITH LIKE DENOMINATORS

You can compare fractions by the size of the fractional parts.
When you compare the number of fractional parts, the numerators are different, but the denominators are the same.

This diagram shows that $\frac{2}{3}$ is greater than $\frac{1}{3}$ because there are more fractional parts in $\frac{2}{3}$ than there are in $\frac{1}{3}$.

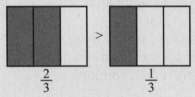

- A fraction with a greater numerator has more fractional parts.
- A fraction with a smaller numerator has fewer fractional parts.

✳ Example

The problem of the day was to write > or < between the fractions $\frac{7}{8}$ and $\frac{5}{8}$. Jason wrote $\frac{7}{8} < \frac{5}{8}$ and Michael wrote $\frac{7}{8} > \frac{5}{8}$.

Who is correct? Justify your answer.

Solution

Michael is correct when he wrote $\frac{7}{8} > \frac{5}{8}$.

Since the denominators are the same (8), you need to compare the numerators.

Since $7 > 5,$ then $\frac{7}{8} > \frac{5}{8}$.

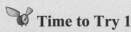 **Time to Try 1**

Jared's homework assignment was to compare fractions using the greater than and less than symbols. These are three of the comparisons Jared made:

$$\frac{5}{5} > \frac{3}{5} \qquad \frac{3}{4} > \frac{4}{4} \qquad \frac{2}{3} > \frac{1}{3}$$

Which comparison is incorrect? Justify your answer.

FRACTIONS WITH UNLIKE DENOMINATORS

Fractions are compared based on the value of their numerators. This comparison can only be done if their denominators are the same. If the denominators are not the same, equivalent fractions must be made first and then the fractions can be compared.

To compare fractions with unlike denominators, follow these steps:
1. Find the lowest common denominator for the given fractions. The lowest common denominator is the lowest common multiple.
2. Make equivalent fractions with the lowest common denominator.
3. Compare the numerators of the equivalent fractions.
   a) The greater the numerator, the greater the fraction.
   b) The smaller the numerator, the smaller the fraction.

Example

Compare the fraction $\frac{4}{6}$ to the fraction $\frac{6}{9}$ using the greater than symbol (>), the less than symbol (<), or the equal to symbol (=). Show your work.

Solution

Step 1
Find the lowest common denominator.

Multiples of 6: 6, 12, <u>18</u>
Multiples of 9: 9, <u>18</u>

The lowest common multiple (18) is the lowest common denominator.

NOTES

Step 2
Make equivalent fractions using the common denominator of 18.

$$\frac{4}{6} = \frac{4 \times 3}{6 \times 3} = \frac{12}{18}$$

$$\frac{6}{9} = \frac{6 \times 2}{9 \times 2} = \frac{12}{18}$$

Step 3
Now that the denominators are the same (18), compare the numerators.

Since $12 = 12$, then $\dfrac{12}{18} = \dfrac{12}{18}$.

Therefore, $\dfrac{4}{6} = \dfrac{6}{9}$

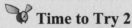 **Time to Try 2**

Compare the fraction $\dfrac{2}{3}$ to the fraction $\dfrac{2}{5}$ using the greater than symbol (>), the less than symbol (<), or the equal to symbol (=). Show your work.

PRACTICE EXERCISES

For each of the following pairs of fractions, compare the first fraction to the second fraction using the greater than symbol (>), the less than symbol (<), or the equal to symbol (=). Show your work.

1. $\dfrac{3}{7}$ and $\dfrac{1}{7}$

2. $\dfrac{3}{4}$ and $\dfrac{3}{5}$

3. $\dfrac{2}{3}$ and $\dfrac{3}{4}$

317

Lesson 5 ORDERING FRACTIONS ON NUMBER LINES

You can order fractions on number lines by using benchmarks like 0, $\frac{1}{2}$, and 1.

FRACTIONS WITH LIKE DENOMINATORS

1. To order fractions with like denominators, order the numerators from least to greatest.
2. Then, place the fractions (according to their numerators) on the number line by counting the ticks from 0 to determine the correct positions.

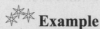 **Example**

$$\frac{5}{8}, \frac{8}{8}, \frac{3}{8}, \frac{1}{8}$$

Place the four fractions in the correct positions on a number line marked in eighths.

Solution

Step 1
Order the fractions from least to greatest.

Since the denominators are the same (8), order the numerators from least to greatest.
1, 3, 5, 8

From least to greatest, the fractions are $\frac{1}{8}$, $\frac{3}{8}$, $\frac{5}{8}$, $\frac{8}{8}$.

Step 2
Order the fractions on the number line.

Since the denominators are eighths, the number line is marked in eighths from 0 to 1, with $\frac{1}{2}$ representing the equivalent fraction $\frac{4}{8}$.

Place $\frac{1}{8}$ on the first tick after the 0.

Place $\frac{3}{8}$ on the third tick after the 0.

Place $\frac{5}{8}$ on the fifth tick after the 0 (one tick after the benchmark fraction $\frac{1}{2}$).

Place $\dfrac{8}{8}$ on the eighth tick after the 0 (on the 1 mark, since $\dfrac{8}{8} = 1$).

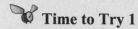

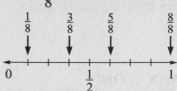

Time to Try 1

$$\dfrac{5}{6}, \ \dfrac{2}{6}, \ \dfrac{3}{6}, \ \dfrac{6}{6}$$

Place the given fractions in the correct positions on the number line marked in sixths.

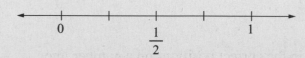

FRACTIONS WITH UNLIKE DENOMINATORS

To place fractions with unlike denominators on a number line, you need to make equivalent fractions first.

Follow these steps to order fractions with unlike denominators:
1. Determine the lowest common denominator.
2. Make equivalent fractions.
3. Order the equivalent fractions by the numerators.
4. Place the equivalent fractions on the number line by counting the ticks from 0 to determine the correct positions.

Example

$$\dfrac{2}{5}, \ \dfrac{9}{10}, \ \dfrac{1}{2}, \ \dfrac{3}{5}$$

Place the four fractions in order on a number line.

Solution

Step 1

Determine the lowest common denominator for the fractions.

Multiples of 2: 2, 4, 6, 8, <u>10</u>,…
Multiples of 5: 5, <u>10</u>,…
Multiples of 10: <u>10</u>, 20,…

The lowest common multiple (10) is the lowest common denominator (10).

NOTES

Step 2

Make equivalent fractions using the common denominator of 10.

$$\frac{2}{5} = \frac{2 \times 2}{5 \times 2} = \frac{4}{10} \qquad \frac{1}{2} = \frac{1 \times 5}{2 \times 5} = \frac{5}{10} \qquad \frac{3}{5} = \frac{3 \times 2}{5 \times 2} = \frac{6}{10}$$

Step 3

Order the four equivalent fractions by the numerators.

$$\frac{4}{10}, \ \frac{5}{10}, \ \frac{6}{10}, \ \frac{9}{10}$$

Step 4

Place the fractions on a number line marked in tenths, where the benchmark fraction $\frac{1}{2}$ represents the equivalent fraction $\frac{5}{10}$.

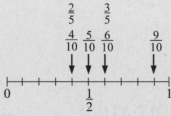

Time to Try 2

$$\frac{2}{3}, \ \frac{3}{4}, \ \frac{1}{2}$$

Place the three fractions in order on the given number line.

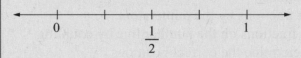

PRACTICE EXERCISES

Place the following sets of fractions in the correct positions on the given number lines.

1. $\dfrac{3}{6}, \dfrac{5}{6}, \dfrac{2}{6}, \dfrac{1}{6}$

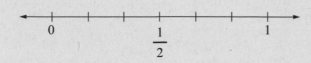

2. $\dfrac{2}{5}, \dfrac{1}{10}, \dfrac{3}{5}, \dfrac{9}{10}$

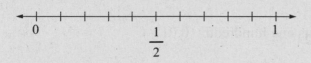

3. $\dfrac{2}{6}, \dfrac{1}{2}, \dfrac{3}{4}, \dfrac{2}{3}$

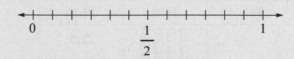

Lesson 6 *REPRESENTING DECIMALS WITH BASE TEN BLOCKS*

A decimal number can be represented with base ten blocks.

When decimal numbers are represented with base ten blocks, the same base ten blocks that are used to represent whole numbers are also used to represent decimal numbers, but they are renamed.

• One larger cube represents the whole number 1.

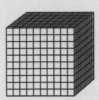

• One flat represents one-tenth: 0.1.

• One rod represents one-hundredth: 0.01

• One small cube represents one-thousandth: 0.001.

✦✧✦ **Example**

O	.	Tth	Hth	Thth
	.			

What decimal number is represented by the given set of base ten blocks? Explain your answer by describing the value of each set of blocks.

Solution

Step 1

Determine the decimal number.

The number represented by the base ten blocks is one and forty-two thousandths: 1.042.

Step 2

Describe the value of each set.

- The one large cube to the left of the decimal point represents the whole number 1 and has a value of 1.
- There is no flat in the tenths position so the tenths have no value: 0.0
- The four rods in the hundredths place (to the right of the blank tenths place) have a value of four-hundredths: 0.04.
- The two units in the thousandths place (to the right of the rods) have a value of two-thousandths: 0.002.

$$1 + 0.04 + 0.002 = 1.042$$

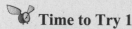 **Time to Try 1**

O	.	Tth	Hth	Thth

What decimal number is represented by the given set of base ten blocks? Explain your answer by describing the value of each set of blocks.

PRACTICE EXERCISES

Write the decimal number that is represented by the base ten blocks. Describe the value of each set of blocks.

1.

O	.	Tth	Hth	Thth
	.			

2.

O	.	Tth	Hth	Thth
	.			

Lesson 7   PLACE VALUE IN DECIMAL NUMBERS

A place value chart can help you see the position of each digit in a decimal number.

The following place value chart shows the relationship between the visual and symbolic representations of the number 1.438.

Ones	•	Tenths	Hundredths	Thousandths
	•			
1	•	0.1	0.01	0.001
1 one	•	4 tenths	3 hundredths	8 thousandths

- The value of 1 is 1.0 (a whole number).
- The value of 4 is four-tenths: 0.4.
- The value of 3 is three-hundredths: 0.03.
- The value of 8 is eight-thousandths: 0.008.

✳ Example

Write the digits of the number 0.458 in the correct positions in a place value chart.

Describe the value of each digit.

Solution

Step 1
Place the digits in their correct positions in the place value chart.

O	.	Tth	Hth	Thth
0	.	4	5	8

Step 2
Describe the value of each digit.
- The value of 0 is zero. There is no whole number.
- The value of 4 is four-tenths: 0.4.
- The value of 5 is five-hundredths: 0.05.
- The value of 8 is eight-thousandths: 0.008.

NOTES

 Time to Try 1

Write the digits of the number 3.506 in the correct positions in the place value chart.

Describe the value of the digits 5 and 6.

O	.	Tth	Hth	Thth

USING EXPANDED NOTATION

You can express the sum of the place values in expanded notation. If there is a digit that has no value (0), the zero is not included in the expanded notation.

 Example

Express the sum of the place values in the number 1.708 in expanded notation.

Solution

Step 1

Determine the value of each digit.

- The number 1 represents the whole number 1 and has a value of 1.
- The number 7 represents seven-tenths and has a value of 0.7.
- The 0 represents zero hundredths. It has no value.
- The number 8 represents eight-thousandths and has a value of 0.008.

Step 2

Express the number in expanded notation.

The expanded form of 1.708 is $1 + 0.7 + 0.008$.

 Time to Try 2

Express the sum of the place values in the number 3.055 in expanded notation.

PRACTICE EXERCISES

1. Write the digits of the number 2.609 in the correct positions in the place value chart. Describe the value of each digit.

O	.	Tth	Hth	Thth

Express the sum of the place values in expanded notation for the following three decimal numbers.

2. 0.853

3. 0.023

4. 4.207

Lesson 8   EQUIVALENT DECIMAL NUMBERS: TENTHS, HUNDREDTHS, THOUSANDTHS

Equivalent decimal numbers have the same value when you compare them.

The following base ten blocks show how 0.4 (4 out of 10) has the same value as 0.40 (40 out of 100), and 0.400 (400 out of 1000).

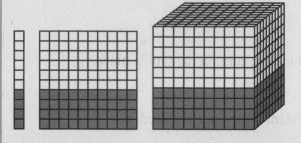

The following place value chart also shows how 0.4 (four-tenths) has the same value as 0.40 (forty-hundredths), and 0.400 (four hundred- thousandths).

O	.	Tth	Hth	Thth
0	.	4		
0	.	4	0	
0	.	4	0	0

Adding a 0 after the last digit of a decimal number does not change the value.

0.4 → 0.400
0.40 → 0.400
0.400 → 0.400

Adding a 0 before the last digit **does** change the value. For example, 0.4 and 0.04 are not equivalent decimals (four out of 10 compared to four out of 100).

EXPRESSING TENTHS AS EQUIVALENT HUNDREDTHS AND THOUSANDTHS

You can express a given tenth as an equivalent hundredth by adding one zero to the right of the tenth.

You can express a given tenth as an equivalent thousandth by adding two zeros to the right of the tenth.

Example

The shaded part of this rod can be represented as the decimal 0.7.

Express the given tenth as an equivalent hundredth and thousandth.

Solution

Step 1
Express the tenth as an equivalent hundredth.

Add a zero to the right of the digit in the tenths place.
$0.7 \rightarrow 0.7\underline{0}$

Seven-tenths is equivalent to seventy-hundredths.
$0.7 = 0.70$

Step 2
Express the given tenth as an equivalent thousandth.

Add two zeros to the right of the digit in the tenths place.
$0.7 \rightarrow 0.7\underline{00}$

Seven-tenths is equivalent to seven hundred-thousandths.
$0.7 = 0.700$

 Time to Try 1

The shaded part of this rod can be represented as the decimal 0.3.

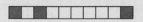

Express the given tenth as an equivalent hundredth and thousandth.

NOTES

EXPRESSING HUNDREDTHS AS EQUIVALENT THOUSANDTHS

You can express a given hundredth as an equivalent thousandth by adding one zero to the right of the digit in the hundredths place.

 Example

The decimal number 0.40 represents the 40 out of 100 squares that are shaded on this flat.

Express the given hundredth as an equivalent thousandth.

Solution

Add one zero to the right of the digit in the hundredths place.
0.40 → 0.40<u>0</u>

Forty-hundredths is equivalent to four hundred-thousandths, as shown by these diagrams.

0.40 = 0.400

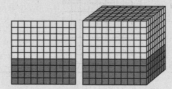

 Time to Try 2

The decimal number 0.09 represents the nine out of 100 squares that are shaded on this flat.

Express the given hundredth as an equivalent thousandth.

PRACTICE EXERCISES

1. Express the decimal number 0.5 as an equivalent hundredth. Explain your answer.

2. Express the decimal number 0.6 as an equivalent thousandth. Explain your answer.

Use the following information to answer the next question.

The shaded part of the flat can be represented as the decimal 0.47.

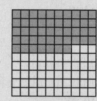

3. Express the given hundredth as an equivalent thousandth. Explain your answer.

Lesson 9   COMPARING AND ORDERING DECIMALS TO THOUSANDTHS

NOTES

You can compare and order decimals by using place value, equivalent decimals, and benchmarks.

USING PLACE VALUE

When comparing decimal numbers, start at the left with the greatest place value. Compare the digits in each place value as you move to the right ($\rightarrow$).

It is much easier to compare the place values if the numbers are organized. One way to organize the numbers is to use a place value chart.
Another way is to make a list, lining up the decimal points.
When the decimal points are lined up, all the place values will also be lined up.

When ordering numbers, you can use the less than symbol (<) and the greater than symbol (>). For example, $0.045 < 0.405 < 0.445$.

ORDERING DECIMALS INCLUDING ONLY TENTHS

When ordering decimals that only include tenths, order the digits in the tenths places from least to greatest (or from greatest to least). The decimals will be ordered in the same sequence.

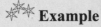 **Example**

0.4, 0.1, 0.7, 0.3
Order the decimal numbers from least to greatest.
Explain your work.

Solution

Step 1
Compare and order the digits in the tenths places.
From least to greatest, the digits are 1, 3, 4, 7.

Step 2
Order the decimal numbers in the same order as the digits.

From least to greatest, the decimals are 0.1, 0.3, 0.4, 0.7.

The order can also be written as $0.1 < 0.3 < 0.4 < 0.7$.

NOTES

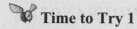 **Time to Try 1**

0.2, 0.9, 0.6, 0.5
Order the decimals from least to greatest. Explain your work.

ORDERING DECIMALS INCLUDING TENTHS AND HUNDREDTHS

When ordering decimals that include hundredths, start by comparing the largest place value, which is the tenths. If the digits in the tenths are the same, for those decimal numbers, move to the right and compare the hundredths.

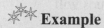 **Example**

0.51, 0.59, 0.17, 0.35
Order the decimals from least value to greatest value.

Use a place value chart to organize the numbers.

Solution

Step 1
Write the numbers in the place value chart.

O	.	Tth	Hth
0	.	5	1
0	.	5	9
0	.	1	7
0	.	3	5

Step 2
Compare the digits in the tenths places.

Since $1 < 3 < 5$, the number with the lowest value is 0.17, and the number with the next lowest value is 0.35.

Step 3
Compare the hundredths for the two numbers that have five-tenths.

Since $1 < 9$, then $0.5\underline{1} < 0.5\underline{9}$.

From least to greatest, the numbers are 0.17, 0.35, 0.51, 0.59.

The order can also be written as $0.17 < 0.35 < 0.51 < 0.59$.

NOTES

 Time to Try 2

0.36, 0.07, 0.28, 0.25
Order the decimals from least value to greatest value.

Use this place value chart to organize the numbers.

O	.	Tth	Hth
	.		
	.		
	.		
	.		

ORDERING DECIMALS INCLUDING TENTHS, HUNDREDTHS, AND THOUSANDTHS

When ordering decimals that include thousandths, start by comparing the tenths, then the hundredths, and then the thousandths.

 Example

0.546, 0.544, 0.645, 0.446
Order the decimals from least to greatest.

Use a place value chart to organize the numbers.

Solution

Step 1

Write the numbers in the place value chart.

O	.	Tth	Hth	Thth
0	.	5	4	6
0	.	5	4	4
0	.	6	4	5
0	.	4	4	6

334

Step 2

Compare the digits in the tenths places.

Since $4 < 5 < 6$, the number with the lowest value is 0.446, and the number with the greatest value is 0.645.

Step 3

Compare the hundredths digits for the two numbers that have five-tenths.

Both numbers have four-hundredths.

Step 4

Compare the thousandths for the two numbers that have five-tenths and four-hundredths.

Since $4 < 6$, then $0.54\underline{4} < 0.54\underline{6}$.

From least to greatest, the numbers are 0.446, 0.544, 0.546, 0.645.

The order can also be written as $0.446 < 0.544 < 0.546 < 0.645$.

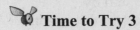 **Time to Try 3**

0.235, 0.254, 0.244, 0.255
Order the decimals from least to greatest.

Use the place value chart to organize the numbers.

O	.	Tth	Hth	Thth
	.			
	.			
	.			
	.			

USING EQUIVALENT DECIMALS

When ordering a set of decimals that includes tenths, hundredths, or thousandths, you first need to make equivalent decimals. Equivalent decimals have the same value.

To make equivalent decimals, add zeros to the right of the last digit for each number so that all the numbers have an equal number of digits (including zeros).

Adding zeros to the right of the digit will not change the value of the decimal.

 Example

0.237, 0.56, 0.9
Order the numbers from least to greatest.

Solution

Step 1
Create equivalent decimals.

Add one zero to the right of 0.56.
$0.56 \rightarrow 0.56\underline{0}$

Add two zeros to the right of 0.9.
$0.9 \rightarrow 0.9\underline{00}$

Step 2
Write the decimals in a place value chart.

O	.	Tth	Hth	Thth
0	.	2	3	7
0	.	5	6	0
0	.	9	0	0

Step 3
Compare the tenths.

Since, $2 < 5 < 9$, then $0.237 < 0.560 < 0.900$

From least to greatest, the decimals are 0.237, 0.56, 0.9

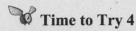 **Time to Try 4**

0.66, 0.6, 0.633

Order the numbers from least to greatest.

Use the place value chart to record the equivalent decimals.

O	.	Tth	Hth	Thth
	.			
	.			
	.			

USING BENCHMARKS

A number line marked in tenths is helpful when putting decimal numbers in order. Using benchmarks like 0, 0.5, and 1 can help you determine where to place the decimal numbers.

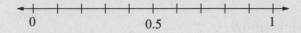

0   0.5   1

To order larger numbers in the hundredths and thousandths, you can still use a number line with the benchmark numbers of 0 and 1. These larger numbers will be ordered according to the number of tenths in the numbers.

✳ **Example**

Order the numbers 0.35, 0.7, and 0.106 on a number line, using the benchmarks of 0, 0.5, and 1.

Solution

Step 1
Identify the tenths place digit in each decimal number.

0.<u>3</u>5

0.<u>7</u>

0.<u>1</u>06

Step 2

Start at the benchmark number 0, and count the ticks until you reach the required tenth.

- For 0.35, count to the third tick. Point the arrow to halfway between the third and fourth ticks.
- For, 0.7, count to the seventh tick. Point the arrow to the seventh tick.
- For 0.106, count to the first tick. Point the arrow just after the first tick.

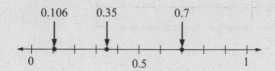

Time to Try 5

0.395, 0.6, 0.85

Place the decimals in the correct positions on the number line.

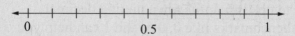

PRACTICE EXERCISES

Use the given place value charts to help you order the next three sets of decimal numbers from least to greatest.

1. 0.413, 0.732, 0.431, 0.634

O	.	Tth	Hth	Thth

2. 0.521, 0.542, 0.5, 0.55

O	.	Tth	Hths	Thth

3. Draw arrows to show the correct placement of the numbers 0.427, 0.75, and 0.19 on the number line. Label each arrow with the correct number.

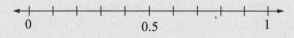

Lesson 10 CONNECTING FRACTIONS AND DECIMALS
(TO THOUSANDTHS)

Decimals can be written in fraction form and fractions can be written in decimal form.

USING PICTORIAL OR CONCRETE REPRESENTATIONS

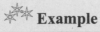 **Example**

O	.	Tth	Hth	Thth
	.			

Write the fraction and decimal represented by the base ten blocks shown in the place value chart.

Solution

Step 1
Count the number of base ten blocks in each place value.

- There are two-tenths (two flats in the tenths position).
- There are five-hundredths (five rods in the hundredths position).
- There are three-thousandths (three units in the thousandths position).

Step 2
Write the decimal represented by the base ten blocks.

The decimal represented by the blocks is 0.253.

Step 3
Write the fraction represented by the base ten blocks.

The fraction represented by the base ten blocks is $\dfrac{253}{1\,000}$.

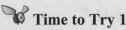 **Time to Try 1**

O	.	Tth	Hth	Thth
	.			

Write the decimal and fraction represented by the base ten blocks in the given place value chart.

WRITING EQUIVALENT FRACTIONS IN DECIMAL FORM

Adding a zero after the last digit of a decimal number does not change the value of the decimal number. For example, the following fractions and related decimals are all equivalent to each other.

- $\dfrac{3}{10} = 0.3$ (three parts out of 10)

- $\dfrac{30}{100} = 0.30$ (thirty parts out of 100)

- $\dfrac{300}{1\,000} = 0.300$ (three hundred parts out of 1 000)

$$\frac{3}{10} = \frac{30}{100} = \frac{300}{1\,000}$$

$$0.3 = 0.30 = 0.300$$

NOTES

FRACTIONS WITH A DENOMINATOR OF 10

If a given fraction has a denominator of 10, the equivalent decimal must have one digit to the right of the decimal point. The digit will be the same as the numerator of the fraction.

 Example

Write the equivalent decimal for the fraction $\frac{3}{10}$. Justify your answer.

Solution

The equivalent decimal is 0.3.

The fraction $\frac{3}{10}$ represents three parts out of 10.

The decimal 0.3 also represents three parts out of 10 parts. This shaded part of this strip represents both the fraction and the decimal.

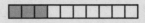

$$\frac{3}{10} = 0.3$$

 Time to Try 2

Write the decimal form of the fraction $\frac{7}{10}$. Justify your answer.

FRACTIONS WITH A DENOMINATOR OF 100

If a given fraction has a denominator of 100, the equivalent decimal must have two digits to the right of the decimal point. The digits will be the same as the numerator of the fraction.

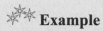 **Example**

Write the decimal form of the fraction $\frac{40}{100}$. Justify your answer.

Solution

The decimal form of $\frac{40}{100}$ is 0.40.

The fraction $\frac{40}{100}$ represents 40 parts out of a total of 100 parts.

The decimal 0.40 also represents 40 parts out of total of 100 parts.

The shaded part of this flat shows that both forms represent the same quantity.

$$\frac{40}{100} = 0.40$$

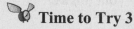 **Time to Try 3**

Write the decimal form of the fraction $\frac{34}{100}$. Justify your answer.

FRACTIONS WITH A DENOMINATOR OF 1 000

If a given fraction has a denominator of 1 000, the equivalent decimal must have three digits to the right of the decimal point. The digits will be the same as the numerator of the fraction.

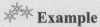 **Example**

Write the equivalent decimal for the fraction $\dfrac{400}{1\ 000}$.

Justify your answer.

Solution

The equivalent decimal form is 0.400.

The fraction $\dfrac{400}{1\ 000}$ represents 400 parts out of a total of 1 000 parts.

The decimal 0.400 also represents 400 parts out of a total of 1 000 parts.

The shaded part of this cube shows how the two forms represent the same quantity.

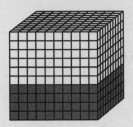

$$\dfrac{400}{1\ 000} = 0.400$$

 Time to Try 4

Write the equivalent decimal for the fraction $\dfrac{520}{1\ 000}$.

Justify your answer.

SAME NUMERATORS WITH DENOMINATORS OF 10, 100, OR 1 000

When you write an equivalent decimal for a fraction, you may need to add one or two zeros **before** the last digit to keep the correct place value.

For example, the following fractions look similar, but they have different decimal values: $\dfrac{2}{10}$, $\dfrac{2}{100}$, and $\dfrac{2}{1\,000}$.

- $\dfrac{2}{10} = 0.2$ (two parts out of 10)

- $\dfrac{2}{100} = 0.02$ (two parts out of 100)

- $\dfrac{2}{1\,000} = 0.002$ (two parts out of 1 000)

ONE-DIGIT NUMERATOR WITH A DENOMINATOR OF 100

If the numerator has one digit and the denominator is 100, place one zero to the left of that digit when you write the equivalent decimal. The zero shows that there are no tenths in the decimal number. The zero is a placeholder.

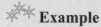 **Example**

Write the decimal form of $\dfrac{9}{100}$. Justify your answer.

Solution

Step 1
Write the equivalent decimal form.

The equivalent decimal form of $\dfrac{9}{100}$ is 0.09.

Step 2
Justify your answer.

Since the denominator is in the hundredths, the equivalent decimal number must have two digits to the right of the decimal point.

Therefore, you need to add one zero to the left of the 9. The zero shows that there are no tenths in the number. The zero is a placeholder.

The shaded part of this flat shows that both forms represent nine parts out of a total of 100 parts.

$$\frac{9}{100} = 0.09$$

 Time to Try 5

Write the equivalent decimal for the fraction $\frac{4}{100}$.

Justify your answer.

TWO-DIGIT NUMERATOR WITH A DENOMINATOR OF 1 000

If the numerator has two digits and the denominator is 1 000, place one zero to the left of the two digits when you write the equivalent decimal. The zero will show you that there are no tenths in the decimal number. The zero is a placeholder.

 Example

Write the decimal form of $\frac{37}{1\,000}$. Justify your answer.

Solution

The equivalent decimal form of the fraction $\frac{37}{1\,000}$ is 0.037

Since the denominator is in the thousandths, the decimal number must have three digits to the right of the decimal point.

Therefore, you need to add one zero to the left of the digits 37. The zero shows that there are no tenths in the number. The zero is a placeholder.

The shaded part of this cube shows that both forms represent 37 parts out of 1 000 parts.

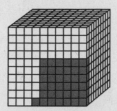

$$\frac{37}{1\ 000} = 0.037$$

Time to Try 6

Write the equivalent decimal form of the fraction $\frac{58}{1\ 000}$.

Justify your answer.

ONE-DIGIT NUMERATOR WITH A DENOMINATOR OF 1 000

If the numeral has one digit and the denominator is 1 000, place two zeros to the left of that digit when you write the equivalent decimal. The two zeros show that there are no tenths or hundredths in the decimal number. The zeros are placeholders.

✳ Example

Write the decimal form of $\frac{9}{1\ 000}$. Justify your answer.

Solution

The decimal form of $\frac{9}{1\ 000}$ is 0.009.

Since the denominator is in the thousandths, the numerator must have three digits to the right of the decimal point.

Therefore, you need to add two zeros to the left of the 9. The two zeros show that there are no tenths or hundredths in the decimal number. The zeros are placeholders.

NOTES

The shaded part of this cube shows that both forms represent nine parts out of a total of 1 000 parts.

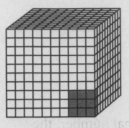

$$\frac{9}{1\ 000} = 0.009$$

 Time to Try 7

Write the equivalent decimal form of $\frac{1}{1\ 000}$. Justify your answer.

WRITING DECIMALS IN FRACTION FORM TO THOUSANDTHS

To write the fraction form of a decimal to the thousandths, follow these steps:

1. Look at the last digit in the decimal number to determine the denominator. If the last digit is in the thousandths place, the denominator is 1 000.
   For example, 0.13<u>2</u>.

2. Determine the numerator by removing the whole number and the decimal. The number you are left with is the numerator.
   For example, $0.132 \rightarrow \frac{132}{1\ 000}$.

Note:
- If the tenths digit is a zero, drop the zero.
  For example, $0.046 \rightarrow \frac{46}{1\ 000}$.

- If the tenths digit and the hundredths digit are both zeros, drop both zeros.
  For example, $0.009 \rightarrow \frac{9}{1\ 000}$

348

Example

Write the equivalent fraction form of 0.003.
Justify your answer.

Solution

The fraction $\dfrac{3}{1\ 000}$ is equivalent to 0.003.

1. Since there are three digits in the decimal number, the denominator of the equivalent fraction is 1 000.
2. Drop the zero in the ones place and the decimal point. You are left with the digits 003.
3. Drop the two zeros in the tenths and hundredths places. You are left with 3, which is the numerator of the fraction.

$$\dfrac{3}{1\ 000}$$

This diagram shows that both forms represent three parts out of a total of 1 000 parts.

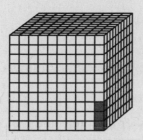

$$0.003 = \dfrac{3}{1\ 000}$$

 Time to Try 8

Write the equivalent fraction for 0.035. Justify your answer.

PRACTICE EXERCISES

Use the following information to answer the next question.

O	.	Tth	Hth	Thth
	.			

1. Write the decimal number and fraction that are represented by the base ten blocks.

Write the decimal equivalents for the following two fractions.

2. $\dfrac{330}{1\,000}$

3. $\dfrac{1}{100}$

Write the fraction forms of the following two decimals.

4. 0.006

5. 0.018

REVIEW SUMMARY

- Equivalent fractions are fractions that represent the same part of a whole or part of a set.
- To create an equivalent fraction, you can use fraction strips or you can multiply or divide the numerator and denominator by the same number.
- To create sets of equivalent fractions, repeatedly multiply the numerator and denominator by the same number.
- To compare fractions with like denominators, compare the numerators. The smaller the numerator, the smaller the fraction.
- To compare fractions with unlike denominators, find the lowest common denominator, and then make equivalent fractions.
- Fractions can be ordered on number lines that use benchmark numbers like 0, $\frac{1}{2}$, and 1.
- Decimal numbers can be represented with base ten blocks:
  - A thousand cube represents the ones.
  - A hundred flat represents the tenths.
  - A ten rod represents the hundredths.
  - A unit represents the thousandths.
- The sum of the place values of a decimal number can be expressed in expanded notation.
  - The tenths are expressed as one digit to the right of the decimal.
  - The hundredths are expressed as two digits to the right of the decimal.
  - The thousandths are expressed as three digits to the right of the decimal.
- To create equivalent decimals, add zeros to the right of the last digit. Adding a zero will not change the value.
- To order decimals using place value, start comparing the greatest place values. Move to the right when digits have the same value.
- To order decimals that include tenths, hundredths, and thousandths, first make equivalent decimals.
- Decimals can be ordered on number lines that use benchmark numbers like 0, 0.5, and 1.

- Fractions and decimals can be equivalent.
  - If the fraction has a denominator of 10, the equivalent decimal must have one digit to the right of the decimal.
  - If the fraction has a denominator of 100, the equivalent decimal must have two digits to the right of the decimal.
  - If the fraction has a denominator of 1 000, the equivalent decimal must have three digits to the right of the decimal.

PRACTICE TEST

Use the following information to answer the next question.

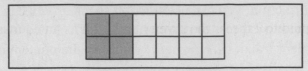

1. Write two equivalent fractions to represent the shaded area of the given figure.

2. Order the fractions $\frac{1}{8}, \frac{7}{8}, \frac{5}{8}, \frac{4}{8}$ on the number line.

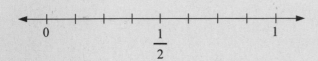

3. Use the strategy of dividing by 3 (÷3) to create a set of three fractions equivalent to $\frac{108}{135}$. Show your work.

4. Order the fractions $\frac{2}{3}, \frac{2}{6}, \frac{1}{2}, \frac{4}{9}$ on the number line.

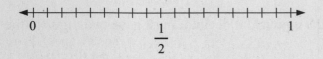

5. Describe the value of each digit in 8.405. Express the sum of the place values in expanded notation.

Use the following information to answer the next question.

The shaded part of the flat can be represented as the decimal 0.58.

Adam and Byron attempted to express the given hundredth as an equivalent thousandth.
- Adam: $0.58 = 0.058$
- Byron: $0.58 = 0.580$

6. Who is correct? Justify your answer.

Use the following information to answer the next question.

The shaded part of the rod can be represented as the decimal 0.9.

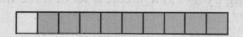

7. Express the given tenth as an equivalent thousandth. Justify your answer.

8. Use the place value chart to help you order the decimal numbers 0.729, 0.498, 0.73, 0.8 from least to greatest.

O	.	Tth	Hth	Thth

9. Write the decimal equivalent for the fraction $\dfrac{7}{100}$. Justify your answer.

Use the following information to answer the next question.

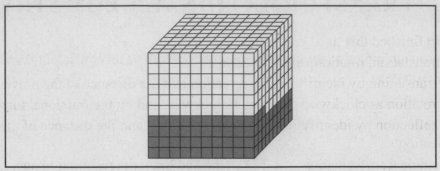

10. Write the fraction and equivalent decimal that represent the shaded parts of the cube.

Use the following information to answer the next question.

O	.	Tth	Hth	Thth
	.			

11. Write the decimal number that is represented by the base ten blocks. Describe the value of each set of blocks.

TRANSFORMATIONAL GEOMETRY

When you are finished this unit, you will be able to…
- identify a translation, rotation, and reflection
- describe a translation by identifying the direction and the distance of the movement
- describe a rotation as clockwise or counter clockwise and by the fractional turn
- describe a reflection by identifying the line of reflection and the distance of the image from the line of reflection
- perform a single transformation of a 2-D shape and draw the resulting image

PREREQUISITE SKILLS AND KNOWLEDGE

Prior to starting this unit, you should be able to…
- demonstrate an understanding of congruency
- demonstrate an understanding of line symmetry

Lesson 1 *IDENTIFYING SINGLE TRANSFORMATIONS*

A transformation is a movement of a figure where the size and shape of the figure do not change. Since the size and shape do not change, the original figure and its transformed image are always congruent.

TRANSLATIONS

A **translation** slides a figure from one location to another without turning the figure. The only thing that changes is that the image is in a different place.

✳ Example

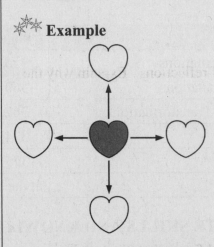

The heart in the middle is shaded to help you see the placement of the original figure. The arrows show you four different translations. Explain why the transformations are translations.

Solution

Each image looks exactly like the original figure, except that it is in a different place. One image moved to the left, one moved upward, one moved to the right, and one moved downward.

🐝 Time to Try 1

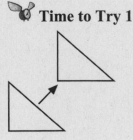

Explain why the transformation of the triangle is a translation.

REFLECTIONS

When a shape is flipped, it looks like it is reflected in a mirror. That is why a flip is called a **reflection**.

The mirror image will always face the opposite direction of the original shape. The two shapes will always be exactly the same distance from the line of reflection.

Sometimes the line of reflection is shown and sometimes it is not shown. The line of reflection is sometimes referred to as a flip line or a mirror line.

 Example

The following figures are examples of reflections. Explain why the transformations are reflections.

Solution

Each image is opposite the original figure, creating a mirror image. One set shows a downward reflection, one shows a reflection to the right, and one shows a reflection to the left.

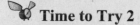 **Time to Try 2**

Darian draws these two figures to illustrate a reflection.

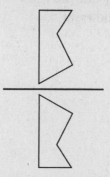

Is Darian's drawing correct? Justify your answer.

ROTATIONS

A **rotation** occurs when a figure is turned around a centre of rotation.

The centre or point of rotation can be a vertex of the shape being rotated. It can also be outside of the shape. When it is outside of the shape, the centre or point of rotation may or may not be shown as a dot.

Note: A rotation diagram often presents the rotation side by side to save space.

 Example

The following figures are examples of three different rotations of the number 6. The centre of rotation is not shown. Explain why each set of figures is a rotation.

Solution

Each set of figures shows the number 6 turning around a vertex. The first rotation shows a quarter turn to the right.

The second rotation shows a half turn to the right so that the rotated figure is below the original figure.

The third rotation shows a three-quarter turn to the right.

Time to Try 3

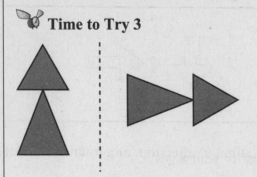

Explain why this set of figures illustrates a rotation.

PRACTICE EXERCISES

Use the following information to answer the next question.

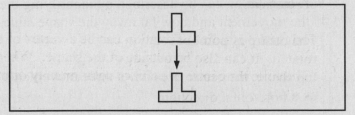

1. Is the transformation a reflection or a translation? Justify your answer.

Use the following information to answer the next question.

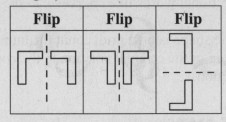

2. Was Josee correct when she identified each transformation as a flip? Justify your answer.

Use the following information to answer the next question.

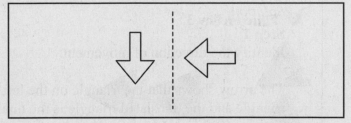

3. Is the transformation a translation, a reflection, or a rotation? Justify your answer.

Lesson 2 *DESCRIBING SINGLE TRANSFORMATIONS*

DESCRIBING TRANSLATIONS

A translation can be described by identifying the direction of the movement and how far away the shape slides from the original position.

The following example shows three movements of the same shape:
- a horizontal direction
- a vertical direction
- a diagonal direction

The movement of a translation can also be described using directional words like *up, down, to the left, to the right*.

If the shape is on a grid, count the number of squares from each vertex in the original position to the corresponding vertex in the new position.

✴ Example

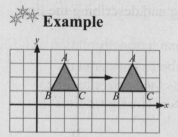

Describe the translation of triangle *ABC*.

Solution

Step 1
Identify the direction of movement.

The arrow shows that the triangle on the left is the original triangle and the translated triangle is the one on its right. The translation was horizontal and to the right.

Step 2
Describe how far the image moves.

Each vertex on the original triangle in the left position moves five squares to the right when the triangle is translated.

✿ Time to Try 1

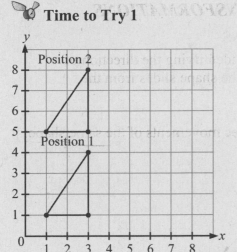

Describe the translation of the triangle from position 1 to position 2.

DESCRIBING REFLECTIONS

A reflection can be described by identifying and describing the line of reflection.

For example, a reflection line can be described as horizontal. The figure flips upward or downward across the horizontal line. A reflection line can be described as vertical. The figure flips to the left or to the right of the vertical line.

If the figure and its reflected image is shown on a grid, the reflection can be described by how far away it is from the line of reflection.

• Count the number of squares between the vertices of the original figure and the flip line.

• Count the number of squares between the vertices of the reflected image and the flip line.

• All the vertices and corresponding vertices of the two figures should be exactly the same distance from the flip line, and opposite each other.

Note: When using grids, primes (′) are often used to indicate a translated image. For example, vertex A' in the reflected image would correspond to vertex A in the original figure.

✴ Example

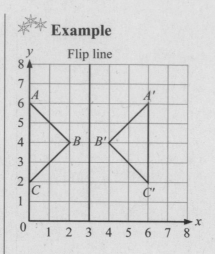

Describe the reflection of the triangle.

Solution

Step 1
Identify the flip line.

The flip line, or line of reflection, is a vertical line, so the image is reflected to the right of the original figure.

Step 2
Describe the distance from the flip line.

The triangle is directly across from its image at all points.
- Vertices A and A' are each three squares from the flip line
- Vertices C and C' are each one square from the flip line.
- Vertices B and B' are each three squares from the flip line.
- The original figure (ABC) is one square to the left of the flip line.
- The reflected image ($A'B'C'$) is one square to the right of the flip line.

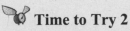 **Time to Try 2**

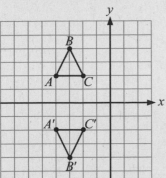

Describe the reflection of triangle *ABC*.

DESCRIBING ROTATIONS

A rotation can be described by the direction of the turn, **clockwise** or **counterclockwise** .

Clockwise

Counterclockwise

A rotation can also be described by the angle of its turn.
Common rotation angles are 90° (quarter turn) and 180° (half turn).

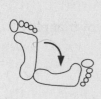

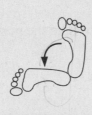

Clockwise quarter turn
90°

Counterclockwise
quarter turn
90°

Clockwise half turn
180°

✳ Example

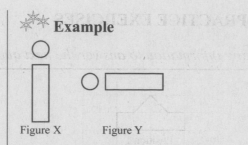

Figure X   Figure Y

Describe the rotation of figure X to figure Y.

Solution
This is one possible solution.

Step 1
Identify the direction of the turn.

Figure X rotates in a counter clockwise direction to result in Figure Y.

Step 2
Describe the angle of the turn.

Since the vertical shape became a horizontal shape, figure X rotated 90° to take the position of figure Y.
It made a quarter turn.

🐝 Time to Try 3

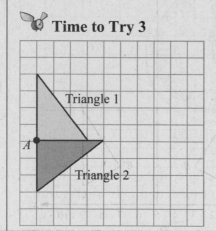

Describe the rotation of triangle 1 to take the position of triangle 2.

PRACTICE EXERCISES

Use the following information to answer the next question.

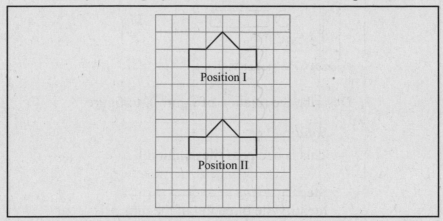

1. Describe the translation of the figure from position I to position II.

Use the following information to answer the next question.

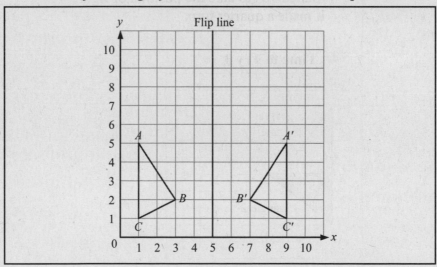

2. Describe the reflection of the triangle.

Use the following information to answer the next question.

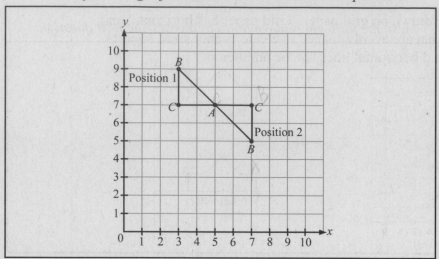

3. Describe the rotation of triangle *ABC* from position 1 to position 2.

Lesson 3   DRAWING IMAGES OF SINGLE TRANSFORMATIONS

Shapes can be drawn on grid paper. Grid paper has horizontal and vertical lines that are evenly spaced to create evenly sized squares. The vertical and horizontal lines can be numbered.

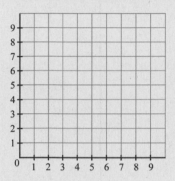

DRAWING TRANSLATED IMAGES

To determine the location in which to draw the translated image, count the given number of squares from each vertex of the figure in the direction given.

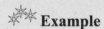 **Example**

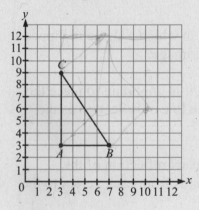

Slide the triangle diagonally (↗) for three squares.

Draw the translated triangle, labelling the vertices *A'B'C'*.

Solution

The translated triangle should look like this:

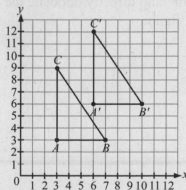

Vertices *A* and *A'* are three squares apart.

Vertices *B* and *B'* are three squares apart.

Vertices *C* and *C'* are three squares apart.

Time to Try 1

Slide the triangle five squares vertically $(\uparrow)$. Draw the translated triangle, labelling the vertices $A'B'C'$.

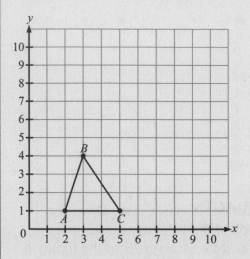

DRAWING REFLECTED IMAGES

A reflection (or flip) is a transformation in which a shape is flipped over a line to form a mirror, or opposite, image.

When drawing the reflection of a shape, it is important to place the flipped image the same distance from the line of reflection as the original shape.

In order to be sure that the image is an exact reflection of the original shape, count the number of squares from each vertex to the line of reflection.

The vertices of the image being drawn must be the same number of squares away from the line of reflection, and directly opposite the corresponding vertices of the original figure.

368

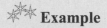 **Example**

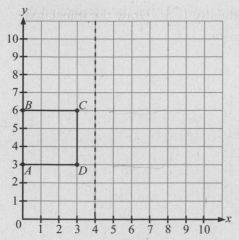

Flip the given shape across the dotted reflection line. Draw the reflected image. Label the vertices $A'B'C'D'$.

Solution

The reflected image should look like this:

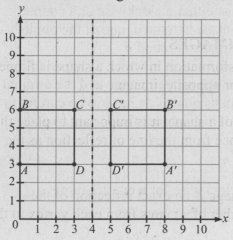

- Vertices A and A' are both four squares from the flip line.
- Vertices B and B' are both four squares from the flip line.
- Vertices C and C' are both one square from the flip line.
- Vertices D and D' are both one square from the flip line.

Time to Try 2

Draw the reflected image of triangle *ABC*. Label the vertices of the reflected image *A'B'C'*.

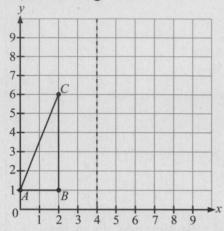

DRAWING ROTATED IMAGES

A rotation is a turn of a shape in either a clockwise or a counter clockwise direction. When a shape is rotated, one of the points remains fixed while the shape rotates around it.

When drawing a rotated image, the rotated image and the original figure must have the same dimensions. You need to be careful to label the vertices of the rotated image correctly.

Example

Rotate figure *ABCD* counter clockwise for a quarter turn. Let vertex *A* be the centre of rotation.

Draw the rotated image. Label the vertices of the rotated rectangle *A'B'C'D'*.

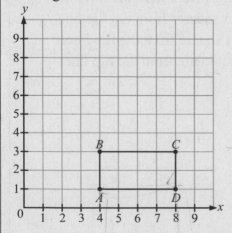

Solution

The rotated rectangle should look like this:

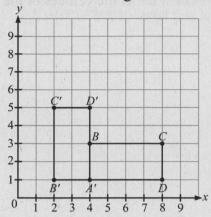

🦋 Time to Try 3

Rotate figure *ABCD* counter clockwise with a quarter turn.
Rotate the figure around vertex *C*.

Draw the rotated image. Label the vertices *A'B'C'D'*.

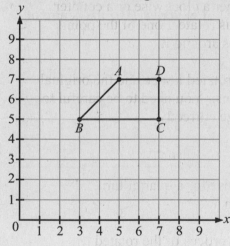

PRACTICE EXERCISES

1. Slide figure *ABCD* diagonally $\left(\nearrow\right)$ for five squares. Draw and label (*A'B'C'D'*) the translated image.

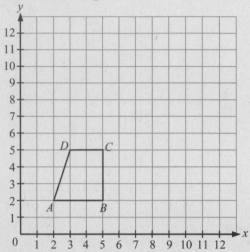

2. Rotate figure *PQRS* counter clockwise for a half turn (180°). Let vertex *P* be the centre of rotation. Draw and label (*P'Q'R'S'*) the rotated image.

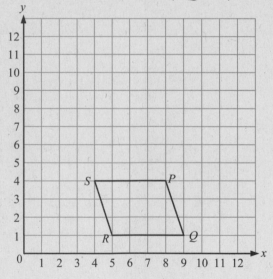

3. Flip figure *STUV* across the dotted reflection line. Draw and label (*S'T'U'V'*) the reflected image.

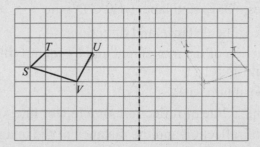

REVIEW SUMMARY

- A translation slides a figure from one location to another without turning or changing the figure.
- In a translation, each vertex of the figure is moved the same distance and direction.
- A translation can be described by identifying the direction of the movement and by identifying how far away the translated image is from the original figure.
- A reflection flips a figure over a line to create an opposite image.
- The line a reflection flips over may be called a flip line, a line of reflection, or a mirror line.
- A reflection can be described by identifying the line of reflection and the distance of the image from the line of reflection.
- A rotation occurs when a figure is turned around a centre of rotation.
- The centre of rotation can be a vertex of the figure being rotated or it can be outside the figure.
- A rotation can be described by the direction it turns (clockwise or counter clockwise) and by the angle it turns (quarter turn, half turn, three-quarter turn).

PRACTICE TEST

Identify the following two transformations. Justify your answers.

1.

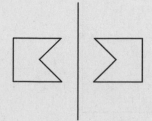

2.

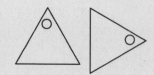

Use the following information to answer the next question.

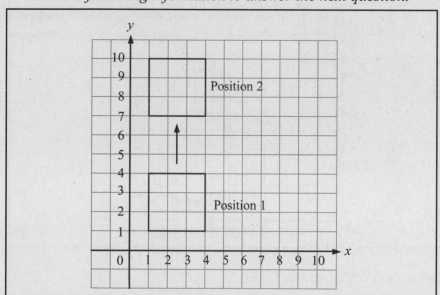

3.   Describe the translation of the square from position 1 to position 2.

Use the following information to answer the next question.

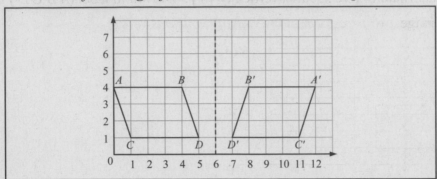

4. Describe the reflection of the parallelogram.

Use the following information to answer the next question.

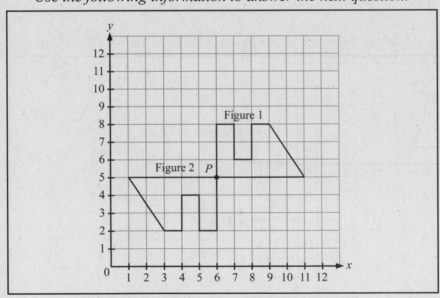

5. Describe the rotation of figure 1 to figure 2.

6. Slide the quadrilateral five squares vertically $(\uparrow)$. Draw and label $(A'B'C'D')$ the translated image.

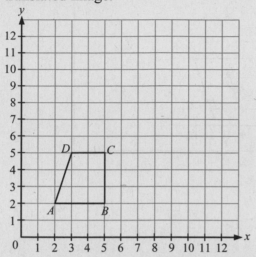

7. Flip the given shape across the dotted reflection line. Draw and label $(L'M'N'O')$ the reflected image.

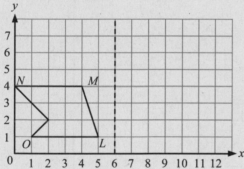

NOTES

VARIABLES AND EQUATIONS

When you are finished this unit, you will be able to...
- explain what a letter variable in a given equation represents
- express a given problem as an equation where the unknown is represented by a letter variable
- create a problem for a given equation where the unknown is represented by a letter variable
- use an inverse operation to determine the number that the letter variable in an equation represents.
- solve problems involving whole numbers and single-variable equations

PREREQUISITE SKILLS AND KNOWLEDGE

Prior to starting this unit, you should be able to...
- demonstrate an understanding that both sides of an equal sign (=) must have the same value
- express a given problem as an equation in which a symbol is used to represent an unknown number
- solve one-step equations involving a symbol

Lesson 1 REPRESENTING AN UNKNOWN NUMBER WITH A LETTER VARIABLE

NOTES

USING AN EQUATION

An equation is a number sentence that uses the equal sign (=) to show that the amount on each side of the equal sign has the same value.

$$3 + 5 = 8$$
$$8 = 8$$

An equation is always written horizontally. If the numbers are written vertically, it is not considered to be an equation.

Equation	Not an Equation
$2 \times 8 = 16$	8 $\times 2$ 16

VARIABLES AS UNKNOWN QUANTITIES

A letter **variable** is a letter that is used in a mathematical expression or equation to represent an unknown quantity. Any letter can be used to represent the same unknown quantity. The choice of letter does not affect or change the solution to a problem.

In a problem, there is always an unknown. An unknown is what you are trying to find out by performing some type of operation (the solution to the problem).

A problem can be written in equation form and the unknown expressed as a letter. The unknown can come anywhere in the equation, as shown in the following examples.

$$r + 3 = 5$$
$$4 + k = 9$$
$$5 + 5 = m$$

Lesson 2 EXPRESSING PROBLEMS AS EQUATIONS WITH ONE UNKNOWN

Follow these steps to express a problem as an equation:
1. Identify the information you know.
2. Identify the unknown in the problem.
3. Choose a letter variable to represent the unknown.
4. Determine which operation will solve the problem.
5. Write the equation.

 Example

Lexie paints one picture every day of the week. She now has a total of 84 pictures. How many weeks has she been painting? Express the problem as an equation.

Solution

Step 1
Start with what you know.

Lexie painted 84 pictures in total. There are seven days in one week, so Lexie painted seven pictures a week.

Step 2
Identify the unknown.

You do not know how many weeks Lexie has been painting pictures. Choose a variable (like the letter P) to represent the unknown.

Step 3
Determine which operation will help you solve the problem.

Since you know the total number (84) and the number in each group (7), one operation you can use is division.

Two ways the problem can be expressed is
$84 \div 7 = P$ and $84 \div P = 9$

 Time to Try 1

Kell and Ryan have the same number of binders. Kell has some red binders and 5 green binders. Ryan has 3 red binders and 4 yellow binders. How many red binders does Kell have?

Write an equation to express this problem. Let the variable k represent the unknown.

PRACTICE EXERCISES

Use the following information to answer the next question.

If the sum of two numbers is 100 and one of the numbers is 63, what is the other number?

1. Write an equation to express the problem. Let the variable N represent the unknown.

Use the following information to answer the next question.

Mrs. Brown made a total of 69 cookies for her daughter to take to school for her birthday. She made enough cookies for each child in her daughter's class to receive three cookies. How many students are in her daughter's class?

2. Write an equation to express the problem. Let the variable c represent the unknown.

Use the following information to answer the next question.

If the product of two numbers is 750 and one of the numbers is 25, what is the other number?

3. Write an equation to express the problem. Let the variable n represent the unknown.

Use the following information to answer the next question.

Ryan and Marina have the same number of erasers. Ryan has some pink erasers and seven white erasers. Marina has five pink erasers and five white erasers. How many pink erasers does Ryan have?

4. Write an equation to express the problem. Let the variable h represent the unknown.

Lesson 3   CREATING PROBLEMS FOR A GIVEN EQUATION

When you are given an equation without an accompanying problem, you can create your own problem to fit the equation.

The first step in writing the problem is to determine what the variable (the unknown) represents. Once you understand what it represents, it will be easier to create a problem.

ADDITION AND SUBTRACTION EQUATIONS

In an addition or subtraction equation, the variable will represent a part or a whole.

    part + part = whole
whole − part = part

 Example

$h + 21 = 37$
Write a problem that can be solved using the given equation.

Solution

Step 1
Determine what the unknown represents.

Since addition is a part + part = whole expression, the variable h represents a part of 37.

Step 2
Create a problem where a part of 37 is added to 21 to equal a total of 37.

After Kaylee finished colouring her picture, she gave her 21 markers to Marlene. Marlene now has 37 markers. How many markers did Marlene have before Kaylee gave her the 21 markers?

 Time to Try 1

$25 = r - 7$
Write a problem that can be solved using the given equation.

NOTES

MULTIPLICATION AND DIVISION EQUATIONS

In a multiplication or division equation, the variable (the unknown) will represent the number of groups, the number in each group, or the total number of items.

number of groups × number in each group = total
total ÷ number of groups = number in each group

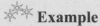 **Example**

$100 = 4C$
Write a problem that can be solved using the given equation.

Solution
Step 1
Determine what the unknown represents.

Since multiplication can be expressed as
total = number of groups × number in each group, the
variable C represents the number in each group.

Step 2
Create a problem where you know the total (100) and you know the number of groups (4), but you do not know the number of items in each group.

Mrs. Kuzyk opened a box of 100 straws. She gave an equal number of straws to four groups of students to use for their bridge-building assignment. How many straws did each group of students get?

 Time to Try 2
$20 \div f = 5$
Write a problem that can be solved using the given equation.

PRACTICE EXERCISES

Write a problem that can be solved by each of the following four equations:

1. $k + 25 = 37$

2. $32 = x - 8$

3. $5 \times 20 = h$

4. $24 \div f = 4$

Lesson 4   *USING INVERSE OPERATIONS TO SOLVE EQUATIONS*

To solve an equation that uses a letter variable, you can use an inverse or opposite operation to determine the value of the variable.

USE ADDITION TO SOLVE SUBTRACTION EQUATIONS

 Example

$35 = m - 9$

Use the inverse operation of addition to determine the value of m. Check your work. If both sides of the equal sign have the same value (35), you know the answer is correct.

Solution

Step 1
Determine the value of m.

If $35 = m - 9$, then $9 + 35 = m$.
Since $9 + 35 = 44$, $m = 44$.

Step 2
Check your work.

Substitute 44 for the variable m in the equation.
$35 = m - 9$
$35 = 44 - 9$
$35 = 35$

 Time to Try 1

$46 = f - 13$

Use the inverse operation of addition to determine the value of f. Check your work.

USE SUBTRACTION TO SOLVE ADDITION EQUATIONS

 Example

$15 + N = 47$

Use the inverse operation of subtraction to determine the value of N. Check your work.

Solution

Step 1

Determine the value of N.

If $15 + N = 47$, then $47 - 15 = N$.
Since $47 - 15 = 32$, $N = 32$.

Step 2

Check your work.

Substitute 32 for the variable N in the equation.
$15 + N = 47$
$15 + 32 = 47$
$47 = 47$

 Time to Try 2

$R + 32 = 86$

Use the inverse operation of subtraction to determine the value of R.
Check your work.

USE DIVISION TO SOLVE MULTIPLICATION EQUATIONS

 Example

$6r = 72$

Use the inverse operation of division to determine the value of r.
Check your work

Solution

Step 1

Determine the value of r.

If $6r = 72$, then $72 \div 6 = r$.
Since $72 \div 6 = 12$, $r = 12$.

Step 2

Check your work.

Substitute 12 for the variable r in the equation.
$6r = 72$
$6 \times 12 = 72$
$72 = 72$

NOTES

 Time to Try 3

$88 = 4b$

Use the inverse operation of division to determine the value of b. Check your work.

USE MULTIPLICATION TO SOLVE DIVISION EQUATIONS

 Example

$N \div 10 = 7$

Use the inverse operation of multiplication to determine the value of N. Explain your work.

Solution

Step 1

Determine the value of N.

If $N \div 10 = 7$, then $7 \times 10 = N$.
Since $7 \times 10 = 70$, $N = 70$.

Step 2

Check your work.

Substitute 70 for the variable N in the equation.

$N \div 10 = 7$
$70 \div 10 = 7$
$7 = 7$

 Time to Try 4

$8 = r \div 9$

Use the inverse operation of multiplication to determine the value of r. Check your work.

PRACTICE EXERCISES

1. $100 = f - 73$

    Use the inverse operation of addition to determine the value of f. Check your work.

2. $15 + N = 79$

    Use the inverse operation of subtraction to determine the value of N. Check your work.

3. $125 = 5x$

    Use the inverse operation of division to determine the value of x. Check your work.

4. $P \div 10 = 11$

    Use the inverse operation of multiplication to determine the value of P. Check your work.

Lesson 5 *SOLVING SINGLE-VARIABLE, ONE-STEP PROBLEMS*

When solving problems, follow this plan:
- Identify the information you know.
- Identify the unknown.
- Determine which operation will solve the problem.
- Write an equation, using a variable to represent the unknown.
- Solve the equation, using a strategy that works best for you.
- Check your work to see that both sides of the equal sign have the same value.

ADDITION AND SUBTRACTION PROBLEMS

The equation you write to represent an addition or subtraction problem can be represented in many ways.

For example, to show that 2 plus an unknown number equals 5, you could write any of these equations:
- $2+k=5$ or $5=2+k$
- $k+2=5$ or $5=k+2$
- $5-2=k$ or $k=5-2$
- $5-k=2$ or $2=5-k$

Regardless of how you express the equation, the unknown is still represented by the variable k, and $k = 3$ in every equation.

 Example

Lily picked some apples off the apple tree in her backyard. After she gave her neighbour 14 apples, she had 9 apples left. How many apples did Lily have before she gave apples to her neighbour?

Let A represent the unknown in the equation you write. Solve the problem. Check your work.

Solution
Step 1
Identify the unknown.

The unknown is the number of apples Lily had before she gave some to her neighbour.

Step 2
Write an equation to express the problem.

One equation you can use to solve the problem is $A-14=9$.

Step 3
Solve the equation.

If $A - 14 = 9$, then $9 + 14 = A$.
Since $9 + 14 = 23$, $A = 23$.

Lily had 23 apples before she gave some to her neighbour.

Step 4
Check your work.

Substitute 23 for the variable A in the equation.
$$A - 14 = 9$$
$$23 - 14 = 9$$
$$9 = 9$$

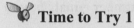 **Time to Try 1**

Corinne baked a total of 75 cookies. She kept 30 cookies at home and sent her brother Jordan to school with the rest so that his class could have a snack at recess. How many cookies did Jordan take to school?

Let the variable C represent the unknown in the equation you write. Solve the problem. Check your work.

MULTIPLICATION AND DIVISION PROBLEMS

The equation you write to represent a multiplication or division problem can be represented in many ways.

For example, to show that 2 multiplied by an unknown number is 6, you can write any of these equations:
- $2 \times r = 6$ or $6 = 2 \times r$
- $r \times 2 = 6$ or $6 = 2 \times r$
- $6 \div 2 = r$ or $r = 6 \div 2$
- $6 \div r = 2$ or $2 = 6 \div r$

Regardless of how you express the equation, the unknown is still represented by the variable r, and $r = 3$ in every equation.

NOTES

 Example

Miss Adams bought six packs of coloured markers for her students to use for a particular assignment. Each pack had the same number of markers. There were a total of 48 markers. How many markers were in each pack?

Let the variable m represent the unknown in the equation you write. Solve the problem. Check your work.

Solution
Step 1
Identify the unknown.

The unknown is the number of markers in each pack.

Step 2
Write an equation to express the problem.

One equation you can use to solve the problem is $m = 48 \div 6$.

Step 3
Solve the problem.

Since $m = 48 \div 6$, $m = 8$.
There were eight markers in each pack.

Step 4
Check your work.

Substitute 8 for the variable m in the equation.
$m = 48 \div 6$
$8 = 48 \div 6$
$8 = 8$

 Time to Try 2

During summer holidays, 54 children enrolled in a baseball camp. The coach separated the children into six baseball teams. Each team had the same number of children. How many children were on each team?

Let the variable s represent the unknown in the equation you write. Solve the problem. Check your work.

392

PRACTICE EXERCISES

Use the following information to answer the next question.

Stephanie baked a batch of cupcakes. After she sent 83 cupcakes to school for the bake sale, she had 17 cupcakes left for her family. How many cupcakes did Stephanie bake?

1. Let the variable *C* represent the unknown in the equation you write. Solve the problem. Check your work.

Use the following information to answer the next question.

Greg opened a box that had 1 000 straws. After Greg used some of the straws to build a tower, there were 378 straws left in the box. How many straws did Greg use to build the tower?

2. Let *T* represent the unknown in the equation you write. Solve the problem. Check your work.

Use the following information to answer the next question.

Mr. Friss ordered some boxes of white art paper for the art room. Each box had eight packages of paper. In total, there were 120 packages. How many boxes of paper were ordered?

3. Let *P* represent the unknown in the equation you write. Solve the problem. Check your work.

REVIEW SUMMARY

- An equation is a number sentence that uses the equal sign (=) to show that the amount on each side of the equal sign has the same value.
- An equation is always written horizontally.
- A letter variable is a letter that is used in a mathematical expression or equation to represent an unknown quantity.
- An unknown is what you are trying to find out by performing some type of operation (the solution to the problem).
- In an addition or subtraction equation, the variable will represent a part or a whole.
- In a multiplication or division equation, the variable will represent the number of groups, the number in each group, or the whole (total number).
- Inverse operations are opposite operations.
  - Addition and subtraction are inverse operations.
  - Multiplication and division are inverse operations.
- You can use inverse operations to solve equations.

394

PRACTICE TEST

Use the following information to answer the next question.

Melissa received a total of 45 medals over the course of her skiing career. Of these, 19 were silver. How many medals were not silver?

---

1. Write an equation to express the problem. Let the variable G represent the unknown.

Use the following information to answer the next question.

Alexis reads for one hour every day of the week. Since she began doing this, she has read for a total of 91 hours. How many weeks has she been reading?

---

2. Write an equation to express the problem. Let the variable R represent the unknown.

3. Write a problem that can be solved using the equation $k + 18 = 40$.

4. $63 = m - 15$

Use the inverse operation of addition to determine the value of m. Check your work.

5. $83 + N = 150$

Use the inverse operation of subtraction to determine the value of N. Check your work.

Use the following information to answer the next question.

> Three moms baked a total of 264 cookies to sell at the school bake sale. They packaged 12 cookies in each box and sold the cookies by the box. How many boxes were used?

6. Let k represent the unknown in the equation you write. Solve the problem. Check your work.

Use the following information to answer the next question.

> A class collected 1 000 pennies to donate to an animal shelter. During recess, Jon and Greg rolled 370 of the pennies. How many pennies still need to be rolled?

7. Let the variable T represent the unknown in the equation you write. Solve the problem. Check your work.

8. $66 = 3h$

Use the inverse operation of division to determine the value of h. Check your work.

9. $P \div 11 = 11$

Use the inverse operation of multiplication to determine the value of P. Check your work.

CAPACITY AND VOLUME

When you are finished this unit, you will be able to…

- describe the relationship between millilitres and litres
- select appropriate referents for millilitres and litres
- estimate capacity using referents
- measure capacity using conversions from millilitres and litres and from litres to millilitres
- order capacities from least to greatest and from greatest to least
- select appropriate referents for cubic centimetres and cubic metres
- estimate volume using referents
- measure volume using referents like cubes and by using formulas
- construct or draw right rectangular prisms

PREREQUISITE SKILLS AND KNOWLEDGE

Prior to starting this unit, you should be able to…

- demonstrate an understanding of what a referent is
- use a referent to measure in non-standard units

Lesson 1   RELATIONSHIPS BETWEEN MILLILITRES AND LITRES

NOTES

The **capacity** of a container is the amount of liquid that the container can hold. Two standard units used for measuring capacity are **litres (L)** and **millilitres (mL).**

A millilitre is a very small unit of measure and is used to measure the capacities of small containers. The relationship between millilitres and litres is that there are 1 000 millilitres in one litre.

1 L = 1 000 mL

Containers with a capacity less than 1 L are usually measured in millilitres. Containers with a capacity greater than 1 L are usually measured in litres.

If the capacity of a container is just over 1 L, millilitres are usually used. For example, a bottle that holds 1 L and 75 millilitres of juice will most likely be labelled as having a capacity of 1 075 mL.

Many containers have a capacity that is less than 1 L but are measured in terms of litres. When you refer to their capacities, you can use fractional words like *one-quarter litre*, *one-half litre*, or *three-quarters of a litre*.

This table shows the relationships between fractional parts of litres and the corresponding millilitres.

$\frac{1}{4}$ L	250 mL
$\frac{1}{2}$ L	500 mL
$\frac{3}{4}$ L	750 mL
$\frac{4}{4}$ L	1 000 mL = 1 L

PRACTICE EXERCISES

For each container shown, write whether it would be best to record the capacity in millilitres (mL) or litres (L).

A bottle of syrup:

1. A full bottle of syrup could have a capacity of 725 _____.

A bathtub:

2. A standard-sized bathtub filled with water could have a capacity of 375 _____.

A cup:

3. A cup of hot chocolate could have a capacity of 200 _____.

Lesson 2   USING APPROPRIATE REFERENTS FOR MILLILITRES AND LITRES

MILLILITRES

When estimating the capacity of a small container, you want to use a referent that is reasonable. It is best to choose a referent that is close in size to the container being measured, and is smaller than the container being measured.

• The larger the referent used to estimate capacity, the fewer number of referents needed.

• The smaller the referent used to estimate capacity, the greater the number of referents needed.

Some referents for millilitres are listed as follows:

A drop of water is about 1 mL.	
One teaspoon holds about 5 mL of liquid.	
One tablespoon holds about 15 mL of liquid.	
A small milk or juice carton holds about 250 mL of liquid.	
Many small water bottles hold about 500 mL.	

 Example

After Jared ate his yogurt for lunch, he decided to measure the capacity of the yogurt container.

Should he use the tablespoon, the eye dropper, or the small water bottle as a referent? Justify your answer.

Solution

Of the three choices, the tablespoon is the most appropriate referent.

Since a tablespoon can hold about 15 mL of water, the tablespoon is a better referent than the eyedropper which holds about 1 mL of water.

Since a lunch yogurt container is smaller than a 500mL bottle, the bottle is too large a referent.

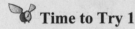 **Time to Try 1**

Laramy used the lid of his thermos bottle as a referent to estimate the capacity of the thermos.

Did Laramy use an appropriate referent? Justify your answer.

LITRES

When estimating the capacity of a large container, you should use a referent that can hold at least 1 L of liquid. For very large containers, you should use referents that are greater than 1 L in capacity.

NOTES

Some referents for litres are listed as follows:

A regular carton of juice holds about 1 L.	
A large bottle of pop holds about 2 L.	
A large jug of milk holds about 4 L.	

✳ Example

Josh wants to measure the amount of water his bathtub could hold. Should Joshua use the 1 L carton from juice, the 2 L pop bottle, of the 4 L jug from milk as a referent? Justify your answer.

Solution

Joshua should use the 4 L jug from milk as a referent.

Since a bathtub is a large container, it would be most appropriate to choose a large referent. You would need fewer jugs of water than if you used the 1 L carton or the 2 L bottle.

🦋 Time to Try 2

Jill uses a 100 mL cup to measure the capacity of the laundry sink. Jill is pouring her 50th cup of water into the sink.

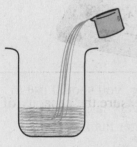

Did Jill use an appropriate referent for estimating the capacity of the sink? Justify your answer.

PRACTICE EXERCISES

Use the following information to answer the next question.

Louise uses an eyedropper to measure the capacity of a beaker.

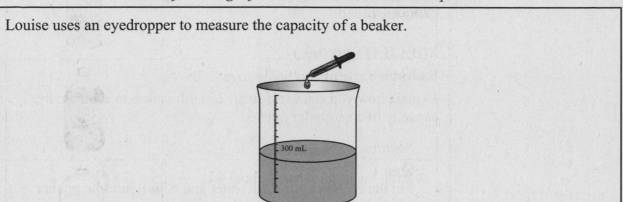

300 mL

1. Is the eyedropper an appropriate referent to use? Justify your answer.

Use the following information to answer the next question.

Debra uses a jar that holds almost 2 L of water to measure the capacity of the sink at the back of the classroom.

2. Is Debra using an appropriate referent to measure the capacity of the sink?
    Justify your answer.

Lesson 3 ESTIMATING CAPACITY USING REFERENTS

When estimating capacity with a referent, you are determining about how many of the referent containers are needed to fill the container being measured.

MILLILITRES (mL)

Example

Explain how you can use a small 250 mL carton to estimate the capacity of a particular pitcher.

Solution

Step 1

Fill the empty carton with water and pour it into the pitcher. Mark the level of the water in the pitcher.

Step 2

Repeat the process, making a mark after each carton of water was poured into the pitcher.

Step 3

When the pitcher is full, determine the estimated capacity.

The capacity of the pitcher is a little more than the total capacity of three cartons: 250 + 250 + 250 = 750 mL. A good estimate of the capacity of the pitcher could be about 800 mL.

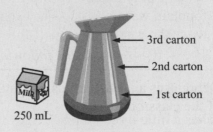

🐛 Time to Try 1

The small pail holds about 220 mL of water.

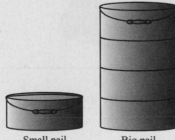

Small pail   Big pail

Estimate the capacity of the big pail. Explain how you used the referent to estimate.

LITRES

Example

Emily used a 1 L carton to estimate the capacity of this juice fountain. She poured 16 cartons of juice into the fountain.

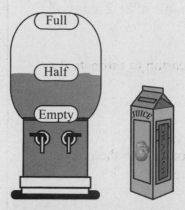

Estimate the capacity of the juice fountain. Explain your answer.

Solution

The capacity of the fountain is about 32 L.

When Emily poured 16 cartons of juice into the fountain, the fountain was half full. The capacity of the fountain when full is twice the capacity of a half-full fountain.
$16 \times 2 = 32$

 Time to Try 2

It takes a little more than 8 L of water to fill the small pail.

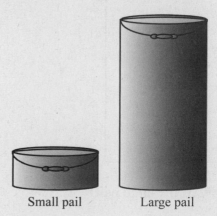

Small pail   Large pail

Estimate the capacity of the large pail. Explain how you can use the referent to estimate the capacity of the large pail.

PRACTICE EXERCISES

Use the following information to answer the next question.

Aspen measures the capacity of a bottle by pouring full cups of water into it. Each cup holds about 100 mL when full. The arrow points to the water level in the bottle after 2 cups of water have been poured into the bottle.

1. Estimate the capacity of the bottle in millilitres. Explain your answer.

Use the following information to answer the next question.

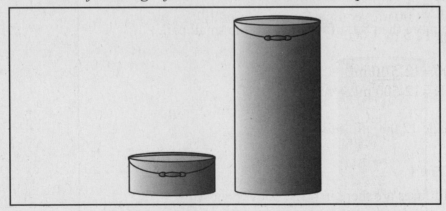

2. If the small pail holds about 33 L of water, what is the capacity of the large pail? Explain your answer.

Lesson 4   MEASURING AND RECORDING CAPACITY

To compare capacities that are measured in different units, you need to convert all the measurements into the same unit. It is usually more practical to convert litres into millilitres when comparing capacities.

CHANGING LITRES INTO MILLILITRES

When you convert litres into millilitres, the number of millilitres will be larger than the number of litres. That means you should multiply the number of litres by 1 000 to find the number of millilitres.

Larger unit to smaller unit → think multiplication.

A quick way to multiply a whole number by 1 000 is to add three zeros to the end of the number. 6 L ×1 000 = 6 <u>000</u> mL

A quick way to multiply a decimal number by 1 000 is to move the decimal point three places to the right. 6.5 L ×1 000 = 6 <u>500</u> mL

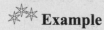 **Example**

Rhonda made 12.5 L of lemonade for a class party. Expressed in millilitres, how much lemonade did Rhonda make?

Solution

Larger unit to smaller unit → think multiplication.

Since 1 L = 1 000 mL, convert 12.5 L into millilitres by multiplying 12.5 by 1 000

12.5×1 000 = 12 <u>500</u> mL
      12.5 L = 12 500 mL

Rhonda made 12 000 mL of lemonade.

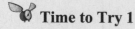 **Time to Try 1**

How many millilitres are there in 4 L? Show your work.

NOTES

CHANGING MILLILITRES INTO LITRES

When you convert millilitres into litres, the number of litres will be smaller than the number of millilitres. That means that you can divide the number of millilitres by 1 000 to find the number of litres.

Smaller unit to larger unit → think division.

- A quick way to divide a whole number by 1 000 is to move the decimal point three places to the left. $7 \text{ L} \times 1 \ 000 = 7 \ \underline{000} \text{ mL}$.

- When the decimal point is not shown, it would be located to the right of the last digit. $2\underline{450} \text{ mL} \div 1 \ 000 = 2.45 \text{ L}$

 Example

How many litres are there in 3 550 millilitres?

Solution

Smaller unit to larger unit → think division.

Since 1 000 mL = 1 L, convert 3 550 mL into litres by dividing 3 550 mL by 1 000.

$3 \ \underline{550} \div 1 \ 000 = 3.55$
   $3 \ 550 \text{ mL} = 3.55 \text{ L}$

 Time to Try 2

A bowl is filled with 1 520 mL of milk. Expressed in litres, how much milk is in the bowl? Show your work.

USING FRACTIONS OF LITRES

This chart shows the relationships between the fractional parts of litres and their equivalent millilitre measures.

$\frac{1}{4}$ L = 250 mL
$\frac{1}{2}$ L = 500 mL
$\frac{3}{4}$ L = 750 mL
$\frac{4}{4}$ L = 1 000 mL

✳✳✳ **Example**

How many glasses of liquid will it take to fill one 1 L carton?
Explain your answer.

Solution

It would take four $\frac{1}{4}$ L glasses to fill the carton.

One-quarter litre is equal to 250 mL.

Since the carton has a capacity of 1 L, it would take four glasses
to equal 1 000 mL (1 L).
250 + 250 + 250 + 250 = 1 000

 Time to Try 3

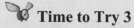

Kaitlyn's milk carton holds one-quarter litre of milk.

Last Monday, 28 Grade 5 students chose to drink a carton of milk at
recess. How many litres of milk did the students drink last Monday?
Explain your answer.

NOTES

RECORDING CAPACITIES FROM LEAST TO GREATEST

When ordering capacities from least to greatest and all the capacities are in the same unit (millilitres or litres), place the numbers in order from least value to greatest value.

If there are millilitre and litre capacities, order the millilitre capacities first (if they are less than 1 000 mL), and then the litre capacities.

If some millilitre capacities are greater than 1 000 mL, convert the litres to millilitres so they are in the same unit. Then, place the numbers in order from least to greatest.

✳ Example

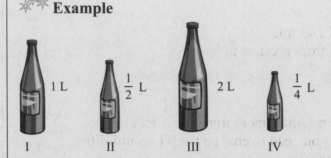

I   1 L   II $\frac{1}{2}$ L   III   2 L   IV $\frac{1}{4}$ L

Order the bottles from least capacity to greatest capacity.

Solution

Since $\frac{1}{4} < \frac{1}{2} < 1 < 2$, the capacities from least to greatest are

$\frac{1}{4}$ L, $\frac{1}{2}$ L, 1 L, 2 L.

In order from least capacity to greatest capacity, the bottles are IV, II, I, III.

🐝 Time to Try 4

4 L, 544 mL, 4.5 L, 454 mL

Order the capacities from least to greatest.

RECORDING CAPACITIES FROM GREATEST TO LEAST

When ordering capacities from greatest to least and all the capacities are in the same unit (millilitre or litres), place the numbers in order from greatest value to least value.

If there are millilitre and litre capacities, order the litre capacities first, and then the millilitre capacities (if they are all less than 1 000 mL).

If some of the millilitre capacities are greater than 1 000 mL, convert the litres to millilitre so the capacities are all in the same unit. Then, order the numbers from greatest to least.

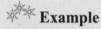 **Example**

9 mL, 9 L, 5 000 mL, 45 mL
Order the capacities from greatest to least.

Solution

Step 1
Since one of the millilitre measurements is greater than
1 000 mL (1 L), you need to change the 9 L to millilitres.
9 L × 1 000 = 9 000 mL

Step 2
Place the numbers in order from greatest to least.
9 000 > 5 000 > 45 > 9
9 000 mL > 5 000 mL > 45 mL > 9 mL.

From greatest to least, the capacities are 9 L, 5 000 mL, 45 mL, 9 mL.

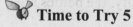 **Time to Try 5**

2 L, 1 200 mL, 950 mL, 1 L

Order the capacities from greatest to least.

PRACTICE EXERCISES

Use the following information to answer the next question.

Each of the bottles shown has a capacity of 2 L.

1. What is the capacity of the bottles in millilitres? Show your work.

2. Melanie prepared 5 500 mL of fruit punch for a party. How many litres of fruit punch did Melanie prepare? Show your work.

Use the following information to answer the next question.

4½ L   1 L   250 mL   1 200 mL   1½ L

3. Order the capacities of the five containers from least to greatest.

4. Order the capacities 540 mL, 450 mL, 1 L, and 0.5 L from greatest to least.

Lesson 5 UNDERSTANDING VOLUME OF PRISMS

Volume is the amount of space that a three-dimensional figure like a rectangular prism takes up.

The black box is bigger than the grey box because it occupies more space. This observation can be verified by using cubes and recreating the boxes.

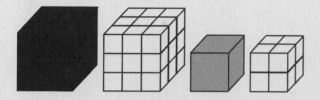

It took three layers of nine cubes to make the black box. It took two layers of four cubes to make the grey box.

The volume of the boxes can be determined by counting up all the cubes that make up each box.

- The black box is made up of 27 cubes. The black box has a volume of 27 units^3.
- The grey box is made up of eight cubes. The grey box has a volume of 8 units^3.

The volume of any rectangular prism can be determined by identifying how many cubes each prism is made up of.

Volume is measured in cubic units (unit^3). A cubic unit is a cube where each side is equal to one unit.

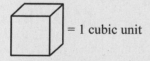 = 1 cubic unit

Cubic units are the most appropriate unit to use for measuring volume because cubes fit side by side without leaving spaces or gaps. Cubes can also be layered without spaces or gaps.

PRACTICE EXERCISES

Use the following information to answer the next question.

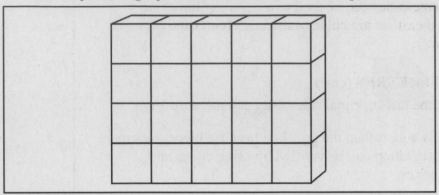

1. What is the volume of this box?

Use the following information to answer the next question.

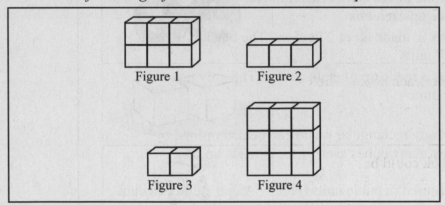

Figure 1

Figure 2

Figure 3   Figure 4

2. Which rectangular prism has the **greatest** volume? Justify your answer.

414

Lesson 6   *USING APPROPRIATE REFERENTS FOR CUBIC CENTIMETRES AND CUBIC METRES*

Although any size cubes can be used to measure volume, the most common measures are cubic centimetres (cm^3) and cubic metres (m^3).

CUBIC CENTIMETRES (cm^3)

A centimetre cube has six equal sides that each measure 1 cm.

1 cm
1 cm
1 cm

You can use referents to help you measure the volume of small right rectangular prisms. A referent for a cubic centimetre is an object that is about 1 cm in height, width, and length.

Some referents for cubic centimetres are listed as follows:

Dice are each about 1 cm^3.	
Sugar cubes are each about 1 cm^3.	
A number block could be about 1 cm^3.	
A child's building block could be about 1 cm^3.	

NOTES

CUBIC METRES (m³)

A metre cube has six equal sides that each measure 1 m (100 cm). It would take 1 000 000 cm³ (100×100×100) to equal the volume of 1 m³.

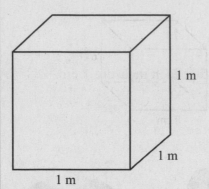

Metre cubes are used to measure large volumes.

For example, the interior of a semi truck would be measured in cubic metres. A storage room would be measured in cubic metres.

A referent for cubic metres could be a cardboard box that is about 1 m long, 1 m wide, and 1 m high.

416

PRACTICE EXERCISES

Use the following information to answer the next question.

Marina wants to estimate the volume of the box shown.

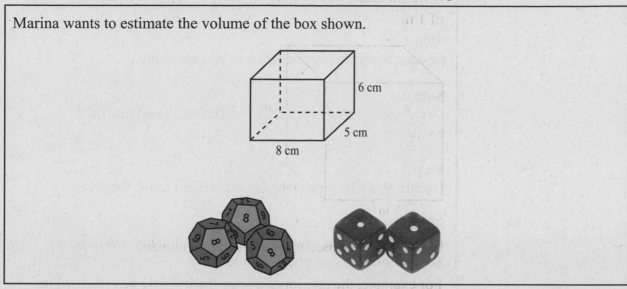

1. Which set of dice would be **best** for her to use to make a good estimate? Justify your answer.

Use the following information to answer the next question.

Sam is using a 1 m^3 referent to estimate the volume of the back of this truck.

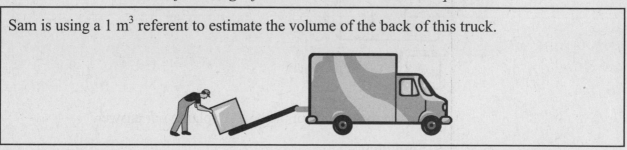

2. Explain why it is more appropriate for Sam to use a 1 m^3 referent than a 1 cm^3 referent.

Lesson 7 *ESTIMATING VOLUME USING REFERENTS*

When you estimate volume, you are deciding about how many cubic units will fill the space of the rectangular prism you are measuring.

Step 1

Choose a referent for the measure you are using.

Step 2

Decide about how many cubes will cover the bottom of the prism.

Step 3

Decide about how many layers are needed to fill the prism.

Step 4

Determine the total number of cubes you think you will need. That will be the estimated volume.

 Example

Jason uses cubic building blocks to help him estimate the volume of the given box. He starts by covering the base of the box with nine blocks: three rows with three blocks in each row.

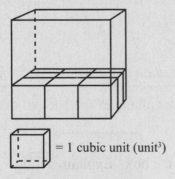

= 1 cubic unit (unit³)

Estimate the volume of the box. Explain your answer.

Solution

Step 1

Estimate the volume.

The volume of the box is around 27 units^3.

Step 2
Explain your answer.

Jason should be able to make two more layers of blocks.

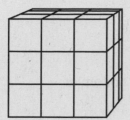

Three layers would result in a total of 27 blocks. $9 + 9 + 9 = 27$

 Time to Try 1

Alex used a connecting cube to represent 1 cm^3.

He used the cube to help him estimate the volume of the box.

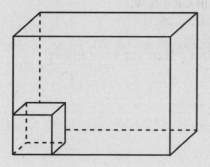

Using the referent, estimate the volume of the box. Explain your answer.

PRACTICE EXERCISES

Use the following information to answer the next question.

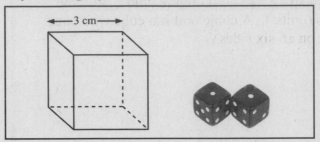

1. Using the dice as referents, estimate the volume of the cube. Explain your answer.

Use the following information to answer the next question.

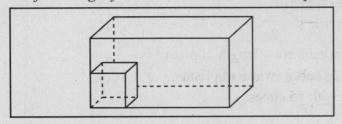

2. Using the 1 cm cube as a referent, estimate the volume of the box. Explain your answer.

Use the following information to answer the next question.

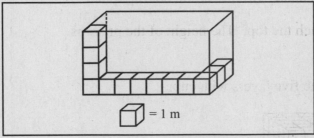

3. Using the 1 m cube as a referent, estimate the volume of the crate. Explain your answer.

Lesson 8   MEASURING AND RECORDING VOLUME

USING REFERENTS (CUBES)

Volume is the amount of space that a 3-D figure holds. Volume is measured in cubic units (units^3). A cubic unit is a cube with equal side lengths of one unit on all six sides.

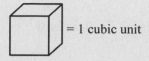 = 1 cubic unit

To find the volume of a rectangular prism, start by counting the number of cubic units needed to fill the base of the prism.

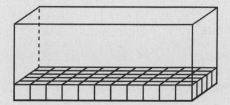

- There are 11 cubes in each row (length of prism).
- There are five rows of cubes (width of prism).
- The base is covered with 55 cubes.

The next step is to determine the number of cubic units needed to reach the top of the prism.

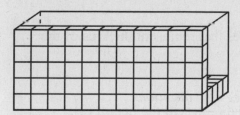

It takes five cubes to reach the top. The height of the prism is five cubes.

The next step is to fill the five layers with cubes.

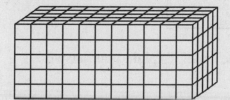

✳✳ **Example**

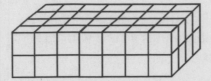

What is the volume of the given rectangular prism? Explain how the cubes can be used to determine the volume.

Solution

Step 1
Determine the volume of the prism.

The volume of the prism is 56 units^3.

Step 2
Explain how the cubes can be used to determine the volume.

Count the number of cubes that represent the length (7).
Count the number of cubes that represent the width (4).

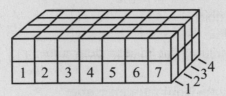

Determine the number of cubes that represent the area of the base of the prism.
$7 \times 4 = 28$ or $7+7+7+7 = 28$

Count the number of cubes that represent the height (2).
To determine the volume, add the two layers of blocks together.
$28 + 28 = 56$

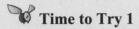 **Time to Try 1**

This rectangular prism was created by stacking congruent layers of connecting cubes.

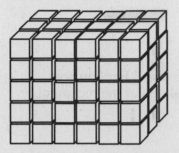

Explain how to find the volume of the rectangular prism using the connecting cubes.

USING A FORMULA

Another way to determine the volume of a rectangular prism is to use the volume formula: $V = l \times w \times h$

volume = length × width × height

- Multiply the length times the width of the base to determine the area of the base.
- Multiply the area of the base by the height to determine the volume.

These diagrams show how the cube method of determining the volume (using a referent) is related to the formula method of determining the volume.

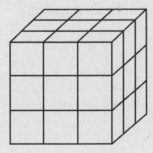 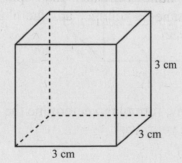

3 cm

3 cm

3 cm

NOTES

✳ Example

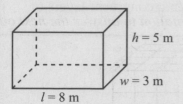

h = 5 m
w = 3 m
l = 8 m

Use the volume formula to determine the volume of the rectangular prism. Show your work.

Solution

Step 1
Identify the volume formula.

The formula for determining the volume of a rectangular prism is $V = l \times w \times h$.

Step 2
Show your work.

Substitute the numbers for the length (8 m), the width (3 m), and the height (5 m) into the formula.

$$V = l \times w \times h$$
$$= 8 \times 3 \times 5$$
$$= 120 \text{ m}^3$$

The volume of the rectangular prism is 120 m^3.

🦋 Time to Try 2

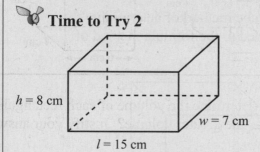

h = 8 cm
w = 7 cm
l = 15 cm

Use the volume formula to determine the volume of the rectangular prism. Show your work.

PRACTICE EXERCISES

Use the following information to answer the next question.

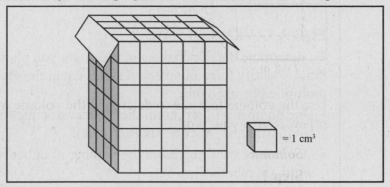

1. Explain how you can use the referent to determine the volume of the box.

Use the following information to answer the next question.

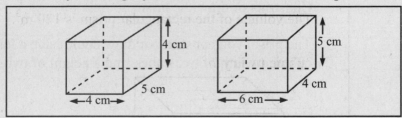

2. Use the volume formula to determine the volume of each rectangular prism. Which of the two prisms has the greater volume? Justify your answer.

Lesson 9   CONSTRUCTING OR DRAWING RIGHT RECTANGULAR PRISMS

NOTES

You can use cubes to construct or draw right rectangular prisms.

FOR A GIVEN VOLUME

To determine the dimensions of the prism you plan to construct or draw, identify three numbers that will equal the given volume when multiplied by each other.

- One number will represent the number of cubes needed for the length (number of cubes in each row).
- One number will represent the number of cubes needed for the width (number of rows).
- One number will represent the number of cubes needed for the height (number of layers).

 Example

Construct or draw a rectangular prism that has a volume of 16 units^3.

Solution

Step 1

Identify three numbers that equal 16 when multiplied by each other.
One set of numbers is $4 \times 2 \times 2 = 16$.

Step 2

Construct or draw the prism.

The prism you construct or draw could have a length of four cubes, a width of two cubes, and a height of two cubes.

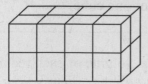

 Time to Try 1

Construct or draw a rectangular prism that has a volume of 27 units^3.

SAME VOLUME, DIFFERENT PRISMS

The same volume can be represented by more than one rectangular prism.

To construct two (or more) rectangular prisms for a given volume, you first need to determine two (or more) sets of three numbers that will equal the given volume when multiplied by each other.

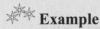 **Example**

Construct or draw two rectangular prisms for a volume of 4 units^3.

Solution

Step 1
Identify three numbers that will equal 4 when multiplied by each other.

One set of numbers is $2 \times 2 \times 1 = 4$.

The prism you construct or draw could have a length of two cubes, a width of two cubes, and a height of one cube.

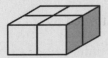

Step 2
Identify another three numbers that will equal 4 when multiplied by each other.
$4 \times 1 \times 1 = 4$

The prism you construct or draw could have a length of four cubes, a width of one cube, and a height of one cube.

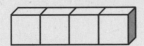

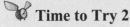 **Time to Try 2**

Draw two rectangular prisms that both have a volume of 8 units^3.

PRACTICE EXERCISES

1. Construct or draw a rectangular prism that has a volume of 24 units^3.

2. Construct or draw three rectangular prisms that each have a volume of 12 units^3.

REVIEW SUMMARY

- Capacity is most commonly measured in millilitres and litres.
- There are 1 000 mL in 1 L.

- Small capacities can be recorded in millilitres or in fractions of litres like 250 mL $\left(\text{or } \dfrac{1}{4} \text{ L} \right)$,

  500 mL $\left(\text{or } \dfrac{1}{2} \text{ L} \right)$, and 750 mL $\left(\text{or } \dfrac{3}{4} \text{ L} \right)$.

- Larger capacities are usually recorded in litres. Capacities just greater than 1 L are often recorded in millilitres.
- The referent you choose for estimating capacity should be appropriate for the size of the container you are measuring.
- To change litres into millilitres, multiply the number of litres by 1 000.
- To change millilitres to litres, divide the number of millilitres by 1 000.
- Volume is the amount of space that a rectangular prism takes up.
- The referent you choose for estimating volume should be appropriate for the size of the rectangular prism you are measuring.
- Volume is measured and recorded in cubic units like cm^3 and m^3.
- You can measure volume by using referents that are cubes. Count the number of cubes that will fill up the prism.
- You can measure volume by using the volume formula: $V = l \times w \times h$.
- To construct or draw a prism for a given volume, first identify three numbers that equal the given volume when multiplied by each other.
  - The three numbers will represent the number of cubes needed for the length, width, and height of the prism.
  - The same volume can be represented by different rectangular prisms.

PRACTICE TEST

Use the following information to answer the next question.

Emma uses an eyedropper to measure the capacity of a cup.

1. Is the eyedropper an appropriate referent to use? Justify your answer.

Use the following information to answer the next question.

Ashley uses a 4 L jug to fill the small pail with water. It takes 15 jugs to fill the small pail.

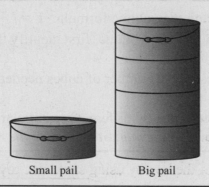

Small pail   Big pail

2. Estimate the capacity of the big pail. Explain your work.

Use the following information to answer the next question.

1 000 mL, 1.5 L, 1 005 mL, 0.5 mL

3. Order the capacities from greatest to least.

Use the following information to answer the next question.

A coach brought five packs of water bottles to soccer practice. Each pack had six bottles. Each bottle contained 300 mL of water.

4. How many litres of water did the coach bring to the practice? Show your work.

Use the following information to answer the next question.

1 200 mL, 2 L, 950 mL, 2 050 mL, 1 L

5. Order the capacities from least to greatest.

Use the following information to answer the next question.

William estimates the volume of the box by using same size toy blocks.

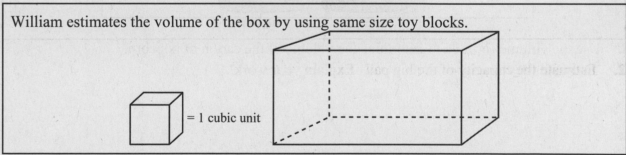

= 1 cubic unit

6. Using the given referent, estimate the volume of the box. Explain how you used the referent.

Use the following information to answer the next question.

Jerome constructed this figure out of blocks to determine the volume of a box that has the same dimensions.

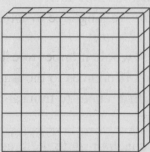

7. What is the volume of the box? Explain how you can use the blocks to determine the volume of the box.

Use the following information to answer the next question.

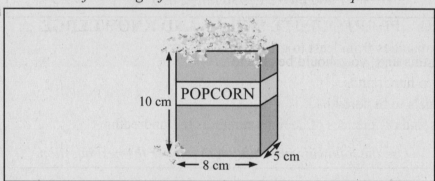

8. Use the volume formula to determine the volume of the carton of popcorn. Show your work.

9. Construct or draw three rectangular prisms that each has a volume of 18 units^3.

ADDITION AND SUBTRACTION OF DECIMALS

When you are finished this unit, you will be able to…

- use front-end estimation and comparative language to estimate sums and differences to thousandths
- round decimal numbers to the nearest whole number to estimate sums and differences
- use algorithms to calculate sums and differences to thousandths
- solve problems involving sums and differences to thousandths

PREREQUISITE SKILLS AND KNOWLEDGE

Prior to starting this unit, you should be able to…

- add decimals to hundredths
- subtract decimals to hundredths
- estimate sums and differences of decimal numbers to hundredths

Lesson 1 ESTIMATING SUMS AND DIFFERENCES TO THOUSANDTHS

USING FRONT-END ESTIMATION AND COMPARATIVE LANGUAGE TO DESCRIBE SUMS

To use front-end estimation, keep the whole number, and drop the decimal point and decimal digits.

The next step is to describe the sum by comparing it to the estimated sum. You can use words or phrases like *is greater than*, *is less than*, *is almost the same as*, and *is about*.

 Example

Using the strategy of front-end estimation, describe the sum of $9.45 + 1.1 + 125.735$.

Solution

Step 1
Use front-end estimation.
$$9.45 \rightarrow 9$$
$$1.1 \rightarrow 1$$
$$125.735 \rightarrow 125$$

Step 2
Calculate the estimated sum.
$$9 + 1 + 125 = 135$$

Step 3
Describe the sum of $9.45 + 1.1 + 125.735$.

Since all three numbers were rounded down, the estimated sum is less than the actual sum.

Therefore, you can describe the sum of $9.45 + 1.1 + 125.735$ as being greater than 135.

 Time to Try 1

Using the strategy of front-end estimation, describe the sum of $120.005 + 12.1 + 0.016 + 24.02$

USING FRONT-END ESTIMATION AND COMPARATICVE LANGUAGE TO DESCRIBE DIFFERENCES

Recall that in front-end estimation, you keep the whole number and drop the decimal point and decimal digits.

Describe the difference by comparing it to the estimated difference, using words or phrases like *is greater than*, *is less than*, *is almost the same as*, and *is about*.

 Example

Using the strategy of front-end estimation, describe the difference of $135.873 - 16.001$.

Solution

Step 1
Use front-end estimation.
$135.873 \rightarrow 135$
$16.001 \rightarrow 16$

Step 2
Calculate the estimated difference.
$135 - 16 = 119$

Step 3
Describe the difference of $135.873 - 16.001$.

Since 135.873 was rounded down and 16.001 is almost the same, the estimated difference will be less than the actual difference.

Therefore, you can describe the difference of $135.873 - 16.001$ as being greater than 119.

 Time to Try 2

Using the strategy of front-end estimation, describe the difference of $163.983 - 10.981$.

ROUNDING TO THE NEAREST WHOLE NUMBER

To round to the nearest whole number, look at the digit in the tenths place.

- If the digit is 5 or greater than 5, round up the digit in the ones place. Drop the decimal point and decimal digits.
- If the digit in the tenths place is less than 5, leave the whole number as it is. Drop the decimal point and decimal digits.

USING THE ROUNDING RULE TO ESTIMATE SUMS

 Example

Using the strategy of rounding to the nearest whole number, estimate the sum of $875.356 + 39.089$. Show your work.

Solution

Step 1
Round the decimal numbers.

$875.\underline{3}56 \rightarrow 875$ because $3 < 5$
$39.\underline{0}89 \rightarrow 39$ because $0 < 5$

Step 2
Add the rounded numbers, regrouping where necessary.

$$\begin{array}{r} 875 \\ +39 \\ \hline 914 \end{array}$$

The estimated sum of $875.356 + 39.089$ is 914.

 Time to Try 3

Using the strategy of rounding to the nearest whole number, estimate the sum of $14.735 + 0.109 + 363.5$. Show your work.

USING THE ROUNDING RULE TO ESTIMATE DIFFERENCES

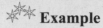 **Example**

Using the strategy of rounding to the nearest whole number, estimate the difference of $892.479 - 694.301$. Show your work.

Solution

Step 1
Round the decimal numbers.
$892.\underline{4}79 \rightarrow 892$ because $4 < 5$
$694.\underline{3}01 \rightarrow 694$ because $3 < 5$

Step 2
Subtract the rounded numbers, regrouping where necessary.

$$
\begin{array}{r}
892 \\
-694 \\
\hline
198
\end{array}
$$

The estimated difference of $892.479 - 694.301$ is 198.

Time to Try 4

Using the strategy of rounding to the nearest whole number, estimate the difference of 605.35 and 295.689. Show your work.

PRACTICE EXERCISES

1. Using the strategy of front-end estimation, describe the sum of $173.123 + 0.27 + 236.051$. Show your work.

2. Using the strategy of front-end estimation, describe the difference of $172.007 - 83.1$. Show your work.

3. Using the strategy of rounding to the nearest whole number, estimate the sum of $398.903 + 172.999 + 18.05$. Show your work.

4. Using the strategy of rounding to the nearest whole number, estimate the difference of $437.448 - 201.8$. Show your work.

Lesson 2 CALCULATING SUMS AND DIFFERENCES TO THOUSANDTHS

Adding or subtracting decimal numbers is similar to adding or subtracting whole numbers.
- You work from right to left.
- Place value is important because only the digits in the same place value position can be added together or subtracted from each other.

When calculating sums and differences involving decimals, it is important to remember these points:
- Line up the decimal points when writing the numbers. Doing this will keep the same place values in line.
- The decimal point in the answer is always placed between the digit in the ones place and the digit in the tenths place. All decimal points should be directly below each other.
- It is easier to calculate when there are the same number of digits to the right of the decimal point.

ADDING THE SAME NUMBER OF DECIMAL PLACE VALUES

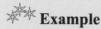 **Example**

Find the sum for $3.780 + 2.134$.

Solution

Remember to line up the decimal points and the same place value digits when writing the numbers below each other.

$$\begin{array}{r} \overset{1}{2.780} \\ +2.134 \\ \hline 5.914 \end{array}$$

Remember to put the decimal in the answer between the ones digit (5) and tenths digit (9).

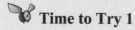 **Time to Try 1**

Find the sum for $17.503 + 52.096$. Show your work.

NOTES

ADDING A DIFFERENT NUMBER OF DECIMAL PLACE VALUES

Recall that you can make equivalent decimals by adding zeros to the ends of decimal numbers without changing their values.

 Example

Find the sum for $4.7 + 5.324 + 1.75$. Show your work.

> *Solution*
>
> **Step 1**
> Add zeros to make equivalent decimals.
> $4.7 \rightarrow 4.700$
> $1.75 \rightarrow 1.750$
>
> **Step 2**
> Show your work.
> $$\begin{array}{r} \overset{1}{4.700} \\ 5.324 \\ +1.750 \\ \hline 11.774 \end{array}$$

Remember to put the decimal in the answer between the ones digit (1) and tenths digit (7).

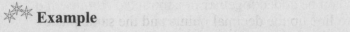 **Time to Try 2**

Find the sum for $34.52 + 176.409 + 1.8$. Show your work.

SUBTRACTING THE SAME NUMBER OF DECIMAL PLACE VALUES

 Example

Find the difference for 3.785 − 2.134

Solution

Remember to line up the decimal points and the same place value digits when writing the numbers below each other.

```
  3.785
− 2.134
  1.651
```

Remember to put the decimal in the answer between the ones digit (1) and tenths digit (6).

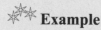 **Time to Try 3**

Find the difference for 83.760 − 2.145. Show your work.

SUBTRACTING A DIFFERENT NUMBER OF DECIMAL PLACE VALUES

Recall that you can make equivalent decimals by adding zeros to the ends of decimal numbers without changing their values.

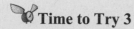 **Example**

Find the difference for 311.458 − 19.14
Show your work.

Solution

Step 1
Make an equivalent decimal for 19.14.
19.14 → 19.140

Step 2

Show your work.

$$\overset{2\ \overset{10}{\cancel{0}}\ 11}{\cancel{3}11}.458$$
$$-1\ 9.140$$
$$\overline{\ 292.318}$$

Remember to put the decimal in the answer between the ones digit (2) and tenths digit (3).

 Time to Try 4

Find the difference for $38.96 - 7.832$. Show your work.

PRACTICE EXERCISES

Find the sums for the next two questions. Show your work.

1. $83.409 + 165.5$

2. $427.4 + 32.056 + 71.23$

Find the differences for the next two questions. Show your work.

3. $426.663 - 14.5$

4. $187.45 - 7.126$

Lesson 3   SOLVING PROBLEMS INVOLVING DECIMALS TO THOUSANDTHS

NOTES

Solving an addition or subtraction problem requires you to read the question carefully and to understand what is being asked.

You need to pay close attention to keywords such as *total*, *in all*, *altogether*, and *sum*. These words are often clues that you may need to add to solve the problem.

Words such as *left*, *how many more*, *fewer*, and *difference* are often clues that you may need to subtract to solve the problem.

GENERAL RULES FOR ADDING AND SUBTRACTING DECIMAL NUMBERS

Step 1
Write the numbers vertically.

Step 2
Line up the decimal points and same place values.

Step 3
Make equivalent decimals so all the digits to the right of the decimal point have the same number of digits.

Step 4
Add or subtract the same as for whole numbers, regrouping where necessary.

Step 5
Place the decimal point in the answer between the ones digit and tens digit.

Example

Jenny ran the first half of a race in 24.35 s and the second half in 34.657 s. How much longer did it take Jenny to run the second half of the race?

Solution

Step 1

Determine the operation that will solve the problem.

The words "how much longer" are a clue that you need to subtract.

Step 2

Subtract the two race times to find the difference.

$$
\begin{array}{r}
34.657 \\
-24.350 \\
\hline
10.307 \\
\end{array}
$$

It took Jenny 10.307 s longer to run the second half of the race than the first half of the race.

 Time to Try 1

Hannah delivered 5.356 kg of papers and 1.786 kg of flyers in one day. What was the total weight of the papers and flyers she delivered that day?

PRACTICE EXERCISES

1. Three students practiced running a relay race. Haley ran her lap in 73.5 s. Brent ran his lap in 70.09 s. Darcey ran her lap in 69.445 s. What was the total time of the practice race?

2. Several girls practiced racing during the lunch hour at their school. Amanda ran around the track in 28.428 s. Her sister Kelly ran around the same track in 34.75 s. How much faster was Amanda than Kelly?

3. For a quilting project, Mrs. Mullen bought 5.8 m of blue material, 9.25 m of striped material, and 12.459 m of flowered material. How much material did Mrs. Mullen buy in all?

4. Paul and Julia both ran for two hours. Paul ran 12.529 km in the first hour and 14.273 km in the second hour. Julia ran 16.728 km in the first hour and 10.087 km in the second hour. How much farther did Julia run than Paul?

REVIEW SUMMARY

- To use front-end estimation, keep the whole number, and drop the decimal point and decimal digits.
- You can describe a sum or difference by comparing it to an estimated sum or difference, using comparative language like *greater than*, *less than*, *almost the same*.
- To round decimal numbers to the nearest whole number, look at the digit in the tenths place.
  - If the digit is five or greater, round up the digit in the ones place, and drop the decimal point and decimal digits.
  - If the digit is less than 5, leave the whole number as it is, and drop the decimal point and decimal digits.
- When adding or subtracting decimal numbers, it is important to line up the decimal points and the place values.
- If the decimal numbers have different values, make equivalent decimals so all numbers have the same number of digits to the right of the decimal points.
- When solving problems, look for clue words to help you determine the operation to use.
- Clue words for subtraction are words such as *how many more*, *fewer*, and *difference*.
- Clue words for addition are words such as *total*, *in all*, *altogether*, and *sum*.

PRACTICE TEST

1. Using the strategy of front-end estimation, describe the sum of $37.56 + 1.392 + 146.5$. Show your work.

2. Using the strategy of rounding to the nearest whole number, estimate the sum of $34.729 + 0.15 + 126.09$. Show your work.

3. Calculate the sum of 120.5, 87.061, and 1.25. Show your work.

4. Katelyn ran the first half of a race in 24.35 s and the second half in 34.657 s. How long did it take her to complete the entire race?

5. Using the strategy of front-end estimation, describe the difference for $198.903 - 72.919$. Show your work.

6. Using the strategy of rounding to the nearest whole number, estimate the difference for $383.427 - 71.61$. Show your work.

7. Calculate the difference of 305.516 and 27.45. Show your work.

Use the following information to answer the next question.

The coach timed five of his best runners at a practice run and recorded their times as follows:
- David came in at 131.05 s.
- Maria came in at 130.99 s.
- Lexie came in at 132.725 s.
- Brent came in at 131.345 s.
- Carol came in at 130.8 s.

8. What is the difference between the fastest recorded time and the slowest recorded time?

450

PROBABILITY

When you are finished this unit, you will be able to…

• describe the likelihood of a single outcome as impossible, possible, or certain

• compare the likelihood of two possible outcomes occurring using words like *less likely*, *more likely*, or *equally likely*

PREREQUISITE SKILLS AND KNOWLEDGE

Prior to starting this unit, you should be able to…

• demonstrate an understanding of the words *impossible*, *possible*, and *certain* as related to everyday life

• demonstrate an understanding of the words *less likely*, *more likely*, and *equally likely* as related to everyday life

Lesson 1 LIKELIHOOD OF A SINGLE OUTCOME: CERTAIN, IMPOSIBLE AND POSSIBLE

NOTES

Probability is the chance of an event happening. An event is something that may or may not happen.

All events have three probable outcomes: certain, impossible, or possible.

A CERTAIN OUTCOME

An event that is certain is one that will *always* happen.

You can conduct the same probability experiment a number of times, and the result will always be the same. The certain outcome will always occur.

 **Example**

Jenna rolls a standard six-sided die with the numbers 1, 2, 3, 4, 5, and 6 on the faces. She is certain that the die will land on a number greater than 0 and less than 7.

Is Jenna correct? Justify your answer.

Solution

Yes, Jenna is correct when she says that the die will always land on a number greater than 0 and less than 7.

Since $0 < 1 < 2 < 3 < 4 < 5 < 6$, each number on the die is greater than zero.

Since $1 < 2 < 3 < 4 < 5 < 6 < 7$, each number on the die is less than 7.

Therefore, every number on the die (1, 2, 3, 4, 5, 6) is greater than 0 and less than 7.

🦋 Time to Try 1

Pascal flips a two-sided coin 10 times. One side of the coin is white, and the other side is brown. Pascal is certain that the coin will land on the white side each time he flips it.

Is Pascal correct? Justify your answer.

AN IMPOSSIBLE OUTCOME

An event that is impossible is one that will *never* happen.

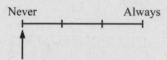

You can conduct the same probability experiment a number of times, and the result will always be the same. The impossible outcome will never occur.

✳ Example

Grayson rolls a regular six-sided die.

Each face of the die has either one dot, two dots, three dots, four dots, five dots, or six dots.

NOTES

Grayson is hoping that if he rolls the die at least 10 times, the outcome will be that the die will land on a face with 8 dots at least one time.

What is the likelihood of the outcome occurring? Justify your answer.

Solution

It is impossible for the outcome to occur.

Since the number of dots on the faces of the die only go from one to six, the die can never land on a face with eight dots. It does not matter how many times the die is rolled, the die can only land on faces with one, two, three, four, five, or six dots.

 Time to Try 2

Joannie has a bag of gumdrops. There are six purple gumdrops, two red gumdrops, and four blue gumdrops in the bag. Joannie puts her hand in the bag and, without looking, pulls out one gumdrop.

What is the likelihood that Joannie will pull out a gumdrop in her favourite colour, which is pink? Justify your answer.

A POSSIBLE OUTCOME

To say that an event is possible means that it *could* happen.

You can conduct the same experiment a number of times, and the result will always be a that possible outcome might occur.

Example

Darian flips a two-sided counter six times. He thinks it is possible for the counter to land on the white side three times and on the black side three times.

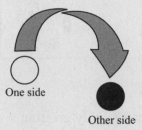

One side

Other side

Is Darian correct? Justify your answer.

Solution

Yes, Darian is correct when he says that the outcome is possible.

There are two possible outcomes. The counter could land on white or on black each time it is flipped.

After six flips, there are all sorts of possibilities of how many times the counter could land on white or on black. Landing an equal number of times on each colour is one of the many possibilities.

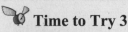 **Time to Try 3**

Describe the likelihood of the spinner landing on yellow as *possible*, *impossible*, or *certain*. Justify your answer.

PRACTICE EXERCISES

Use the following information to answer the next question.

Shabir rolls a six-sided number cube with the numbers 1, 2, 3, 4, 5, and 6 on the faces. He predicts that the cube will land on a single-digit number.

1. Describe Shabir's predicted outcome as *certain*, *possible*, or *impossible*. Justify your answer.

Use the following information to answer the next question.

Before Jordyn spins the spinner, she predicts that it will land on a number greater than 3 and less than 5.

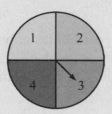

2. Describe Jordyn's predicted outcome as *certain*, *possible*, or *impossible*. Justify your answer.

Use the following information to answer the next question.

Megan rolls a six-sided number cube with the numbers 1, 2, 3, 4, 5, and 6 on the faces. When Megan rolls the cube, she hopes the cube lands on an odd number greater than 5.

3. What is the likelihood of the outcome occurring? Justify your answer.

Lesson 2   COMPARING THE LIKELIHOOD OF TWO POSSIBLE OUTCOMES

Possible outcomes can be described as *likely to occur*, *less likely to occur*, or *equally likely to occur*.

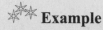

Impossible   Less likely   More likely   Certain

MORE AND MOST LIKELY OUTCOMES

An outcome is more likely when there are more chances or opportunities for the outcome to occur compared to other outcomes.

The most likely outcome is the outcome that has the greatest chance of occurring.

✸✸✸ Example

Dayton spins this spinner 10 times and records the number of times the spinner stops on each colour.

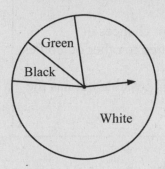

On which color is the spinner **more likely** to stop? Justify your answer.

Solution

Step 1
Identify the most likely outcome.

The most likely outcome is for the spinner to stop on white more times than on green or black.

Step 2
Justify your answer.

The white part of the spinner takes up more than $\frac{3}{4}$ of the circle.

NOTES

Even if the spinner is spun 10 times, the spinner will still most likely stop on white more times than on green or black because the green and black parts are so small compared to the size of the white part.

Time to Try 1

Miss Hailes places 10 cards with numbers on them face down on her desk. She then calls a student to pick one of the cards.

Which number will the student **most likely** pick? Justify your answer.

LESS AND LEAST LIKELY OUTCOMES

An outcome is less likely when there are fewer chances or opportunities for the outcome to occur compared to other outcomes.

The least likely outcome is an outcome that is possible but has the least chance of occurring.

 Example

Daria has a bag that contains five lemon candies, three cherry candies, and two mint candies. She puts her hand into the bag and, without looking, pulls out a candy.

Which type of candy is Daria **less likely** to pick? Justify your answer.

Solution

Step 1
Determine the least likely outcome.

The least likely outcome is for Daria to pick a mint candy.

Step 2
Justify your answer.

There are five lemon candies, three cherry candies, and two mint candies. This means that the most likely outcome is pulling out a lemon candy.

Therefore, it is less likely to pick a cherry candy than a lemon candy. It is less likely to pick a mint candy than a lemon or cherry candy.

The least likely outcome is pulling out a mint candy because there are fewer mint candies than there are cherry or lemon candies.

 Time to Try 2

Jennifer says it is less likely that the spinner will stop on red than on yellow. Emma says it is less likely that the spinner will stop on yellow than on red.

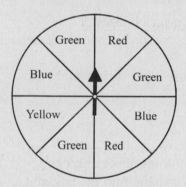

Who is correct? Justify your answer.

EQUALLY LIKELY OUTCOMES

In a probability experiment, two outcomes are equally likely if both outcomes have the same chance of occurring.

 Example

Jaymeson and Shaylah roll a regular six-sided number cube with the numbers 1, 2, 3, 4, 5, and 6 on its faces. They each roll the cube 10 times. Jaymeson gets a point every time an even number is rolled.

Shaylah gets a point every time an odd number is rolled. Are the two possible outcomes equally likely? Justify your answer.

NOTES

Solution

Yes, it is equally likely to roll an odd number or an even number.

There are three even numbers: 2, 4, and 6
Jaymeson has a 3 out of 6 chance of rolling an even number.

There are three odd numbers: 1, 3, 5
Shaylah has a 3 out of 6 chance of rolling an odd number.

Since they both have three chances out of six chances, the two outcomes are equally likely.

 Time to Try 3

Jason drew this spinner for a game he made that he will play with Ryan.

Jason will get a point every time the spinner lands on white.
Ryan will get a point every time the spinner lands on grey.

Ryan says the spinner is not fair and he will lose the game.
Jason says the spinner is fair.

Who is correct? Explain your answer, using probability language.

PRACTICE EXERCISES

Use the following information to answer the next question.

Scott put six blue tiles and five green tiles into a bag. He then pulled a tile out of the bag, recorded the colour, and put the tile back in the bag. He did this 12 times.

1. Are the outcomes of this experiment **equally likely**? Justify your answer.

Use the following information to answer the next question.

Lora and Darcy play a game with a spinner. When the spinner stops on a white part, Lora gets a point. When the spinner stops on a shaded part, Darcy gets a point.

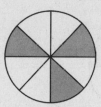

2. Who will **most likely** win the game? Justify your answer.

Use the following information to answer the next question.

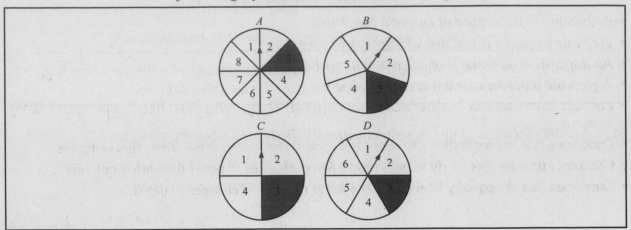

3. If all four spinners were spun at the same time, which spinner would be **least likely** to stop on 3? Justify your answer.

REVIEW SUMMARY

- Probability is the chance of an event happening.
- A certain outcome is one that will *always* happen.
- An impossible outcome is one that will *never* happen.
- A possible outcome is one that *could* happen.
- Possible outcomes can be described as more (most) likely, less (least) likely, and equally likely to occur.
- Outcomes that are more likely to occur have more chances to occur than other outcomes.
- Outcomes that are less likely to occur have fewer chances to occur than other outcomes.
- Outcomes that are equally likely have the same number of chances to occur.

PRACTICE TEST

Use the following information to answer the next question.

Students are playing a game using two spinners: spinner G and spinner H.

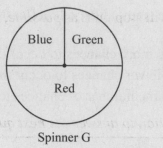

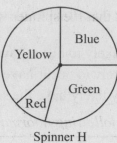

Spinner G   Spinner H

1. On which spinner are the students **more likely** to land on green than on blue? Justify your answer.

Use the following information to answer the next question.

Chung made this spinner to illustrate the probability of a particular outcome.

2. Was Chung illustrating an outcome that is *possible*, *impossible*, or *certain*? Justify your answer.

Use the following information to answer the next question.

A spinner has five equal sections labeled A, B, C, D, E. After James spun the spinner 14 times, he realized that the spinner stopped on A, B, C, and D several times, but never stopped on E.

3. Describe the likelihood that the spinner will stop on E as *possible*, *impossible*, or *certain*. Justify your answer.

Use the following information to answer the next question.

Students use this spinner for a game. Each student is assigned a shape, and the winner of the game is the student whose shape the spinner lands on most frequently.

4. In order for all the players to have an equal chance of winning the game, which shape must go in the blank space? Justify your answer.

Use the following information to answer the next question.

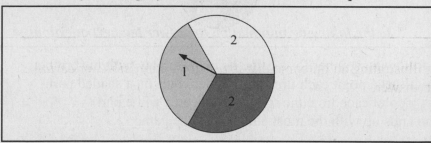

5. Use the terms *more likely*, *less likely*, and *equally likely* to describe all the outcomes for this spinner. Justify your descriptions.

Use the following information to answer the next question.

Maria rolls a standard six-sided number cube with the numbers 1, 2, 3, 4, 5, and 6 on the faces.

6. Is it **more likely** that the number cube will stop on a number greater than 3 or less than 3? Justify your answer.

Use the following information to answer the next question.

The math problem of the day was to draw a spinner that was most likely to land on a 6, least likely to land on a 2, and could possibly land on 4.

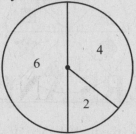

7. Is the spinner drawn correctly? Justify your answer.

Use the following information to answer the next question.

Kell made the following spinner for a game he plans to play with his brother Dayton. Kell will get a point each time the spinner lands on a shaded part. Dayton will get a point each time the spinner lands on a white part. The person who ends up with the most points wins the game.

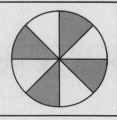

8. Will Kell and Dayton have an equal chance of winning the game? Justify your answer.

SNAP

Student Notes and Problems

ANSWERS AND SOLUTIONS

CASTLE ROCK
RESEARCH CORP

PATTERN RULES

Lesson 1—Understanding Pattern Rules

✿ TIME TO TRY ✿
ANSWERS AND SOLUTIONS

1. **Step 1**
Verify the pattern.

Since the pattern rule says to subtract 6 from each term to get the next term, subtract 6 from each number in the pattern.
$54 - 6 = 48$
$48 - 6 = 42$
$42 - 6 = 36$
$36 - 6 = 30$

Dayton's pattern is incorrect.

Step 2
Justify your answer.

The pattern is incorrect because it does not follow the pattern rule for the entire pattern. When 6 is subtracted from 36, the answer is 30, not 32.

PRACTICE EXERCISES
ANSWERS AND SOLUTIONS

1. **Step 1**
Verify the pattern.
$12 + 9 = 21$
$21 + 9 = 30$
$30 + 9 = 39$
$39 + 9 = 48$

Peter's pattern is correct.

Step 2
Justify your answer.

The pattern is correct because it follows the pattern rule of adding 9 to each number to get the next number.

3. **Step 1**
Verify Olivia's pattern.
$12 \times 2 = 24$
$24 \times 2 = 48$
$48 \times 2 = 96$
$96 \times 2 = 192$

Olivia's pattern is correct.

Verify Sam's pattern.
$14 \times 2 = 28$
$28 \times 2 = 56$
$56 \times 2 = 112$
$112 \times 2 = 224$

Sam's pattern is correct.

Step 2
Justify your answer.

Both patterns are correct because they both follow the pattern rule of multiplying each term by 2 to get the next term.

Lesson 2—Expressing Pattern Rules as Expressions

✿ TIME TO TRY ✿
ANSWERS AND SOLUTIONS

1. **Step 1**
Determine how the numbers change from term to term.
$2 \times 2 = 4$
$4 \times 2 = 8$
$8 \times 2 = 16$
$16 \times 2 = 32$

The pattern rule used is to start with 2 and multiply each term by 2 to get the next term.

Step 2
State the pattern rule as an expression.

One way to express the rule is ×2.
Another way is $n \times 2$ (choosing any letter).

PRACTICE EXERCISES
ANSWERS AND SOLUTIONS

1. **Step 1**
Since the pattern of numbers is growing (increasing), count up from any number to the number on its right to see how it is increasing.
$$55 + 6 = 61$$
$$61 + 6 = 67$$
$$67 + 6 = 73$$
$$73 + 6 = 79$$

The pattern rule used is to start at 55 and add 6 to each term to get the next term.

Step 2
State the pattern rule as an expression in two ways.

One way to express the rule is +6.
Another way is $n + 6$ (choosing any letter).

3. **Step 1**
Determine how the numbers change from term to term.
$$13 \times 10 = 130$$
$$130 \times 10 = 1\ 300$$
$$1\ 300 \times 10 = 13\ 000$$

The pattern rule used is to start with 13 and multiply each term by 10 to get the next term.

Step 2
State the pattern rule as an expression in two ways.

One way to express the rule is ×10.
Another way is $n \times 10$ (choosing any letter).

Lesson 3—Using Mathematical Language to Describe Pattern Rules

TIME TO TRY
ANSWERS AND SOLUTIONS

1. **Step 1**
Determine how each row of stars changes from row 1 to row 5.

One way to do this is to count the number of stars in each row and compare the numbers.

Row	Number of Stars
1	16
2	14
3	12
4	10
5	8

Step 2
Describe the pattern rule using mathematical language.

The pattern rule is that there are two fewer stars in each row than in the previous row.

2. **Step 1**
Determine how the numbers change from term to term.

One way you can do this is by counting up from each number to the number on its right.
$$24 + 6 = 30$$
$$30 + 6 = 36$$
$$36 + 6 = 42$$

Each number increases by 6 to get the next number.

Step 2
Express the pattern rule using mathematical language.

Since this is a growing pattern, the pattern rule is that each number is six greater than the previous number.

PRACTICE EXERCISES
ANSWERS AND SOLUTIONS

1. **Step 1**
Determine how each figure changes from the previous figure.

You can do this by counting the number of square tiles in each figure and comparing the numbers.

Figure	Number of Square Tiles
1	1
2	3
3	5
4	7

Step 2

Express the pattern rule using mathematical language.

Two more tiles are added to each figure to make the next figure.

3. **Step 1**

Determine how the numbers change from term to term.
$4 \times 3 = 12$
$12 \times 3 = 36$
$36 \times 3 = 108$

Each number is multiplied by 3.

Step 2

Express the pattern rule using mathematical language.

Each number is three times greater than the previous number.

Lesson 4—Using Pattern Rules to Extend Growing Patterns

❧ TIME TO TRY ❧
ANSWERS AND SOLUTIONS

1. **Step 1**
Identify the pattern rule.

Count the number of circles in each figure.

Figure 1 has two circles.
Figure 2 has four circles. $2 + 2 = 4$
Figure 3 has six circles. $4 + 2 = 6$

Each succeeding figure adds two more circles to the previous figure. This pattern rule can be expressed as +2.

Step 2

Apply the pattern rule of +2 to determine the number of circles that should be in the next two figures.

Figure 4 will have eight circles.
$6 + 2 = 8$
Figure 5 will have ten circles.
$8 + 2 = 10$

Figures 4 and 5 are shown as follows:

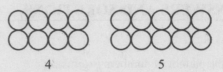

4   5

2. **Step 1**
Determine how the numbers change from term to term.

One way to do this is to subtract any two consecutive numbers.
$22 - 7 = 15$
$37 - 22 = 15$
$52 - 37 = 15$

The pattern rule is to add 15 to each term to get the next term. The pattern rule can be expressed as +15 or $n + 15$.

Step 2
Apply the pattern rule of +15 for two more terms.
$52 + 15 = 67$
$67 + 15 = 82$

When the pattern is extended, the next two terms will be 67 and 82.

3. **Step 1**
Determine how the numbers change from term to term.
$3 \times 2 = 6$
$6 \times 2 = 12$
$12 \times 2 = 24$

The pattern rule for the given numbers is to start with 3 and multiply each number by 2 to get the next number. The rule can be expressed as ×2 or $n \times 2$.

Step 2
Continue the pattern rule of ×2 for two more terms.
$24 \times 2 = 48$
$48 \times 2 = 96$

If the given pattern is extended, the next two numbers will be 48 and 96.

PRACTICE EXERCISES
ANSWERS AND SOLUTIONS

1. **Step 1**
Count the number of squares in each figure.

Figure 1 has one row of 5 squares.
Figure 2 has two rows of 5 squares.
Figure 3 has three rows of 5 squares.

The pattern rule is to add one row of 5 squares to each figure to make the next figure.
Step 2
Apply the pattern rule of +1 row of 5 squares to determine the number of squares that should be in the next two figures.

Figure 4 will have four rows of 5 squares.
Figure 5 will have five rows of 5 squares

Figures 4 and 5 are shown as follows:

     4   5

Step 2
Apply the pattern rule of +7 for two more terms.
$77 + 7 = 84$
$84 + 7 = 91$

When the pattern is extended, the next two terms will be 84 and 91.

3. **Step 1**
Determine how the numbers change from term to term.
$9 \times 2 = 18$
$18 \times 2 = 36$
$36 \times 2 = 72$
Since each number is two times greater than the previous number, the pattern rule is to multiply each term by the constant 2 to get the next term.

Step 2
Apply the pattern rule of ×2 for two more terms.
$72 \times 2 = 144$
$144 \times 2 = 288$

When the given pattern is extended, the next two terms will be 144 and 288.

Lesson 5—Using Pattern Rules to Extend Shrinking Patterns

🦋 TIME TO TRY 🦋
ANSWERS AND SOLUTIONS

1. **Step 1**
Examine how the number of triangles changes from row to row.

Row 1 has 15 triangles.
Row 2 has 12 triangles; three fewer triangles than row 1.
Row 3 has 9 triangles; three fewer triangles than row 2.

Since there are three fewer triangles in each row, the pattern rule is to remove three triangles from each row to make the next row. The rule can be expressed as –3.

Step 2
Apply the rule of –3 for the next two rows.

Row 4 will have 6 triangles.
$9 - 3 = 6$

Row 5 will have 3 triangles.
$6 - 3 = 3$

When the given pattern is extended, the next two rows will have six and three triangles.

Row 4   △ △ △ △ △ △
Row 5   △ △ △

2. **Step 1**
Determine how the numbers change from term to term.

You can do this by subtracting each set of consecutive numbers.
$123 - 117 = 6$
$117 - 111 = 6$
$111 - 105 = 6$

Each number is six less than the previous number. The pattern rule used can be expressed as –6 or $n - 6$.

Step 2
Apply the pattern rule of -6 for two more terms.
$105 - 6 = 99$
$99 - 6 = 93$

If the pattern is extended for two more terms, the next two terms will be 99 and 93.

3. **Step 1**
Determine how the numbers change from term to term.
$625 \div 5 = 125$
$125 \div 5 = 25$

Since each number is one-fifth the value of the previous number, the pattern rule is to divide each term by 5 to get the next term. The rule can be expressed as $\div 5$ or $n \div 5$.

Step 2
Apply the pattern rule of $\div 5$ for two more terms.
$25 \div 5 = 5$
$5 \div 5 = 1$

When the given pattern is extended, the next two terms will be 5 and 1.

PRACTICE EXERCISES
ANSWERS AND SOLUTIONS

1. **Step 1**
Examine how the number of rectangles changes from row to row.

Row 1 has 11 rectangles.
Row 2 has 10 rectangles, one less rectangle than row 1.
Row 3 has 9 rectangles, one less rectangle than row 2.

Since there is one less rectangle in each row than the previous row, the pattern rule is to remove one rectangle from each row to make the next row. The rule can be expressed as -1 or $n - 1$.

Step 2
Apply the rule of -1 for the next two rows.

Row 4 will have 8 rectangles.
$9 - 1 = 8$

Row 5 will have 7 rectangles.
$8 - 1 = 7$

When the pattern of rectangles is extended, the next two rows will have eight and

seven rectangles.

Row 4
Row 5

3. **Step 1**
Determine how the numbers change from term to term.
$243 \div 3 = 81$
$81 \div 3 = 27$

Since each number is one-third the value of the previous number, the pattern rule is to divide each term by 3 to get the next term. The rule can be expressed as $\div 3$ or $n \div 3$.

Step 2
Apply the pattern rule of $\div 3$ for two more terms.
$27 \div 3 = 9$
$9 \div 3 = 3$

When the given pattern is extended, the next two terms will be 9 and 3.

Lesson 6—Determining Pattern Rules for Patterns in Charts and Tables

🦋 TIME TO TRY 🦋
ANSWERS AND SOLUTIONS

1. **Step 1**
Determine how the numbers change from term to term.

Starting at the number 30, subtract two consecutive shaded numbers to see how each number changes to result in the next number.
$30 - 24 = 6$
$24 - 18 = 6$
$18 - 12 = 6$
$12 - 6 = 6$

Each number decreases in value by 6.

Step 2
Express the pattern rule in words and as an expression.

In words: Start at thirty and subtract six from each term (number) to get the next term (number).

As an expression: -6 or $n - 6$ (using any letter).

2. **Step 1**
Determine how each "in" number changes into its corresponding "out" number.

One way to do this is to subtract the "in" numbers from the corresponding "out" numbers.

$15 - 7 = 8$
$11 - 3 = 8$
$21 - 13 = 8$
and so on.

The number 8 is added to each "in" number to result in the corresponding "out" number.

Step 2
Express the pattern rule in words and as an expression.

In words: Add eight to each "in" number to get the resulting "out" number.

As an expression: $+8$ or $n + 8$ (using any letter).

PRACTICE EXERCISES
ANSWERS AND SOLUTIONS

1. **Step 1**
Determine how the numbers change from term to term.

Starting at the number 31, subtract two consecutive circled numbers to see how each number changes to result in the next number.
$31 - 24 = 7$
$24 - 17 = 7$
$17 - 10 = 7$
$10 - 3 = 7$

When you start at 31, each number decreases in value by 7. (31, 24, 17…)

Step 2
Express the pattern rule in words and as an expression.

In words: Start at thirty-one and subtract seven from each term to get the next term.

As an expression: -7 or $n - 7$ (using any letter).

3. **Step 1**
Determine how each "in" number changes into its corresponding "out" number.
$2 \div 2 = 1$
$24 \div 2 = 12$
$8 \div 2 = 4$
$100 \div 2 = 50$

Each "in" number was divided by 2 to result in the corresponding "out" number.

Step 2
Express the pattern rule in words and as an expression.

In words: Divide each "in" number by two to get the resulting "out" number.

As an expression: $\div 2$ or $n \div 2$ (using any letter).

Lesson 7—Using Pattern Rules to Make Predictions

✤ TIME TO TRY ✤
ANSWERS AND SOLUTIONS

1. **Step 1**
Count the number of squares in each of the rows, and enter the numbers in the chart.

Row	Number of Squares
1	9
2	8
3	7

Step 2
Determine the pattern rule.

Since each row has one less square than the previous row, the pattern rule is to subtract one square from each row to get the next row.
The rule can be expressed as -1 or $n - 1$.

Step 3
Apply the pattern rule of –1 for the next four terms in the chart to determine the number of squares that will be in the seventh row.

Row	Number of Squares
4	$7-1=6$
5	$6-1=5$
6	$5-1=4$
7	$4-1=3$

The seventh row will have three squares.

2. **Step 1**
Place the first three terms in a table of values to the right of their corresponding term numbers.

Term Number	Term
1	47
2	60
3	73

Step 2
Determine the pattern rule.

Examine the numbers to see how they change from term to term.

One way to do this is to subtract each group of two consecutive numbers.
$60-47=13$
$73-60=13$

Since each term is 13 more than the previous term, the pattern rule is to add 13 to each term to get the next term. The rule can be expressed as +13 or $n+13$.

Step 3
Apply the pattern rule of +13 for the next three terms in the table of values to predict the sixth term.

Term Number	Term
4	$73+13=86$
5	$86+13=99$
6	$99+13=112$

If the pattern continues, the sixth term will be 112.

3. **Step 1**
Place the first four terms of the pattern in the table of values to the right of their corresponding term numbers.

Term Number	Term
1	5
2	10
3	20
4	40

Step 2
Determine the pattern rule.

Examine the numbers to see how they change from term to term.
$5\times2=10$
$10\times2=20$
$20\times2=40$

Since each number is doubled (two times greater than the previous number), the pattern rule is to multiply each term by 2 to get the next term.

The rule can be expressed as ×2 or $n\times2$.

Step 3
Apply the pattern rule of ×2 for the next three terms in the table of values to predict the seventh term.

Term Number	Term
5	$40\times2=80$
6	$80\times2=160$
7	$160\times2=320$

If the pattern continues, the seventh term will be 320.

4. **Step 1**
Place the first three terms of the pattern in the table of values to the right of their corresponding term numbers.

Term Number	Term
1	139
2	129
3	119

Step 2

Determine the pattern rule.

One way to determine how the numbers change is to subtract each set of consecutive numbers.
$139 - 129 = 10$
$129 - 119 = 10$

Since each term is 10 less than the previous term, the pattern rule is to subtract 10 from each term to get the next term. The rule can be expressed as -10 or $n - 10$.

Step 3

Apply the pattern rule for the next three terms in the table of values to predict the sixth term.

Term Number	Term
4	$119 - 10 = 109$
5	$109 - 10 = 99$
6	$99 - 10 = 89$

If the pattern continues, the sixth term will be 89.

5. **Step 1**

Place the first four terms of the pattern in the table of values to the right of their corresponding term numbers.

Term Number	Term
1	256
2	128
3	64
4	32

Step 2

Determine the pattern rule.

It looks like each consecutive number is decreasing by half. Check if this is correct by dividing each term by two.
$256 \div 2 = 128$
$128 \div 2 = 64$
$64 \div 2 = 32$

Since each term is half the previous term, the pattern rule is to divide each term by 2 to get the next term. The rule can be expressed as $\div 2$ or $n - 2$.

Step 3

Apply the pattern rule of $\div 2$ for the next three terms to predict the seventh term.

Term Number	Term
5	$32 \div 2 = 16$
6	$16 \div 2 = 8$
7	$8 \div 2 = 4$

If the pattern continues, the seventh term will be 4.

PRACTICE EXERCISES
ANSWERS AND SOLUTIONS

1. **Step 1**

Count the number of stars in each of the five rows, and enter the numbers in the chart.

Row	Number of Stars
1	16
2	14
3	12
4	10
5	8

Step 2

Determine the pattern rule.

Since each row has two fewer stars than the previous row, the pattern rule is to subtract 2 stars from each row to get the next row.
The rule can be expressed as -2 or $n - 2$.

Step 3

Apply the pattern rule of -2 for the next three terms in the chart to determine the number of stars in the eighth row.

Row	Number of Stars
6	$8 - 2 = 6$
7	$6 - 2 = 4$
8	$4 - 2 = 2$

If the pattern continues, there will be two stars in the eighth row.

3. **Step 1**

Place the first four terms of the pattern in the table of values to the right of their corresponding term numbers.

Term Number	Term
1	1
2	3
3	9
4	27

Step 2
Determine the pattern rule.

Since each term is three times greater than the previous term, the pattern rule is to multiply each term by 3 to get the next term. The rule can be expressed as ×3 or $n \times 3$.

Step 3
Apply the pattern rule of ×3 for the next three terms.

Term Number	Term
5	$27 \times 3 = 81$
6	$81 \times 3 = 243$
7	$243 \times 3 = 729$

The seventh term will be 729.

5. **Step 1**
Place the first four terms of the pattern in the table of values to the right of their corresponding term numbers.

Term Number	Term
1	320
2	160
3	80
4	40

Step 2
Determine the pattern rule.

Since each term is one-half the value of the previous term, the pattern rule is to divide each term by 2 to get the next term. The rule can be expressed as ÷2 or $n \div 2$.

Step 3
Apply the pattern rule of ÷2 for the next three terms to predict the seventh term.

Term Number	Term
5	$40 \div 2 = 20$
6	$20 \div 2 = 10$
7	$10 \div 2 = 5$

The seventh term will be 5.

Lesson 8—Verifying Predictions Visually

🦋 TIME TO TRY 🦋
ANSWERS AND SOLUTIONS

1. **Step 1**
Determine the pattern rule.

The pattern starts with 16, and each term decreases in value by 2. (–2)

Therefore, the fourth term will be 10.
$(12 - 2 = 10)$

The fifth term will be 8. $(10 - 2 = 8)$

Step 2
Verify the rule with a diagram.

This set of stars represents the pattern:
16, 14, 12, 10, 8

Row 1 ☆☆☆☆☆☆☆☆☆☆☆☆☆☆☆☆

Row 2 ☆☆☆☆☆☆☆☆☆☆☆☆☆☆

Row 3 ☆☆☆☆☆☆☆☆☆☆☆☆

Row 4 ☆☆☆☆☆☆☆☆☆☆

Row 5 ☆☆☆☆☆☆☆☆

2. **Step 1**
Determine the pattern rule used.

Each number is doubled to get the next number. The rule can be expressed as ×2.

Step 2
Verify the prediction.

Make a table of values for the given pattern, extending it for two terms.

Term Number	Term
1	1
2	2
3	4
4	8
5	16
6	$16 \times 2 = 32$
7	$32 \times 2 = 64$

Joshua's prediction was correct.

PRACTICE EXERCISES
ANSWERS AND SOLUTIONS

1. **Step 1**
Determine if the prediction is correct.

Yes, Kerrie's prediction is correct.

Step 2
Verify the prediction.

The pattern starts with 1, and each term increases in value by 2 (+2).

This set of squares represents the pattern: 1, 3, 5, 7, 9

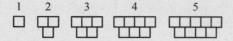

3. **Step 1**
Determine if the prediction is correct.

No, Marina's prediction is incorrect.

Step 2
Verify the prediction.

Each number is decreased in value by 7. The rule can be expressed as −7.

Term Number	Term
1	67
2	60
3	53
4	46
5	$46 - 7 = 39$
6	$39 - 7 = 32$
7	$32 - 7 = 25$

The seventh term is 25, not 28.

Lesson 9—Using Pattern Rules to Solve Problems

❀ TIME TO TRY ❀
ANSWERS AND SOLUTIONS

1. **Step 1**
Make a table of values to organize the numbers and to make it easier to see the given terms and their term numbers.

Term Number	Term
1	
2	
3	118
4	
5	124
6	127

Step 2
Determine the pattern rule.

Only 124 and 127 are consecutive numbers.

You can see that 3 is added to 124 to get 127. That means that the pattern rule is to add 3 to each term to get the next term. The rule can be expressed as +3.

Step 3
Verify the pattern rule by completing the given pattern.

Term Number	Term
1	112
2	115
3	118
4	121
5	124
6	127

Step 4
Verify the prediction by extending the table of values.

Apply the pattern rule of +3 to predict the tenth term.

Term Number	Term
7	$127+3=130$
8	$130+3=133$
9	$133+3=136$
10	$136+3=139$

The tenth term of the sequence of numbers will be 139.

2. **Step 1**
Determine the pattern rule.

The pattern starts with four (circles).

For each succeeding square, the pattern grows by three more circles.

The pattern rule is to start with 4 and add 3 to each term to get the next term.

The rule can be expressed as +3.

Step 2
Apply the rule of +3.

Make a table of values to help you predict the fifth term. The number of squares will be the term numbers. The number of circles will be the terms.

Term Number	Term
1	4
2	4+3 = 7
3	7+3 = 10
4	10+3 = 13
5	13+3 = 16

Jaz drew 16 circles in the fifth square.

3. **Step 1**
Make a table of values.

The table of values will help you keep track of the term numbers and their corresponding terms as you apply the pattern rule of ×2.

Term Number	Term
1	5
2	10
3	20
4	40
5	80
6	160

Step 2
This pattern generated by the given rule is
5, 10, 20, 40, 80, 160

The sixth term has a value of 160.

PRACTICE EXERCISES
ANSWERS AND SOLUTIONS

1. **Step 1**
Determine the pattern rule.

The consecutive numbers are 3 and 9.

Here, the number 3 is multiplied by 3 to get the number 9.

The pattern rule is to multiply each term by 3 to get the next term.

The rule can be expressed as ×3.

Step 2
Verify the pattern rule by completing the given pattern.

Term Number	Term
1	1
2	3
3	9
4	27
5	81

Step 3
Apply the pattern rule of ×3 to predict the seventh term.

Term Number	Term
6	$81 \times 3 = 243$
7	$243 \times 3 = 792$

The seventh term of the sequence is 792.

3. The pattern generated by the given rule is
100, 91, 82, 73, 64, 55

Term Number	Term
1	100
2	$100 - 9 = 91$
3	$91 - 9 = 82$
4	$82 - 9 = 73$
5	$73 - 9 = 64$
6	$64 - 9 = 55$

The fourth term of the pattern has a value of 73.

Practice Test

ANSWERS AND SOLUTIONS

1. Verify the pattern by adding 13 to each number in the pattern.
$$5 + 13 = 18$$
$$18 + 13 = 31$$
$$31 + 13 = 44$$
$$44 + 13 = 57$$

The pattern is incorrect because it does not follow the pattern rule throughout the sequence of numbers. When 13 is added to 44, the sum is 57, not 55.

Adam's pattern is incorrect.

3. **Step 1**
Determine the pattern rule used.

One way to determine how the numbers change from term to term is to subtract each set of two consecutive numbers.
$$25 - 5 = 20$$
$$45 - 25 = 20$$
$$65 - 45 = 20$$
$$85 - 65 = 20$$

A value of 20 is added to each number.

Step 2
Express the pattern rule using mathematical language.

The pattern starts with five and then twenty is added to each term to result in the next term.

5. **Step 1**
Determine how the numbers change from term to term.

One way to do this is to count up from each number to the number on its right.
$$4 + 5 = 9$$
$$9 + 5 = 14$$
$$14 + 5 = 19$$
$$19 + 5 = 24$$
$$24 + 5 = 29$$

Each number is 5 more than the number before it.

Step 2
Express the pattern rule in words and as an expression.

In words: Start at four and add five to each term to get the next term.

As an expression: $+5$ or $n + 5$ (using any letter).

7. Andrew will need 21 square tiles to make the sixth figure.

Step 1
Count the number of squares used in each figure. Enter the numbers in the chart.

Figure	Number of Tiles
1	1
2	5
3	9
4	13

Step 2
Determine the pattern rule.

Since each figure has four more squares than the previous figure, the pattern rule is to start with one square and then add four more squares to each figure to make the next figure.

The rule can be expressed as $+4$ or $n + 4$.

Step 3
Apply the pattern rule of $+4$ for the next two terms in the chart.

Figure	Number of Tiles
1	1
2	5
3	9
4	13
5	$13 + 4 = 17$
6	$17 + 4 = 21$

9. These are the five terms of the pattern:
31, 24, 17, 10, 3

Step 1
Determine the pattern rule.

The pattern starts with 31, and each term decreases in value by 7.
$$31 - 7 = 24$$
$$24 - 7 = 17$$

Step 2

Apply the pattern rule of –7 to determine the next two terms.

$17 - 7 = 10$

$10 - 7 = 3$

These rows of circles verify the pattern rule of –7 and the prediction of the fifth term.

Row 1

Row 2

Row 3 ○○○○○○○○○○
○○○○○○○

Row 4 ○○○○○○○○○○

Row 5 ○○○

Corinne's prediction is correct.

REPRESENTING WHOLE NUMBERS TO ONE MILLION

Lesson 1—Place Value and Period Names

🦋 TIME TO TRY 🦋
ANSWERS AND SOLUTIONS

1. To solve the problem, you need to count the number of place values that you move.
   - The digit 2 in the hundreds place in the ones period has a value of 200.
   - The digit 2 in the ones place in the thousands period is one place value to the left, so it has a value of $200 \times 10 = 2\ 000$.
   - The digit 2 in the hundred thousands place in the thousands period is two places to the left of 2 000, so it has a value of $2\ 000 \times 10 \times 10 = 200\ 000$.

PRACTICE EXERCISES
ANSWERS AND SOLUTIONS

1. The 4 in the ones period has a value of 4. It needs to be multiplied by 10 for each place value that it moves to the left.

   Since it moves 4 places to the left to get to the digit 4 in the ten thousands place, it needs to be multiplied by 10 four times.
   $4 \times 10 \times 10 \times 10 \times 10 = 40\ 000$

3. The 8 in the hundreds place in the ones period has a value of 800. It needs to be multiplied by 10 for each place value that it moves to the left.

   Since it moves three places to the left to get to the digit 8 in the hundred thousands place, it needs to be multiplied by 10 three times.
   $800 \times 10 \times 10 \times 10 = 800\ 000$

Lesson 2—Using Place Value Charts

🐝 TIME TO TRY 🐝
ANSWERS AND SOLUTIONS

1.

Thousands			Ones		
H	**T**	**O**	**H**	**T**	**O**
9	0	2	0	3	0

- The digit 3 is in the tens position. Its value is 3×10, or 30.
- The digit 2 is in the thousands position. Its value is $2 \times 1\ 000$, or 2 000.
- The digit 9 is in the hundred thousands position. Its value is $9 \times 100\ 000$, or 900 000.

PRACTICE EXERCISES
ANSWERS AND SOLUTIONS

1. The digit 8 in the hundreds place in the thousands period has a value of 800 000. One hundred thousand is represented by the numeral 100 000. Therefore, eight hundred thousands is represented by $8 \times 100\ 000 = 800\ 000$.

Thousands			Ones		
H	**T**	**O**	**H**	**T**	**O**
8	0	0	0	0	0

3. The digit 4 is in the tens position in the ones period. To determine its value, multiply 4 by 10.
$4 \times 10 = 40$

The digit 3 is in the hundreds position in the ones period. To determine its value, multiply 3 by 100.
$3 \times 100 = 300$

The digit 5 is in the ones position in the thousands period. To determine its value, multiply 5 by 1 000.
$5 \times 1\ 000 = 5\ 000$

The digit 2 is in the hundreds position in the thousands period. To determine its value, multiply 2 by 100 000.
$2 \times 100\ 000 = 200\ 000$

Remember: The zeros in the ten thousands position and the ones position have no values. They are placeholders.

Lesson 3—Using Expanded Notation

🐝 TIME TO TRY 🐝
ANSWERS AND SOLUTIONS

1. Step 1
Start at the left, and write the value of each digit in the number.

- 1 has a value of 100 000. $(1 \times 100\ 000)$
- 0 indicates that there are no ten thousands.
- 7 has a value of 7 000. $(7 \times 1\ 000)$
- 0 indicates that there are no hundreds.
- 6 has a value of 60. (6×10)
- 3 has a value of 3. (3×1)

Step 2
Start at the left, and write the values horizontally with a + sign between each pair of values.
$100\ 000 + 7\ 000 + 60 + 3$

Remember: The zeros are not included in expanded notation.

Another way of writing the expanded notation is to show each digit being multiplied by its place value position.
$(1 \times 100\ 000) + (7 \times 1\ 000) + (6 \times 10) + (3 \times 1)$

2. Step 1
Place the values shown in the expanded notation in a place value chart.

Thousands			Ones		
H	**T**	**O**	**H**	**T**	**O**
9	5	4	3		1

Step 2
Since there are no tens in the expanded notation, you need to place a zero in the tens place as a placeholder.

Thousands			Ones		
H	**T**	**O**	**H**	**T**	**O**
9	5	4	3	0	1

The expanded notation
$900\ 000 + 50\ 000 + 4\ 000 + 300 + 1$ represents the number 954 301.

PRACTICE EXERCISES
ANSWERS AND SOLUTIONS

1. **Method 1**
   $40\ 000 + 5\ 000 + 600 + 80 + 7$

   Method 2
   $(4 \times 10\ 000) + (5 \times 1\ 000) + (6 \times 100)$
   $+ (8 \times 10) + (7 \times 1)$

3. **Step 1**
   Place the values shown in the expanded notation in a place value chart.

Thousands			Ones		
H	T	O	H	T	O
4	5	4	8		

   Step 2
   Use zeros as placeholders in the tens and ones positions.

Thousands			Ones		
H	T	O	H	T	O
4	5	4	8	0	0

   The expanded notation
   $400\ 000 + 50\ 000 + 4\ 000 + 800$ represents the numeral 454 800.

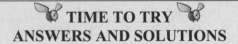

Lesson 4—Reading and Writing Numbers to One Million

🐝 TIME TO TRY 🐝
ANSWERS AND SOLUTIONS

1. **Step 1**
   Enter the number into a place value chart so you can see the place value positions of each digit.

Thousands Period			Ones Period		
H	T	O	H	T	O
1	2	0	9	4	5

   Step 2
   Read the number.

   Start at the left, and say the words for the digits in the thousands period followed by the word *thousand*: 120 is read as one hundred twenty thousand.

Then, say the words for the digits in the ones period: 945 is read as nine hundred forty-five.

Putting the two periods together, you would say "one hundred twenty thousand nine hundred forty-five." (Do not say the word *and*.)

Step 3
Write the number in words.

Start at the left, and write the thousands period: one hundred twenty thousand.

Follow the thousands period with the ones period: nine hundred forty-five.

Putting the two periods together, write 120 945 in words as one hundred twenty thousand nine hundred forty-five.

2. **Step 1**
   Start with the thousands period.

   Enter the digits that represent the words *three hundred twenty-six* into the chart.

Thousands Period			Ones Period		
H	T	O	H	T	O
3	2	6			

   Step 2
   Move to the ones period.

   Enter the digits that represent the words *eight hundred three* into the chart.

Thousands Period			Ones Period		
H	T	O	H	T	O
3	2	6	8	0	3

   Written as a numeral, the number three hundred twenty-six thousand eight hundred three is 326 803.

PRACTICE EXERCISES
ANSWERS AND SOLUTIONS

1. Start with the digits in the thousands period.

   Write the words for 872 followed by the word *thousand*.
   872 → eight hundred seventy-two thousand

   Write the words for the ones period.

835 → eight hundred thirty-five

Put the two parts together.

872 835 is written in words as eight hundred seventy-two thousand eight hundred thirty-five.

3. Start with the thousands period.

Place the digits that represent the words *two hundred ninety-six* into the chart.

Thousands Period			Ones Period		
H	T	O	H	T	O
2	9	6			

Move to the ones period.

Place the digits that represent the word *twelve* into the chart.

Thousands Period			Ones Period		
H	T	O	H	T	O
2	9	6	0	1	2

The numeral form of the number two hundred ninety-six thousand twelve is 296 012.

Lesson 5—Comparing and Ordering Numbers up to One Million

TIME TO TRY
ANSWERS AND SOLUTIONS

1. **Step 1**
Organize the numbers so that the place values line up. You can use a place value chart to do this.

Thousands			Ones		
H	T	O	H	T	O
4	4	8	2	0	1
4	3	8	2	0	0
3	3	8	0	2	0

Step 2
Compare the digits in the greatest place value position, which is the hundred thousands position.

Since $4 > 3$, you only need to compare the numbers 448 201 and 438 200.

Step 3
Compare the digits in the ten thousands position. Since $4 > 3$, you now know that
4_48 201 > 4_38 200 .

The number with the greatest value is 448 201.

2. **Step 1**
Organize the numbers, lining up the place values.

One way to do this is to write the numbers one below the other.
707 990
770 909
907 709

Step 2
Compare the digits in the greatest place value position, which is the hundred thousands.

Since $9 > 7$, the number with the greatest value is 907 709.

Step 3
Compare the digits in the ten thousands position for the numbers 7_07 990 and 7_70 909 .

Since $7 > 0$, 7_70 909 > 7_07 990 .

Written in descending order (greatest to least), the numbers are 907 709, 770 909, 707 990.

Another way of writing the numbers in descending order is to use the greater than (>) symbol.
907 709 > 770 909 > 707 990 .

PRACTICE EXERCISES
ANSWERS AND SOLUTIONS

1. Organize the numbers, lining up the place values.
418 134
398 432
389 413

Start at the left, and compare the digits in the hundred thousands position.
4_18 134
3_98 432
3_89 413

Since $4 > 3$, you only need to continue comparing 398 432 and 389 413.
Compare the digits in the ten thousands position.

3<u>9</u>8 432
3<u>8</u>9 413

Since $8 < 9$, the number 389 413 has the least value.

3. The digits in the chart should look like this:

Thousands			Ones		
H	T	O	H	T	O
4	3	5	9	2	3
4	4	5	2	3	4
2	3	4	5	3	4

Compare the digits in the hundred thousands position.

Since $2 < 4$, the number with the least value is 234 534

Compare the digits in the ten thousands position for 4<u>3</u>5 923 and 4<u>4</u>5 234 .

Since $3 < 4$, the greatest number is 445 324.
234 534 < 435 923 < 445 234

Written in order from least to greatest, the numbers are 234 534, 435 923, 445 234.

Lesson 6—Understanding the Magnitude of Numbers to One Million

✂ TIME TO TRY ✂
ANSWERS AND SOLUTIONS

1. **Step 1**
Think of a relationship that could help you.

For example, since 24 hours = 1 day, you could divide 1 000 000 hours by 25 hours (compatible numbers) to determine about how old the person is in days.
$1\ 000\ 000 \div 25 = 40\ 000$

The person is about 40 000 days old.

Step 2
Think of another relationship that could help you.

For example, since 365 days = 1 year, you could use your calculator to divide 40 000 by 360 (compatible numbers).
$40\ 000 \div 360 = 111.111$

If the person was about 1 000 000 hours old, he or she was about 111 years old.

PRACTICE EXERCISES
ANSWERS AND SOLUTIONS

1. **Step 1**
Determine the number of pens a box can hold.

Since there are eight pens in a package and there are 25 packages in a box, multiply 8 by 25.
$8 \times 25 = 200$

Step 2
Determine the number of boxes needed to package 1 000 000 pens.

Divide 1 000 000 by 200.
$$\frac{1\ 000\ 000}{200} = \frac{10\ 000}{2}$$
$$= 5\ 000$$

The company would need 5 000 boxes to package 1 000 000 pens.

3. To determine the number of thousands cubes needed, divide 1 000 000 by 1 000.
$$\frac{1\ 000\ 000}{1\ 000} = \frac{1\ 000}{1}$$
$$= 1\ 000$$

It would take 1 000 of these cubes to represent the number 1 000 000.

Practice Test

ANSWERS AND SOLUTIONS

1. The 1 in the ones place in the ones period has a value of 1. $(1 \times 1 = 1)$

It needs to be multiplied by 10 for each place value that it moves to the left. Since it moves three places to the left, it needs to be multiplied by 10 three times.
$1 \times 10 \times 10 \times 10 = 1\ 000$

3. The digits in the chart should look like this:

Thousands			Ones		
H	T	O	H	T	O
4	6	2	3	6	2
4	6	1	1	9	2
4	6	1	1	5	5

Start at the left, and compare the digits in the same place values.

Since each number has 4 hundred thousands and 6 ten thousands, compare the digits in the thousands place.
46$\underline{2}$ 362
46$\underline{1}$ 192
46$\underline{1}$ 155

Since $1 < 2$, you only need to continue comparing 461 192 and 461 155.

Since there is 1 hundred in both numbers, compare the digits in the tens places.
461 1$\underline{9}$2
461 1$\underline{5}$5

Since $5 < 9$, the number with the least value is 461 155.

5. **Method 1**
   $700\ 000 + 70\ 000 + 7\ 000 + 70$

   Method 2
   $(7 \times 100\ 000) + (7 \times 10\ 000)$
   $+ (7 \times 1\ 000) + (7 \times 10)$

7. Start with the thousands period.

Place the digits that represent the words *three hundred twenty-six* into the chart.

Thousands Period			Ones Period		
H	T	O	H	T	O
3	2	6			

Move to the ones period.

Place the digits representing the word *fifteen* into the chart.

Thousands Period			Ones Period		
H	T	O	H	T	O
3	2	6	0	1	5

The numeral form of the number three hundred twenty-six thousand fifteen is 326 015.

9. **Step 1**
Determine the number of pens in each box.

Since there are 12 pens in a package and 20 packages in a box, multiply 12 by 20.
$12 \times 20 = 240$

Step 2
Change 240 to a number that is close to 240 but compatible with 1 000 000.
$240 \rightarrow 250$

Step 3
Determine the number of boxes needed to package 1 000 000 pens.

Divide 1 000 000 by 250.
$$\frac{1\ 000\ 00\!\!\!/0}{25\!\!\!/0} = \frac{10\ 0000}{25}$$
$$= 4\ 000$$

The company would need close to 4 000 boxes to package 1 000 000 pens.

11. The digit 4 in the hundreds place in the thousands period has a value of 400 000.

One hundred thousand is represented by the numeral 100 000. Four hundred thousands is represented by $4 \times 100\ 000 = 400\ 000$.

Thousands			Ones		
H	T	O	H	T	O
4	0	0	0	0	0

ESTIMATION STRATEGIES

Lesson 1—Understanding Estimation

PRACTICE EXERCISES
ANSWERS AND SOLUTIONS

1. The teacher only wants to know about how many cubes were used, so an exact answer is not needed.

2. If the estimated product and the actual product are close, Nelson will know that $37 \times 43 = 591$ is a reasonable solution.

   If the estimated product and the actual product are far apart, Nelson will know that $37 \times 43 = 591$ is not reasonable and needs to be recalculated.

3. Since the situation is dealing with a purchase, it is best to overestimate. Lynette needs to have enough money to pay for both items, so an underestimate would not give her enough money. As well, if she needs to pay a tax on the clothes, she then needs to have enough money to pay the tax as well.

Lesson 2—Using Front-End Estimation

❧ TIME TO TRY ❧
ANSWERS AND SOLUTIONS

1. **Step 1**
   Determine the operation needed to solve the problem.

   Since you need to determine the total number of cards, you need to multiply.

   Step 2
   Use front-end estimation for the number of packages and the number of cards in each package.
   $93 \rightarrow 90$
   $25 \rightarrow 20$

   Step 3
   Multiply the two estimated amounts.
   $90 \times 20 = 1\ 800$

   Abraham has about 1 800 hockey cards in his collection.

PRACTICE EXERCISES
ANSWERS AND SOLUTIONS

1. **Step 1**
   Determine the operation needed to solve the problem.

   The clue words "in total" let you know that you need to add.

   Step 2
   Use front-end estimation.
   $142 \rightarrow 100$
   $167 \rightarrow 100$
   $201 \rightarrow 200$

   Step 3
   Add the three estimated numbers.
   $100 + 100 + 200 = 400$

   The boys have about 400 autographs in total.

3. **Step 1**
   Determine the operation needed to solve the problem.

   The clue words "12 … into each package" and "placed 492 … into packages" let you know that you need to divide.

   Step 2
   Use front-end estimation.
   $492 \rightarrow 400$
   $12 \rightarrow 10$

   Step 3
   Divide the two estimated numbers.
   $400 \div 10 = 40$

   Kevin made about 40 packages on Monday.

Lesson 3—Using Comparative Language

❧ TIME TO TRY ❧
ANSWERS AND SOLUTIONS

1. **Step 1**
   Use front-end estimation for the two numbers.
   $105 \rightarrow 100$
   $610 \rightarrow 600$

Step 2
Use comparative language to describe the sum of $105 + 610$.

Since both numbers were rounded down but both numbers were very close to the rounded amounts, the actual sum will also be close to the estimated sum.

You can describe the sum of $105 + 610$ as being **close to** the sum of $100 + 600 = 700$.

2. **Step 1**
Use front-end estimation for the two numbers.
$699 \rightarrow 600$
$208 \rightarrow 200$

Step 2
Use comparative language to describe the difference of $699 - 208$.

One number is rounded down and is very close to its estimation. $(208 \rightarrow 200)$

The other number is rounded down, but it is rounded down a lot. $(699 \rightarrow 600)$

The given number is actually closer to its nearest hundred (700). This will cause the estimated difference to be quite a bit less than the actual difference.

You can describe the difference of $699 - 208$ as being quite a bit **greater than** the difference of $600 - 200 = 400$

3. **Step 1**
Use front-end estimation for the two factors.
$11 \rightarrow 10$
$81 \rightarrow 80$

Step 2
Use comparative language to describe the product of 11×81.

Since both factors were rounded down and both factors were very close to the rounded factors, the actual product will also be close to the estimated product.

You can describe the product of 11×81 as being **close to** the product of $10 \times 80 = 800$.

4. **Step 1**
Use front-end estimation for the dividend.
$707 \rightarrow 700$

Since the divisor is a one-digit number, it will stay as 4.

Step 2
Use comparative language to describe the quotient of $707 \div 4$.

Since the actual dividend is rounded down but is very close to the rounded number $(707 \rightarrow 700)$, the actual quotient will also be very close to the estimated quotient.

You can describe the quotient of $707 \div 4$ as being **almost the same** as the quotient of $700 \div 4 = 175$.

PRACTICE EXERCISES
ANSWERS AND SOLUTIONS

1. **Step 1**
Use front-end estimation for the three numbers.
$301 \rightarrow 300$
$409 \rightarrow 400$
$502 \rightarrow 500$

Step 2
Use comparative language to describe the sum of $301 + 409 + 502$.

Since the numbers were rounded down but all three numbers were very close to the rounded amounts, the actual sum will also be very close to the estimated sum.

The sum of $301 + 409 + 502$ is **very close to** the sum of $300 + 400 + 500 = 1\ 200$.

3. **Step 1**
Use front-end estimation for the two factors.
$51 \rightarrow 50$
$61 \rightarrow 60$

Step 2
Use comparative language to describe the product of 51×61.

Since both factors were rounded down and both factors were very close to the rounded factors, the actual product will also be close to the estimated product.
The product of 51×61 is **almost the same as** the product of $50 \times 60 = 3\ 000$.

Lesson 4—Using Compensation

🦋 TIME TO TRY 🦋
ANSWERS AND SOLUTIONS

1. **Step 1**
    Use front-end estimation for the first
    two numbers.
    $654 \rightarrow 600$
    $509 \rightarrow 500$

    Use front-end estimation +1 for the third number.
    $753 \rightarrow 800 \ (7+1)$

    Step 2
    Add the three estimations.
    $600 + 500 + 800 = 1\ 900$

    There are about 1 900 coloured counting chips in
    the pail.

PRACTICE EXERCISES
ANSWERS AND SOLUTIONS

1. **Step 1**
    Use front-end estimation for the first
    two numbers.
    $920 \rightarrow 900$
    $449 \rightarrow 400$

    Use front-end estimation +1 for the third number.
    $738 \rightarrow 800 \ (7+1)$

    Step 2
    Add the three estimations.
    $900 + 400 + 800 = 2\ 100$

    Step 3
    Determine the actual sum.
    $920 + 449 + 738 = 2\ 107$

    Step 4
    Compare the estimated sum to the actual sum.

    The estimated sum of 2 100 is very close to the
    actual sum of 2 107. There is a difference of only
    7 between the two sums.

3. **Step 1**
    Use front-end estimation for the first
    two numbers.
    $317 \rightarrow 300$
    $156 \rightarrow 100$

    Use front-end estimation +1 for the third number.

    $144 \rightarrow 200 \ (1+1)$

    Step 2
    Add the three estimations.
    $300 + 100 + 200 = 600$

    About 600 people bought tickets for the
    spring concert.

Lesson 5—Using Compatible Numbers

🦋 TIME TO TRY 🦋
ANSWERS AND SOLUTIONS

1. **Step 1**
    Determine compatible numbers for 42 and 26.

    Since 40 is close to 42, let 40 represent 42.
    Since 26 is close to 25 and all numbers that end in
    5 are compatible with numbers that end in 0, let 25
    represent 26.

    The compatible numbers for 42 and 26 can be 40
    and 25.

    Step 2
    Multiply the compatible numbers.
    40×25

    Since $4 \times 25 = 100$, just add a 0 to the end of 100.
    $100 \rightarrow 1\ 00\underline{0}$

    Using the strategy of compatible numbers, the
    estimated product of 42×26 is 1 000.

2. **Step 1**
    Determine the operation needed to solve this
    problem.

    Since you need to determine the number of
    students in each group (grade), you need to divide.

Step 2
Think of a number close to 356 that can be easily divided by 6.
356 → 360

Since 36 can be easily divided by 6, 360 and 6 are compatible numbers.

Step 3
Divide 360 by 6.
360 ÷ 6 = 60

There are about 60 students in each grade.

PRACTICE EXERCISES
ANSWERS AND SOLUTIONS

1. **Step 1**
    Determine compatible numbers for 39 and 21.

    Since 40 is close to 39, let 40 represent 39.
    Since 20 is close to 21, let 20 represent 21.

    The compatible numbers for 39 and 21 can be 40 and 20.

    Step 2
    Multiply the compatible numbers.
    $40 \times 20 = 800$

    Using the strategy of compatible numbers, the product of 39×21 is about 800.

3. **Step 1**
    Think of numbers close to 58 and 37 that can be compatible numbers.

    Since 58 is close to 60, and 37 is close to 40, 60 and 40 are compatible numbers.

    Step 2
    Calculate the sum of the compatible numbers.
    460 + 840 = 1 300

    Using the strategy of compatible numbers, the sum of 458 + 837 is close to the sum of
    460 + 840 = 1 300 .

Lesson 6—Using the Rounding Rule

❦ TIME TO TRY ❦
ANSWERS AND SOLUTIONS

1. **Step 1**
    Round both numbers to the nearest thousand.
    6 1 98 → 6 000 because 1 < 5
    2 7 02 → 3 000 because 7 > 5

    Step 2
    Subtract the two estimated amounts to determine the estimated number of white buttons.
    6 000 – 3 000 = 3 000

    Since almost half of the buttons (3 000) were black, almost half of the buttons (3 000) would have to be white.

    Trina's calculation of 4 496 white buttons is not close to the estimated number of 3 000; therefore, it is not a reasonable solution.

    She should recheck her calculation.

PRACTICE EXERCISES
ANSWERS AND SOLUTIONS

1. **Step 1**
    Determine the operation needed to solve this problem.

    Since you need to determine the total number of vehicles, you need to add.

    Step 2
    Round each number to its greatest place value (hundreds):
    4 0 8 → 400 because 0 < 5
    5 1 2 → 500 because 1 < 5
    1 6 5 → 200 because 6 > 5

    Step 3
    Add the rounded numbers to determine the estimated number of vehicles.
    400 + 500 + 200 = 1 100

    There were about 1 100 vehicles in the parking lot.

---

3. **Step 1**
    Determine the operation needed to solve the problem.

    Since you know the number of buns in each package and you want to know the total, you need to multiply.

    Step 2
    Round both numbers to the nearest tens.
    $1\underline{2} \rightarrow 10$ because $2 < 5$
    $1\underline{7} \rightarrow 20$ because $7 > 5$

    Step 3
    Multiply the two rounded numbers.
    $10 \times 20 = 200$

    There will be about 200 dinner buns in 17 packages.

Practice Test

ANSWERS AND SOLUTIONS

1. **Step 1**
    Determine the operation needed to solve the problem.

    The clue words "in total" let you know that you need to add.

    Step 2
    Use front-end estimation.
    $\underline{8}39 \rightarrow 800$
    $\underline{4}59 \rightarrow 400$

    Step 3
    Add the two estimated numbers.
    $800 + 400 = 1\ 200$

    In total, the two boys have about 1 200 hockey cards.

3. **Step 1**
    Determine the operation needed to solve this problem.

    Since you need to determine the total number of tulips, you need to multiply.

    Step 2
    Determine the compatible numbers.

    Since 30 is close to 28, use 30 to represent 28.
    Since 50 is close to 53, use 50 to represent 53.

The compatible numbers for 28×53 can be 30×50.

Step 3
Multiply the compatible numbers.

Since $3 \times 5 = 15$, add two zeros to the right of 15.
$30 \times 50 = 1\ 5\underline{00}$

There are about 1 500 tulips in the basket.

5. **Step 1**
    Use front-end estimation for the dividend.
    $\underline{2}79 \rightarrow 200$

    Since the divisor is a one-digit number, it will stay as 5.

    Step 2
    Use comparative language to describe the quotient of $279 \div 5$.

    Since the actual dividend is rounded down $(279 \rightarrow 200)$ the actual quotient will be more than the estimated quotient.

    The quotient of $279 \div 5$ can be described as **more than** $200 \div 5 = 40$.

7. **Step 1**
    Determine the operation needed to solve this problem.

    Since you need to estimate the total number of vehicles, you need to add.

    Step 2
    Use front-end estimation for the first two numbers.
    $\underline{5}38 \rightarrow 500$
    $\underline{3}12 \rightarrow 300$

    Use front-end estimation +1 for the third number.
    $\underline{4}95 \rightarrow \underline{5}00\ (4+1)$

    Step 3
    Add the estimated numbers.
    $500 + 300 + 500 = 1\ 300$

    There were about 1 300 vehicles in the theatre's parking lot.

9. **Step 1**
Use front-end estimation for the first two numbers.
$476 \rightarrow 400$
$228 \rightarrow 200$

Use front-end estimation +1 for the third number.
$215 \rightarrow 300 \ (2+1)$

Step 2
Add the three estimations.
$400 + 200 + 300 = 900$

Mrs. Rabou travelled about 900 metres.

Step 3
Explain the reason for compensation.

Compensation gives a more accurate estimation than front-end estimation.

Since two numbers are rounded down and the third number is rounded up, the estimation of 900 is closer to the actual sum of 919 than the front-end estimation of 800 $(400 + 200 + 200)$.

MENTAL STRATEGIES

Lesson 1—Relating Division Facts to Multiplication Facts

TIME TO TRY
ANSWERS AND SOLUTIONS

1. A fact family uses the same three numbers to represent a given grouping. (The related multiplication fact that represents the same grouping is $7 \times 4 = 28$.)

The two division facts that can also represent the given grouping of circles are $28 \div 7 = 4$ and $28 \div 4 = 7$.

PRACTICE EXERCISES
ANSWERS AND SOLUTIONS

1. Determine the related division facts.

Since $6 \times 2 = 12$, then $12 \div 2 = 6$ (12 books sorted into two groups with six books in each group).

Since $2 \times 6 = 12$, then $12 \div 6 = 2$ (12 books sorted by placing six books into each group, making two groups).

The two related division facts are $12 \div 2 = 6$ and $12 \div 6 = 2$.

3. There are six rows of triangles with eight triangles in each row. There are a total of 48 triangles.

This fact family represents the grouping of triangles:
$6 \times 8 = 48$
$8 \times 6 = 48$
$48 \div 6 = 8$
$48 \div 8 = 6$

Lesson 2—Relating the Zero Property to Multiplication and Division Facts

PRACTICE EXERCISES
ANSWERS AND SOLUTIONS

1. Six groups of zero equals zero because there is nothing in the groups. This diagram shows six groups with nothing in them.

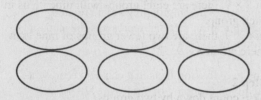

3. Multiplication and division are opposite operations.

   If $6 \div 0 = 0$, then $0 \times 0 = 6$.

   This is not possible, because any number multiplied by 0 is 0.
   $0 \times 0 = 0$

   Therefore, it is impossible to divide a number by 0. There is no answer.

Lesson 3—Skip Counting Up from a Known Fact

🐝 TIME TO TRY 🐝
ANSWERS AND SOLUTIONS

1. **Step 1**
   Compare the two facts.

   In 6×8, there are six groups with eight items in each group.
   In 7×8, there is one more group of eight than there is in 6×8.

   Step 2
   Skip count up by one group.

   Since $6 \times 8 = 48$, then 7×8 is equal to $48 + 8$ (one more group 8).

   Since $6 \times 8 = 48$, then $7 \times 8 = 56$.

2. **Step 1**
   Compare the two facts.

   In 4×6, there are four groups with six items in each group.

   In 6×6, there are two more groups of six than there are in 4×6.

   Step 2
   Skip count up for two groups.

   Since $4 \times 6 = 24$, then 6×6 is equal to $24 + 6 + 6$ (two more groups of 6).

   Since $4 \times 6 = 24$, then $6 \times 6 = 36$.

PRACTICE EXERCISES
ANSWERS AND SOLUTIONS

1. **Step 1**
   Compare the two facts.

   In 8×7, there are eight groups with seven items in each group.

   In 9×7, there is one more group of seven than there is in 8×7.

   Step 2
   Skip count up by one group.

   Since $8 \times 7 = 56$, then 9×7 is equal to $56 + 7$ (one more group of 7).

   Therefore, $9 \times 7 = 63$.

3. **Step 1**
   Compare the two facts.

   In 4×8, there are four groups with eight items in each group.
   In 6×8, there are two more groups of eight than there are in 4×8.

   Step 2
   Skip count up by two groups.

   Since $4 \times 8 = 32$, then 6×8 is equal to $32 + 8 + 8$ (two more groups of 8).

   Therefore, $6 \times 8 = 48$.

Lesson 4—Skip Counting Down from a Known Fact

🦋 TIME TO TRY 🦋
ANSWERS AND SOLUTIONS

1. **Step 1**
    Compare the two facts.

    In 9×7, there are nine groups with seven items in each group.
    In 8×7, there is one less group of seven than there is in 9×7.

    Step 2
    Skip count down by one group.

    Since $9 \times 7 = 63$, then 8×7 is equal to $63 - 7$ (one less group of 7).

    Since $9 \times 7 = 63$, then $8 \times 7 = 56$.

2. **Step 1**
    Compare the two facts.

    In 8×8, there are eight groups with eight items in each group.
    In 6×8, there are two fewer groups of eight than there are in 8×8.

    Step 2
    Skip count down by two groups.

    Since $8 \times 8 = 64$, then 6×8 is equal to $64 - 8 - 8$ (two fewer groups of 8).

    Since $8 \times 8 = 64$, then $6 \times 8 = 48$.

PRACTICE EXERCISES
ANSWERS AND SOLUTIONS

1. **Step 1**
    Compare the two facts.

    In 9×9, there are nine groups with nine items in each group.
    In 8×9, there is one less group of nine than there is in 9×9.

    Step 2
    Skip count down by one group.

    Since $9 \times 9 = 81$, then 8×9 is equal to $81 - 9$ (one less group of 9).

    Therefore, $8 \times 9 = 72$.

3. **Step 1**
    Compare the two facts.

    In 8×9, there are eight groups with nine items in each group.
    In 6×9, there are two fewer groups of nine than there are in 8×9.

    Step 2
    Skip count down by two groups.

    Since $8 \times 9 = 72$, then 6×9 is equal to $72 - 9 - 9$ (two fewer groups of 9).

    Therefore, $6 \times 9 = 54$.

Lesson 5—Using Doubling and Repeated Doubling

🦋 TIME TO TRY 🦋
ANSWERS AND SOLUTIONS

1. Since 6 is a double of 3 ($3 + 3 = 6$), you can double the answer of 3×4 to determine the answer of 6×4.

    Since $3 \times 4 = 12$, then $6 \times 4 = 12 + 12$.
    Since $3 \times 4 = 12$, then $6 \times 4 = 24$.

2. Start with an easier fact like $2 \times 4 = 8$.

    Step 1
    Double $2 \times 4 = 8$.

    When 2 is doubled, it becomes 4. ($2 + 2 = 4$)

    Since $2 \times 4 = 8$, then $4 \times 4 = 8 + 8$.
    Since $2 \times 4 = 8$, then $4 \times 4 = 16$.

    Step 2
    Double $4 \times 4 = 16$.

    When 4 is doubled, it becomes 8. ($4 + 4 = 8$)

    Since $4 \times 4 = 16$, then $8 \times 4 = 16 + 16$.
    Since $4 \times 4 = 16$, then $8 \times 4 = 32$.

PRACTICE EXERCISES
ANSWERS AND SOLUTIONS

1. Since 4 is a double of 2, Susan started with the easier fact of $2 \times 7 = 14$.

   Since $2 \times 7 = 14$, then $4 \times 7 = 14 + 14$.
   Since $2 \times 7 = 14$ then $4 \times 7 = 28$.

3. **Step 1**
   Double $2 \times 2 = 4$.

   When 2 is doubled, it becomes 4.

   Since $2 \times 2 = 4$, then $4 \times 2 = 4 + 4$.

   Step 2
   Double $4 \times 2 = 8$.

   When 4 is doubled, it becomes 8 $(4 + 4 = 8)$.
   Since $4 \times 2 = 8$, then $8 \times 2 = 8 + 8$.
   Since $4 \times 2 = 8$, then $8 \times 2 = 16$.

Lesson 6—Using Halving and Repeated Halving

🦋 TIME TO TRY 🦋
ANSWERS AND SOLUTIONS

1. **Step 1**
   Divide the larger group into two smaller but equal groups.

   Half of 6 is 3, so half of 6×7 is 3×7.

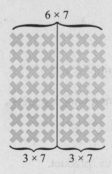

   Step 2
   Solve the problem.

   Multiply 3 by 7.
   $3 \times 7 = 21$

Double the product.
$21 + 21 = 42$

Therefore, $6 \times 7 = 42$.

2. **Step 1**
   Divide the larger group into two smaller and equal groups.

   Half of 8 is 4, so half of 8×5 is 4×5.

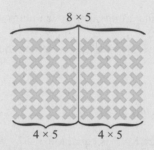

Step 2
Divide each smaller group into two smaller and equal groups.

Half of 4 is 2, so half of 4×5 is 2×5.

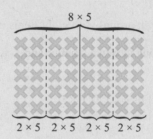

Step 3
Solve the problem.

Multiply 2 by 5.
$2 \times 5 = 10$

Double the product.
$10 + 10 = 20$

Double the new product.
$20 + 20 = 40$

Therefore, $8 \times 5 = 40$.

PRACTICE EXERCISES
ANSWERS AND SOLUTIONS

1. **Step 1**
   Divide the larger group into two smaller but equal groups.

   Half of 4 is 2, so half of 4×6 is 2×6.

   4×6

   $2 \times 6 \quad 2 \times 6$

   Step 2
   Solve the problem.

   Multiply 2 by 6.
   $2 \times 6 = 12$

   Double the product.
   $12 + 12 = 24$

   Therefore, $4 \times 6 = 24$.

3. **Step 1**
   Divide the larger group into two smaller and equal groups.

   Half of 8 is 4, so half of 8×3 is 4×3.

   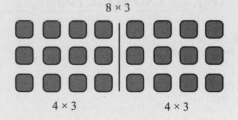
   8×3

   $4 \times 3 \qquad 4 \times 3$

   Step 2
   Divide each smaller group into two smaller and equal groups.

   Half of 4 is 2, so half of 4×3 is 2×3.

   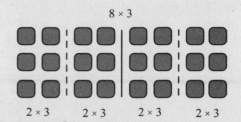
   8×3

   $2 \times 3 \quad 2 \times 3 \quad 2 \times 3 \quad 2 \times 3$

Step 3
Solve the problem.

Multiply 2 by 3.
$2 \times 3 = 6$

Double the product.
$6 + 6 = 12$

Double the sum.
$12 + 12 = 24$

Therefore, $8 \times 3 = 24$.

Lesson 7—Using Patterns in the Nines Facts

🐝 TIME TO TRY 🐝
ANSWERS AND SOLUTIONS

1. One pattern seen in the nines facts is that the sum of the digits in the product always equals 9. Therefore, the product of 36 is the correct answer because 3 + 6 = 9, whereas 3 + 2 = 5.

2. Since 9 is one less than 10, the nines fact of 9×7 will be one less group of seven than the tens fact of 10×7.
   $9 \times 7 = ?$
   $10 \times 7 = 70$
   $70 - 7 = 63$
   $9 \times 7 = 63$

PRACTICE QUESTIONS
ANSWERS AND SOLUTIONS

1. **Step 1**
   Determine the multiplier.

   In the problem 9×5, the multiplier is 5.

   Therefore, the answer will start with 4, one less than 5.

   Step 2
   Determine the next digit in the product.

   Since the digits of the product must add up to 9, the next digit will be 5. $(4 + 5 = 9)$
   $9 \times 5 = 45$

---

3. Since 9 is one less than 10, the nines fact 4×9 will be one group of four less than the tens fact of 4×10.

$4\times9 = ?$
$4\times10 = 40$
$40 - 4 = 36$
$4\times9 = 36$

Lesson 8—Annexing, Then Adding Zero

TIME TO TRY
ANSWERS AND SOLUTIONS

1. Drop the zero from 70.
$70 \rightarrow 7$

Multiply the remaining fact.
$7\times9 = 63$

Add the dropped zero to the end of the product.
$63 \rightarrow 63\underline{0}$

Therefore, $70\times9 = 630$.

2. Drop the two zeros from 200.
$200 \rightarrow 2$

Multiply the remaining fact.
$5\times2 = 10$

Add the two dropped zeros to the end of the product.
$10 \rightarrow 1\,0\underline{00}$

Therefore, $5\times200 = 1\,000$.

3. Drop the three zeros from 5 000.
$5\,000 \rightarrow 5$

Multiply the remaining fact.
$5\times7 = 35$

Add the three dropped zeros to the end of the product.
$35 \rightarrow 35\,\underline{000}$

Therefore, $5\,000 \times 7 = 35\,000$.

PRACTICE EXERCISES
ANSWERS AND SOLUTIONS

1. Drop the zero from 60.
$60 \rightarrow 6$

Multiply the remaining fact.
$8\times6 = 48$

Add the dropped zero to the end of the product.
$48 \rightarrow 48\underline{0}$

Therefore, $8\times60 = 480$.

3. Drop the three zeros from 7 000.
$7\,000 \rightarrow 7$

Multiply the remaining fact.
$7\times7 = 49$

Add the three dropped zeros to the end of the product.
$49 \rightarrow 49\,\underline{000}$

Therefore, $7\,000\times7 = 49\,000$.

Lesson 9—Halving One Factor and Doubling the Other Factor

TIME TO TRY
ANSWERS AND SOLUTIONS

1. Double the 15.
$15\times2 = 30$

Halve the 6.
$6\div2 = 3$

The expression 30×3 has the same value as 15×6.

Since $30\times3 = 90$, then $15\times6 = 90$.

PRACTICE EXERCISES
ANSWERS AND SOLUTIONS

1. Double the 5.
$5 \times 2 = 10$

Halve the 46.
$46 \div 2 = 23$
The expression 10×23 has the same value as 5×46.

Since $10 \times 23 = 230$, then $5 \times 46 = 230$.

3. Double the 25.
$25 \times 2 = 50$

Halve the 6.
$6 \div 2 = 3$

The expression 50×3 has the same value as 25×6.

Since $50 \times 3 = 150$, then $25 \times 6 = 150$.

Lesson 10—Using the Distributive Property

☙ TIME TO TRY ❧
ANSWERS AND SOLUTIONS

1. **Step 1**
Think of the number 34 in expanded notation.
$34 = 30 + 4$

Step 2
Multiply each place value by the factor 6.
$(6 \times 30) + (6 \times 4)$

Step 3
Perform the calculations.
$(6 \times 30) + (6 \times 4)$
$= 180 + 24$
$= 204$

$6 \times 34 = 204$

2. **Step 1**
Think of the number 37 as a subtraction fact using a multiple of 10.
$37 = 40 - 3$

Step 2

Multiply each place value by the factor 9.
$(9 \times 40) - (9 \times 3)$

Step 3
Perform the calculations.
$(9 \times 40) - (9 \times 3)$
$= 360 - 27$
$= 333$

$9 \times 37 = 333$

PRACTICE EXERCISES
ANSWERS AND SOLUTIONS

1. **Step 1**
Think of the number 54 in expanded notation.
$54 = 50 + 4$

Step 2
Multiply each place value by the factor 2.
$(2 \times 50) + (2 \times 4)$

Step 3
Perform the calculations.
$(2 \times 50) + (2 \times 4)$
$= 100 + 8$
$= 108$

$2 \times 54 = 108$

3. **Step 1**
Think of the number 29 as a subtraction fact, using a multiple of 10.
$29 = 30 - 1$

Step 2
Multiply each place value of the subtraction fact by 8.
$(8 \times 30) - (8 \times 1)$

Step 3
Perform the calculations.
$(8 \times 30) - (8 \times 1)$
$= 240 - 8$
$= 232$

$8 \times 29 = 232$

Practice Test

ANSWERS AND SOLUTIONS

1. Drop the zero from 20.
$$20 \rightarrow 2$$

Multiply the remaining fact.
$$7 \times 2 = 14$$

Add the dropped zero to the end of the product.
$$10 \rightarrow 14\underline{0}$$

Therefore, $7 \times 20 = 140$.

3. **Step 1**
Double $2 \times 4 = 8$.

When 2 is doubled, it becomes 4.

Since $2 \times 4 = 8$, then $4 \times 4 = 8 + 8$.

Step 2
Double 4×4.

When 4 is doubled, it becomes 8 (4 + 4 = 8).

Since $4 \times 4 = 16$, then $8 \times 4 = 16 + 16$.
$$2 \times 4 = 8$$
$$4 \times 4 = 16 \ (8 + 8)$$
$$8 \times 4 = 32 \ (16 + 16)$$

5. **Step 1**
Compare the two facts.

In 6×6, there are six groups with six items in each group.

In 4×6, there are four groups of six with six items in each group (two fewer groups).

Step 2
Skip count down by two groups.

Since $6 \times 6 = 36$, then 4×6 is equal to $36 - 6 - 6$ (two fewer groups of 6).

Therefore, $4 \times 6 = 24$.

7. Since 9 is one less than 10, the nines fact 9×7 will be one group of seven less than the tens fact of 10×7.

$$9 \times 7 = ?$$
$$10 \times 7 = 70$$
$$70 - 7 = 63$$
$$9 \times 7 = 63$$

9. **Step 1**
Think of the number 32 in expanded notation.
$$32 = 30 + 2$$

Step 2
Multiply each place value by the factor 6.
$$(6 \times 30) + (6 \times 2)$$

Step 3
Perform the calculations.
$$(6 \times 30) + (6 \times 2)$$
$$= 180 + 12$$
$$= 192$$
$$6 \times 32 = 192$$

11. There are three rows of balls with six balls in each row. There are a total of 18 balls.

The multiplication fact that is related to $3 \times 6 = 18$ is $6 \times 3 = 18$.

The two related division facts are $18 \div 6 = 3$ and $18 \div 3 = 6$.

13. **Step 1**
Compare the two facts.

In 7×7, there are seven groups with seven items in each group.

In 9×7, there are nine groups of seven with seven items in each group (two more groups).

Step 2
Skip count up by two groups.

Since $7 \times 7 = 49$, then 9×7 is equal to $49 + 7 + 7$ (two more groups of 7).

Therefore, $9 \times 7 = 63$.

15. Step 1
Divide the larger group into two smaller and equal groups.

Half of 8 is 4, so half of 8×5 is 4×5.

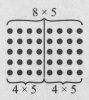

8×5

4×5 4×5

Step 2
Divide each smaller group into two smaller and equal groups.

Half of 4 is 2, so half of 4×5 is 2×5.

8×5

2×5 2×5 2×5 2×5

Step 3
Solve the problem.

Multiply 2 by 5.
$2 \times 5 = 10$

Double the product.
$10 + 10 = 20$

Double the sum.
$20 + 20 = 40$

Therefore, $8 \times 5 = 40$.

MEASUREMENT

Lesson 1—Identifying 90° Angles

❧ TIME TO TRY ❧
ANSWERS AND SOLUTIONS

1. Step 1
Identify the angles that belong in group 1: 90° angles.

Only this angle is a 90° angle:

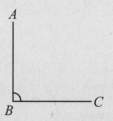

It forms a square corner where the two sides (rays) meet.

90°

Step 2
Identify the angles that belong in group 2: no 90° angles.

These two angles do not have square corners, so they are not 90° angles:

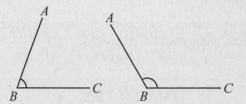

2. Recall that a 90° angle forms a square corner.

The "No Parking" sign has four right angles. Each corner of the rectangular shape is a 90° angle.

The "Walk" sign has two right angles. The two bottom corners of the sign form square corners, which are 90° angles.

PRACTICE EXERCISES
ANSWERS AND SOLUTIONS

1. Yes, the staircase is a good example of 90° angles.

    Each horizontal step and each vertical back of the step create square corners where they meet. The undersides of the stairs also make 90° angles.

    This diagram shows three of the many 90° angles formed.

2. Carlton made one 90° angle in shape B, the triangle, as shown by the square corner.

    He made two 90° angles in the bottom left trapezoid, shape C, as shown by the square corners.

    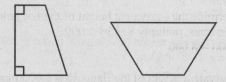

Lesson 2—Sketching and Labelling 90° Angles

🐝 TIME TO TRY 🐝
ANSWERS AND SOLUTIONS

1. Draw a horizontal line and vertical line that meet at a square corner.

    Draw a square corner or arc to mark the 90° angle.

    Choose three letters to name the angle. The middle letter will label the square corner or arc.

The angle you draw could look like this:

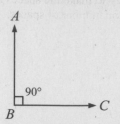

PRACTICE EXERCISES
ANSWERS AND SOLUTIONS

1. Draw a horizontal line and a vertical line that meet at a square corner.

    Draw a square corner to mark the 90° angle. Label it V. Label the end of one line with a U and the end of the other line with a W.

    The angle you draw should have this position. The letter V will label the 90° angle.

    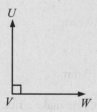

Lesson 3—Using Referents to Measure Length

🐝 TIME TO TRY 🐝
ANSWERS AND SOLUTIONS

1. You could stack about five dimes to measure the width of the paperclip.

     5 dimes

    The width of the paperclip is about 5 mm.

3. Since the dog's height is about 1 m, make a tick on the line for each metre. Try to make the spaces as equal as possible. Count the number of spaces.

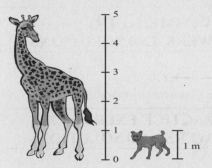

The height of the giraffe is about 5 m.

PRACTICE EXERCISES
ANSWERS AND SOLUTIONS

1. You would need to stack about 10 dimes to equal the height of the die.

10 dimes

The height of the die is about 10 mm.

3. Since the dog's height is about 1 m, make a tick on the line for each metre. Count the number of equally sized spaces on the line.

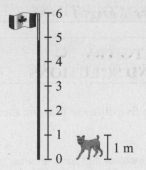

1 m

The height of the flagpole is about 5 m.

Lesson 4—Using Equivalent Measures for Millimetres

🦋 TIME TO TRY 🦋
ANSWERS AND SOLUTIONS

1. Since 1 cm = 10 mm, you need to multiply 3 cm by 10 to determine the equivalent number of millimetres.
$3 \times 10 = 30$

The equivalent length of each side of the stamp is 30 mm.

2. Since 1 000 mm = 1 m, 2 000 mm are equivalent to 2 m.
$2 \times 1\ 000 = 2\ 000$

Marc was correct when he said that there are 2 000 mm in 2 m.

PRACTICE EXERCISES
ANSWERS AND SOLUTIONS

1. 10 mm = 1 cm
To determine the equivalent measure in millimetres, multiply 6 cm by 10.
$6 \times 10 = 60$

The equivalent length of the protractor is 60 mm.

3. 1 000 mm = 1 m.
To determine the equivalent height of the flagpole in millimetres, multiply 8 m by 1 000.
$8 \times 1\ 000 = 8\ 000$

The equivalent height of the flagpole is 8 000 mm.

Lesson 5—Using Millimetres as the Unit of Measure

🦋 TIME TO TRY 🦋
ANSWERS AND SOLUTIONS

1. **Step 1**
Since 10 mm = 1 cm, count by 10s as you pass the 1 cm tick.
10

Step 2
Count by 5s to the mid-tick after 10.
10, 15

Step 3
Count the ticks after 15 by 1s.
10, 15, 16

The pencil sharpener is 16 mm wide.

PRACTICE EXERCISES
ANSWERS AND SOLUTIONS

1. **Step 1**
Since 10 mm = 1 cm, count by 10s as you pass each numbered centimetre.
10, 20, 30

Step 2
Count the ticks that represent each millimetre.

Count by 1s.
10, 20, 30, 31, 32, 33

The key is 33 mm long.

Lesson 6—Understanding the Relationship between Area and Perimeter

🦋 TIME TO TRY 🦋
ANSWERS AND SOLUTIONS

1. When a whole wall is painted, the entire surface of the wall is covered with paint. Therefore, Sarah's dad needs to calculate the area of the wall so that he knows how much paint he needs to buy to cover that surface.

PRACTICE EXERCISES
ANSWERS AND SOLUTIONS

1. A border goes around the edges of the quilt. Mrs. Mullen needs to know the perimeter of the quilt.

3. Since the fence will go around the pen, it would be most useful for Shawn and his dad to know the perimeter of the pen.

Lesson 7—Constructing Rectangles for a Given Area

🦋 TIME TO TRY 🦋
ANSWERS AND SOLUTIONS

1. **Step 1**
Determine all the factors that equal 6 when multiplied by each other.
$1 \times 6 = 6$
$2 \times 3 = 6$

The combinations of numbers that equal 6 when multiplied by each other are the dimensions of the rectangles.

Step 2
Draw and label the rectangles that have an area of 6 units^2.

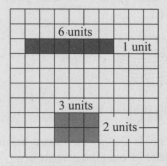

PRACTICE EXERCISES
ANSWERS AND SOLUTIONS

1. **Step 1**
Determine all the factors that equal 15 when multiplied by each other.
$1 \times 15 = 15$
$3 \times 5 = 15$

Step 2
Draw and label the rectangles that have an area of 15 units^2.

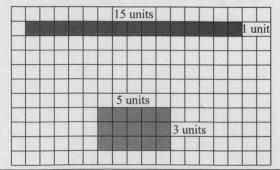

Lesson 8—Constructing Rectangles for a Given Perimeter

🦋 TIME TO TRY 🦋
ANSWERS AND SOLUTIONS

1. Determine all the possible lengths and widths.

    Divide the perimeter by 2.
    $12 \div 2 = 6$.

    Think of all the numbers that add up to 6:
    $1 + 5 = 6$
    $2 + 4 = 6$
    $3 + 3 = 6$

    The number combinations become the lengths and widths of the rectangles you can draw. There are three different rectangles that could each have a perimeter of 12 units.

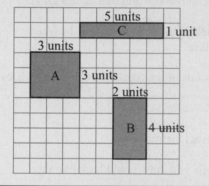

PRACTICE EXERCISES
ANSWERS AND SOLUTIONS

1. **Step 1**
    Determine all the possible lengths and widths.

    Divide the perimeter by 2.
    $8 \div 2 = 4$

    Think of all the numbers that add up to 4.
    $1 + 3 = 4$
    $2 + 2 = 4$

Step 2
Draw the rectangles.

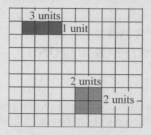

2. **Step 1**
    Determine all the possible lengths and widths.

    Divide the perimeter by 2.
    $18 \div 2 = 9$

    Think of all the numbers that add up to 9.
    $1 + 8 = 9$
    $2 + 7 = 9$
    $3 + 6 = 9$
    $4 + 5 = 9$

Step 2
Draw and label the four rectangles.

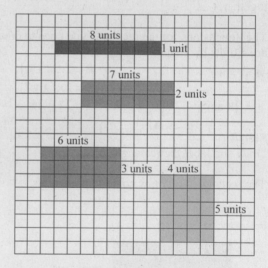

Lesson 9—Constructing Rectangles When Area and Perimeter Are Given

🐝 TIME TO TRY 🐝
ANSWERS AND SOLUTIONS

1. **Step 1**
   Determine all the possible lengths and widths that will equal 28 units^2 when multiplied by each other.
   $1 \times 28 = 28$
   $2 \times 14 = 28$
   $4 \times 7 = 28$

   Step 2
   Identify which length and width will equal 11 (half the perimeter, which is 22 units) when added together.
   $1 + 28 = 29$
   $2 + 14 = 16$
   $4 + 7 = 11$

   Step 3
   Select the length and width that equal 28 when multiplied by each other, and 11 when added together.

   The dimensions for the rectangle you need to draw are 4 units by 7 units.

   $$A = l \times w \qquad\qquad P = 2 \times (l + w)$$
   $$= 4 \times 7 \qquad\qquad\quad = 2 \times (4 + 7)$$
   $$= 28 \text{ units}^2 \qquad\quad = 22 \text{ units}$$

   Step 4
   Draw and label the rectangle.

   The rectangle you draw could look like this:

   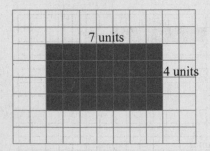

PRACTICE EXERCISES
ANSWERS AND SOLUTIONS

1. **Step 1**
   Determine all the possible lengths and widths that will equal 24 units^2 when multiplied by each other.
   $1 \times 24 = 24$
   $2 \times 12 = 24$
   $3 \times 8 = 24$
   $4 \times 6 = 24$

   Step 2
   Identify which length and width will equal 11 (half of the perimeter, which is 22 units) when added together.
   $1 + 24 = 25$
   $2 + 12 = 13$
   $3 + 8 = 11$
   $4 + 6 = 8$

   Step 3
   Select the length and width that equals 24

   when multiplied by each other, and 11 when added together.

   The dimensions of the rectangle will be 8 units by 3 units.

   Step 4
   Draw and label the rectangle.

   The rectangle you draw could look like this:

   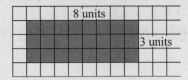

3. **Step 1**
   Determine all the possible lengths and widths that will equal 18 units^2 when multiplied by each other.
   $1 \times 18 = 18$
   $2 \times 9 = 18$
   $3 \times 6 = 18$

   Step 2
   Identify which length and width will equal 9 (half of the perimeter, which is 18 units) when added together.
   $1 + 18 = 19$
   $2 + 9 = 11$
   $3 + 6 = 9$

Step 3
Select the length and width that equals 18 when multiplied by each other, and 9 when added together.

The dimensions of the rectangle will be 6 units by 3 units.

Step 4
Draw and label the rectangle.

The rectangle you draw could look like this:

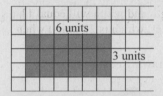

6 units

3 units

Lesson 10—Describing Shapes That Result in the Greatest and Least Areas for a Given Perimeter

❧ TIME TO TRY ❧
ANSWERS AND SOLUTIONS

1. **Step 1**
    Determine all the possible dimensions for a rectangle with a perimeter of 14 units.

    Divide the perimeter by 2:
    $14 \div 2 = 7$

    Think of all the numbers that equal 7 when added together:
    $1 + 6 = 7$
    $2 + 5 = 7$
    $3 + 4 = 7$

    Step 2
    Draw the rectangles.

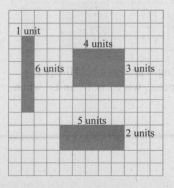

1 unit
4 units
6 units
3 units
5 units
2 units

Step 3
Determine the areas of the three rectangles:
$A = l \times w$
$A = 1 \times 6 = 6 \text{ units}^2$
$A = 2 \times 5 = 10 \text{ units}^2$
$A = 3 \times 4 = 12 \text{ units}^2$

Step 4
Describe the shapes.

The least area is 6 units^2. The rectangle with the least area has a long and narrow shape.

The greatest area is 12 units^2. The rectangle with the greatest area has a shape that is almost like a square.

PRACTICE EXERCISES
ANSWERS AND SOLUTIONS

1. **Step 1**
    Determine all the possible dimensions for a rectangle with a perimeter of 16 units.

    Divide the perimeter by 2.
    $16 \div 2 = 8$

    Think of all the numbers that equal 8 when added together.
    $1 + 7 = 8$
    $2 + 6 = 8$
    $3 + 5 = 8$
    $4 + 4 = 8$

    Step 2
    Draw the rectangles.

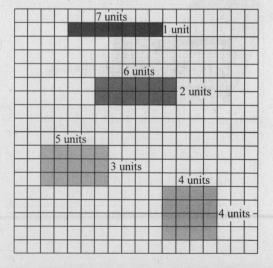

7 units
1 unit
6 units
2 units
5 units
3 units
4 units
4 units

Step 3
Determine the areas of the rectangles.
$A = l \times w$
$A = 1 \times 7 = 7 \text{ units}^2$
$A = 2 \times 6 = 12 \text{ units}^2$
$A = 3 \times 5 = 15 \text{ units}^2$
$A = 4 \times 4 = 16 \text{ units}^2$

Step 4
Describe the shapes.

The least area is 7 units^2. The rectangle with the least area has a long and narrow shape.

The greatest area is 16 units^2. The rectangle with the greatest area has the shape of a square.

Practice Test

ANSWERS AND SOLUTIONS

1. Look for the angle that forms a square corner where the two rays meet. Only the figure on the far right forms a square corner.

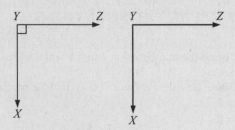

3. The book is about as thick as the height of 11 dimes.

11 dimes

Therefore, the thickness of the book is about 11 mm.

5. **Step 1**
Determine Lee's height in mm.
$1 \text{ m} = 1\ 000 \text{ mm}$
$1.54 \text{ m} = 1.54 \times 1\ 000$
$1.54 \text{ m} = 1\ 540 \text{ mm}$

An easy way to multiply by 1 000 is to move the decimal point three places to the right.
$1.54 \rightarrow 1\ \underline{540}$

Step 2
Compare the two heights.

Jaimie's height is 1 490 mm and Lee's height is 1 540 mm.

Since $1\ 490 < 1\ 540$, Jaimie is shorter than Lee.

7. One way to estimate is to draw the dice side-by-side to determine how many dice would equal the width of the sunglasses.

Try to make each drawing equal in size.

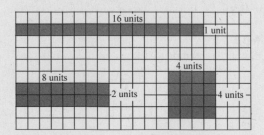

The glasses are about 10 cm in width

9. **Step 1**
Determine all the factors that equal 16 when multiplied by each other.
$1 \times 16 = 16$
$2 \times 8 = 16$
$4 \times 4 = 16$
Step 2
Draw and label the rectangles.

The rectangles you draw can look like this:

16 units / 1 unit / 4 units / 8 units / 2 units / 4 units

11. **Step 1**
Determine all the possible lengths and widths that will equal 8 units^2 when multiplied by each other.
$1 \times 8 = 8$
$2 \times 4 = 8$

Step 2
Identify which length and width will equal 6 (half of the perimeter, which is 12 units) when added together.
$1 + 8 = 9$
$2 + 4 = 6$

Step 3
Select the length and width that equal 8 when multiplied by each other, and 6 when added together.

The dimensions of the rectangle will be 4 units by 2 units.

Step 4
Draw the rectangle with an area of 8 units^2 and a perimeter of 12 units.

MULTIPLICATION OF TWO 2-DIGIT FACTORS

Lesson 1—Using Expanded Notation to Show Partial Products

TIME TO TRY
ANSWERS AND SOLUTIONS

1. **Step 1**
Write each factor in expanded notation.
$77 \rightarrow (70 + 7)$
$39 \rightarrow (30 + 9)$

Step 2
Place a multiplication sign between the two expanded notations.
$(70 + 7) \times (30 + 9)$

The partial product of 77 × 39 is
$(70 + 7) \times (30 + 9)$.

PRACTICE EXERCISES
ANSWERS AND SOLUTIONS

1. No, Ben is not correct.

This is how Ben should have determined the partial product of 66 × 37.

Step 1
Write each factor in expanded notation.
$66 \rightarrow (60 + 6)$
$37 \rightarrow (30 + 7)$

Step 2
Place a multiplication sign between the two expanded notations.
$(60 + 6) \times (30 + 7)$

The partial product of 66 × 37 is
$(60 + 6) \times (30 + 7)$, not $(60 + 6) + (30 + 7)$.

3. **Step 1**

Write each factor in expanded notation.

$69 \rightarrow (60+9)$

$33 \rightarrow (30+3)$

Step 2

Place a multiplication sign between the two expanded notations.

$(60+9)\times(30+3)$

Caleb can write the partial product of 69 × 33 as $(60+9)\times(30+3)$.

Lesson 2—Applying the Distributive Properly to Partial Products

TIME TO TRY
ANSWERS AND SOLUTIONS

1. **Step 1**

Determine the partial product using expanded notation.

$18 \rightarrow (10+8)$

$42 \rightarrow (40+2)$

The partial product of 18 × 42 is $(10+8)\times(40+2)$.

Step 2

Apply the distributive property to the partial product.

- Multiply 10 by 40 and 10 by 2, placing a + sign between the partial products.
  $(10\times40)+(10\times2)$

- Multiply 8 by 40 and 8 by 2, placing a + sign between the partial products.
  $(8\times40)+(8\times2)$

- Place a + sign between the two sets of partial products.
  $(10\times40)+(10\times2)+(8\times40)+(8\times2)$

Step 3

Add the products.

$(10\times40)+(10\times2)+(8\times40)+(8\times2)$

$=400+20+320+16$

400
20
320
$\underline{+16}$
756

$18 \times 42 = 756$

2. **Step 1**

Simplify the expression by placing brackets around the multiplication facts.

$(60\times30)+(60\times6)+(3\times30)+(3\times6)$

Step 2

Complete the multiplication. Then, add the products.

$(60\times30)+(60\times6)+(3\times30)+(3\times6)$

$=1\,800+360+90+18$

$1\,800$
360
90
$\underline{+18}$
$2\,268$

$63 \times 36 = 2\,268$

PRACTICE EXERCISES
ANSWERS AND SOLUTIONS

1. **Step 1**

Determine the partial product using expanded notation.

$24 \rightarrow (20+4)$

$19 \rightarrow (10+9)$

The partial product of 24 × 19 is $(20+4)\times(10+9)$.

Step 2

Apply the distributive property to the partial product.

- Multiply 20 by 10 and 20 by 9, placing a + sign between the partial products.
  $(20\times10)+(20\times9)$

- Multiply 4 by 10 and 4 by 9, placing a + sign between the partial products.
  $(4\times10)+(4\times9)$

- Place a + sign between the two sets of partial products.
  $(20\times10)+(20\times9)+(4\times10)+(4\times9)$

Step 3

Complete the multiplication. Then, add

the products.

$(20\times10)+(20\times9)+(4\times10)+(4\times9)$
$=200+180+40+36$
$=456$

$24\times19=456$

3. **Step 1**
    Simplify the expression by placing brackets around the multiplication facts.
    $(40\times50)+(40\times7)+(1\times50)+(1\times7)$

    Step 2
    Complete the multiplication. Then, add the products.
    $(40\times50)+(40\times7)+(1\times50)+(1\times7)$
    $=2\,000+280+50+7$
    $=2\,337$

    $41\times57=2\,337$

Lesson 3—Using Models to Illustrate 2-Digit Multiplication

🐝 **TIME TO TRY** 🐝
ANSWERS AND SOLUTIONS

1. **Step 1**
    Write the multiplication fact as partial products using expanded notation.
    $(10+5)\times(20+1)$

    Step 2
    Apply the distributive property to the partial products.
    $(10\times20)+(10\times1)+(5\times20)+(5\times1)$

    Step 3
    Use base ten blocks to illustrate each product.

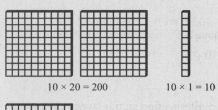

$10 \times 20 = 200$ $10 \times 1 = 10$

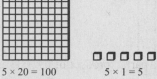

$5 \times 20 = 100$ $5 \times 1 = 5$

Step 4
Add the four sets of base ten blocks to show the product of 15 × 21.

Three hundred flats plus one ten rod plus five units equals 315.

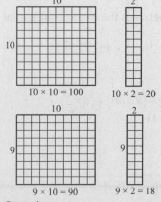

$15 \times 21 = 315$

2. **Step 1**
    Write the multiplication fact as partial products using expanded notation.
    $(10+9)\times(10+2)$

    Step 2
    Apply the distributive property to the partial products.
    $(10\times10)+(10\times2)+(9\times10)+(9\times2)$

    Step 3
    Use grids to illustrate each product.

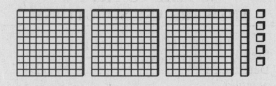

$10 \times 10 = 100$ $10 \times 2 = 20$

$9 \times 10 = 90$ $9 \times 2 = 18$

Step 4
Add the four sets of grids together to form

a rectangle.

The rectangle formed will be 19 squares by 12 squares (19×12).

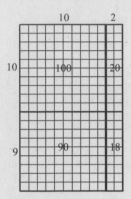

$100 + 90 + 20 + 18 = 228$
$19 \times 12 = 228$

PRACTICE EXERCISES
ANSWERS AND SOLUTIONS

1. **Step 1**
   Write the multiplication fact as partial products using expanded notation.
   $(10 + 2) \times (10 + 1)$

   Step 2
   Apply the distributive property to the partial products.
   $(10 \times 10) + (10 \times 1) + (2 \times 10) + (2 \times 1)$

   Step 3
   Use base ten blocks to illustrate each product.

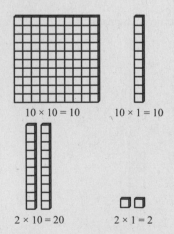

$10 \times 10 = 10$ $10 \times 1 = 10$

$2 \times 10 = 20$ $2 \times 1 = 2$

   Step 4
   Add the four sets of base ten blocks to show the

product of 12×11.

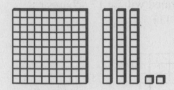

One hundred flat plus three ten rods plus two units equals 132.
$12 \times 11 = 132$

3. **Step 1**
   Write the multiplication fact as partial products using expanded notation.
   $(10 + 7) \times (10 + 1)$

   Step 2
   Apply the distributive property to the partial products.
   $(10 \times 10) + (10 \times 1) + (7 \times 10) + (7 \times 1)$

   Step 3
   Use grids to illustrate each product.

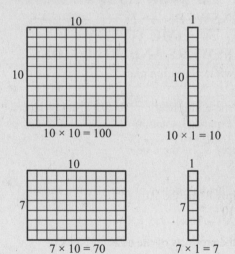

$10 \times 10 = 100$ $10 \times 1 = 10$

$7 \times 10 = 70$ $7 \times 1 = 7$

   Step 4
   Add the four sets of grids together to form a rectangle that shows the product of 17×11.

The rectangle formed will be 17 squares by 11 squares (17 × 11) .

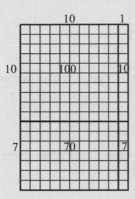

$$100 + 70 + 10 + 7 = 187$$
$$17 \times 11 = 187$$

Lesson 4—Using Algorithms to Multiply Two 2-Digit Factors

TIME TO TRY
ANSWERS AND SOLUTIONS

1. **Step 1**
   Follow the algorithm plan.

   Think of the multiplier (18) in expanded notation. (10 + 8)

   Multiply 81 by the 8 ones.
   81 × 8

   Multiply 81 by the 10.
   81 × 10

   Add the products of the ones and tens.

   Step 2
   Show your work.

   ```
     81
   ×18
    648
    810
   1 458
   ```
   $81 \times 18 = 1\ 458$

1. **Step 1**
   Follow the algorithm plan.

   Think of 31 as (30 + 1).
   Multiply 24 by the ones.
   Multiply 24 by the tens.
   Add the products.

   Step 2
   Show your work.

   ```
     24
   ×31
     24
    720
    744
   ```
   $24 \times 31 = 744$

   $64 \times 23 = 1\ 472$

3. **Step 1**
   Follow the algorithm plan.

   Think of 28 as (20 + 8).
   Multiply 82 by the ones.
   Multiply 82 by the tens.
   Add the products.

   Step 2
   Show your work.

   ```
      1
     82
   ×28
    656
   1 640
   2 296
   ```
   $82 \times 28 = 2\ 296$

Lesson 5—Solving Multiplication Problems in Context

🦋 TIME TO TRY 🦋
ANSWERS AND SOLUTIONS

1. **Step 1**
    Decide which multiplication strategy you will use to solve this problem.

    Step 2
    One example of a strategy you can use is an algorithm.

    $$\begin{array}{r} 50 \\ \times 12 \\ \hline 100 \\ 500 \\ \hline 600 \end{array}$$

    There were 600 chairs in the auditorium.

2. **Step 1**
    Write a problem using the given information.

    Here is an example of a problem that uses the given information:

    There are 25 books on the table at the back of the classroom. Each book has 75 pages. How many pages do the 25 books have in total?

    Step 2
    Solve the problem using a strategy that works for you.

    Here, the problem is solved using the distributive property:

    Write the multiplication fact 25×75 in expanded notation.
    $(20+5)\times(70+5)$

    Apply the distributive property.
    $(20\times70)+(20\times5)+(5\times70)+(5\times5)$

    Add the products.
    $1\ 400+100+350+25=1\ 875$

    There were 1 875 pages in total.

PRACTICE EXERCISES
ANSWERS AND SOLUTIONS

1. **Step 1**
    Choose a strategy to solve the problem.

    One strategy you can use is to apply the distributive property.

    Step 2
    Solve the problem.

    Write the multiplication fact of 35×15 in expanded notation.
    $(30+5)\times(10+5)$

    Apply the distributive property.
    $(30\times10)+(30\times5)+(5\times10)+(5\times5)$

    Do the multiplication facts, and then add the products.
    $300+150+50+25=525$

    Fifteen books would cost $525.

3. **Step 1**
    Choose a strategy to solve the problem.

    One way of solving the problem is to use an algorithm.

    Step 2
    Follow the algorithm plan.

    Think of 13 as (10 + 3).
    Multiply 45 by the ones.
    Multiply 45 by the tens.
    Add the products.

    $$\begin{array}{r} 45 \\ \times 13 \\ \hline 135 \\ 450 \\ \hline 585 \end{array}$$

    In 13 days, Katelyn spends 585 minutes in a dance class.

Practice Test

ANSWERS AND SOLUTIONS

1. Write each number in expanded notation.
$$86 \rightarrow (80+6)$$
$$28 \rightarrow (20+8)$$

Place a multiplication sign between the two expanded notations.
$$(80+6)\times(20+8)$$

The partial product of 86 × 28 is
$$(80+6)\times(20+8).$$

3. **Step 1**
Write the multiplication fact as partial products using expanded notation.
$$(10+3)\times(20+1)$$

Step 2
Apply the distributive property to the partial products.
$$(10\times20)+(10\times1)+(3\times20)+(3\times1)$$

Step 3
Use base ten blocks to illustrate each product.

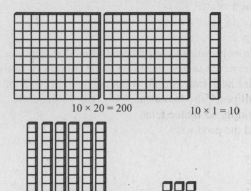

$10 \times 20 = 200$ $10 \times 1 = 10$

$3 \times 20 = 60$ $3 \times 1 = 3$

Step 4
Add the four sets of base ten blocks to show the product of 13 × 21.

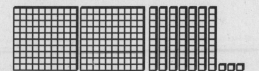

Two hundred flats plus seven ten rods plus three units equals 273.
$$13 \times 21 = 273$$

5. **Step 1**
Follow the algorithm plan.

Think of 13 as (10 + 3).
Multiply 46 by the ones.
Multiply 46 by the tens.
Add the products.

Step 2
Show your work.

$$
\begin{array}{r}
\overset{1}{4}6 \\
\times 13 \\
\hline
138 \\
460 \\
\hline
598 \\
\end{array}
$$

$$46\times13 = 598$$

7. **Step 1**
Choose a strategy to solve the problem.

One strategy you can use is to apply the distributive property to 45 × 15.

Step 2
Solve the problem.

Write the multiplication fact in expanded notation.
$$(40+5)\times(10+5)$$

Apply the distributive property.
$$(40\times10)+(40\times5)+(5\times10)+(5\times5)$$

Step 3
Complete the multiplication. Then, add the products.
$$(40\times10)+(40\times5)+(5\times10)+(5\times5)$$
$$=400+200+50+25$$
$$=675$$

Mrs. Star sold a total of 675 cupcakes.

DATA MANAGEMENT

Lesson 1—Differentiating Between First-Hand and Second-Hand Data

❧ TIME TO TRY ❧
ANSWERS AND SOLUTIONS

1. Since Jared was collecting all the information himself, without any help from other people or other sources, he was collecting first-hand data.

PRACTICE EXERCISES
ANSWERS AND SOLUTIONS

1. **Step 1**
   Identify the data.

   Miss Martin was collecting first-hand data.

   Step 2
   Justify your answer.

   Since Miss Martin was collecting all the information herself, without any help from other people or other sources, she was collecting first-hand data.

Lesson 2—Asking Appropriate Questions to Collect Data

❧ TIME TO TRY ❧
ANSWERS AND SOLUTIONS

1. Nathan needs to ask a question that is broad, or general enough so that he can collect all sorts of data about all the different kinds of things the students learn from the show.

   Asking a question like "What facts have you learned from the show?" would be a good way for Nathan to find out exactly what kind of information his classmates have learned from the show. The data he collects will be wide and varied.

2. Jordyn needs to ask questions that are specific to the kind of information she needs. Since she needs information about North American animals that eat only plants, her questions should be limited to plant-only eating animals from North America. She could ask questions like these:

   - What animals in North America eat only plants?
   - Do any North American animals eat only plants?
   - Which plant-only eating animals live in North America?

PRACTICE EXERCISES
ANSWERS AND SOLUTIONS

1. **Step 1**
   The students could ask questions like these:
   - Which is your favourite city in Canada?
   - Which of these Canadian cities is your favourite? (Listing some choices)

   Step 2
   Explain your answer.

   The students want to collect information about which Canadian city is the most popular among the students at their school so the question asked must limit the choices of cities to those located in Canada.

3. **Step 1**
   Sam could ask questions like these:
   - Where do birds that migrate go for the winter?
   - Do all birds migrate for the winter?
   - How far away do birds fly when they migrate?

   Step 2
   Explain your answer.

   Sam only wants to learn about birds that migrate, so he needs to ask questions about migratory birds. Since he is not specific about particular breeds of birds or locations, his questions can be general about those subjects.

Lesson 3—Identifying Attributes of Double Bar Graphs

🦋 TIME TO TRY 🦋
ANSWERS AND SOLUTIONS

1. **Step 1**
   Identify the missing attribute.

   The graph does not have a title.

   Step 2
   Explain the importance of including a title.

   The title tells you what the graph is about. Without a title, the graph loses its meaning.

   Since this graph does not have a title, you have no idea what the numbers of azalea and wildflower plants are referring to. They could be the number of plants planted. They could be the number of plants eaten by animals. They could be the number of plants blooming in a particular week. Without a title, you can only guess.

PRACTICE EXERCISES
ANSWERS AND SOLUTIONS

1. **Step 1**
   Determine who is correct.

   Katie is correct when she says that one attribute is missing.

   Step 2
   Justify your answer.

   The y-axis is not labelled, so it is not clear what the numbers refer to.

   They could refer to the number of animals that are female or male, or they could refer to the number of boys and girls who voted for their favourite animal, or the number of favourite animals owned by boys and girls.

   Without a label, the data is confusing.

Lesson 4—Interpreting Double Bar Graphs to Draw Conclusions

🦋 TIME TO TRY 🦋
ANSWERS AND SOLUTIONS

1. **Step 1**
   Draw a conclusion from the data presented.

   One conclusion you can draw is that the boys and girls have very different preferences for shoelace colours.

   Step 2
   Justify your conclusion.

   There is not one single colour that both the boys and girls chose in equal numbers.

   The colours that the boys liked the most (black and orange), the girls liked the least.

   The colours that the girls liked the most (purple and white), the boys liked the least.

   According to the data, boys and girls have very different tastes in the colours of shoelaces they would like the principal to buy.

PRACTICE EXERCISES
ANSWERS AND SOLUTIONS

1. When you compare the kinds of medals won, you can conclude that the boys were able to win more medals than the girls at the silver and bronze levels, but the girls were able to win more medals than the boys at the gold level.

2. **Conclusion 1**
   When you compare the heights of the bars, you can see that the bar representing the girls is higher than the bar representing the boys for each grade.

   Therefore, you can conclude that girls in grades 1 to 6 generally do more homework than boys do.

   Conclusion 2
   When you compare the heights of the bars for each grade level, you can see that each grade level is higher than the grade level before it.
   Therefore, you can conclude that students (both boys and girls) do more homework as each year goes by.

Lesson 5—Constructing a Double Bar Graph

🐝 TIME TO TRY 🐝
ANSWERS AND SOLUTIONS

1. The double bar graph you draw and label could look like this:

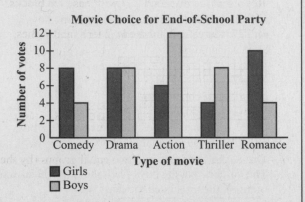

PRACTICE EXERCISES
ANSWERS AND SOLUTIONS

1. The double bar graph you draw could look like this:

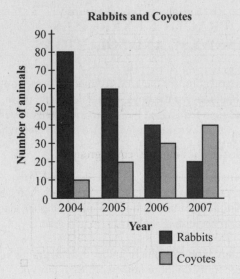

Practice Test

ANSWERS AND SOLUTIONS

1. **Step 1**
    Identify the missing attribute.

    The *y*-axis is not labelled.

    Step 2
    Explain the importance of labelling the *y*-axis.

    The numbers on the *y*-axis are not labelled; therefore, you do not know what they represent.

    The numbers could represent the number of people eating at the restaurant, or the number of tables or chairs at the restaurant, or even the cost of the lunches or dinners.

    Without proper labels, the data is confusing.

3. Since Edmund only needs information about the life span of dogs, his questions should be limited to dogs and not other animals. As well, his questions should be limited to life spans and not other topics like food or shelter.

    Edmund could ask questions like these:
    *   What is the average life span of a dog?
    *   Can a dog's life span be greater than 50 years?
    *   How long do most dogs live?
    *   Do big dogs have a longer life span than small dogs?

5. The graph you draw and label could look like this:

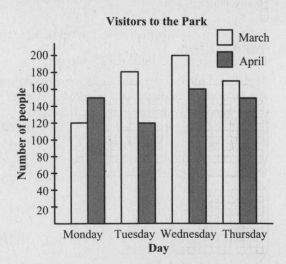

DIVISION OF 3-DIGIT BY 1-DIGIT NUMBERS

Lesson 1—Using Models to Illustrate the Process of Equal Sharing

🐰 **TIME TO TRY** 🐰
ANSWERS AND SOLUTIONS

1. **Step 1**
   Represent the dividend 312 with base ten blocks.

   In 312, there are 3 hundreds, 1 ten, and 2 ones.

   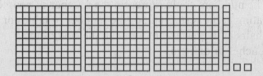

   Step 2
   Divide the hundreds into three equal groups (by the divisor 3).

   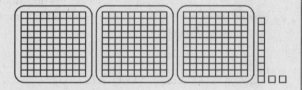

   Step 3
   Regroup the ten rod into 10 units.

   Step 4
   Divide the units into three equal groups.

   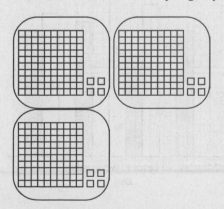

   Step 5
   Determine the quotient.

   Each group has 1 hundred flat (100) and 4 units (4).
   $100 + 4 = 104$

   $312 \div 3 = 104$

2. **Step 1**
   Represent the dividend 227 with base ten blocks.

   In 227, there are 2 hundreds, 2 tens, and 7 ones.

   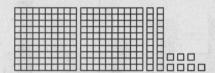

   Step 2
   Divide the hundreds into two equal groups (by the divisor 2).

   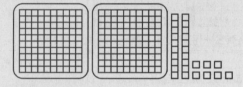

   Step 3
   Divide the tens into two equal groups.

   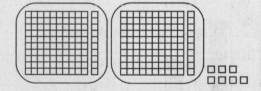

   Step 4
   Divide the ones into two equal groups.

   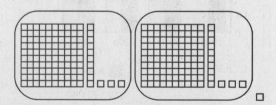

   Step 5
   Determine the quotient.

   Each group has 1 hundred flat (100), 1 ten rod (10), and 3 units (3).
   $100 + 10 + 3 = 113$

   Therefore, $227 \div 2 = 113$ with a remainder of 1.
   $227 \div 2 = 113 \text{ R}1$

PRACTICE EXERCISES
ANSWERS AND SOLUTIONS

1. Step 1
Represent 236 with base ten blocks.

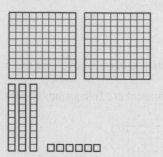

Step 2
Divide the hundreds into two equal groups (by the divisor 2).

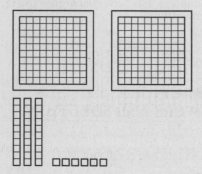

Step 3
Divide the tens into two equal groups.

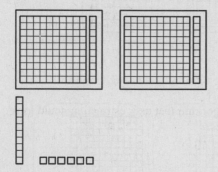

Step 4
Regroup the single ten rod into 10 units.

Step 5
Divide the ones (units) into two equal groups.

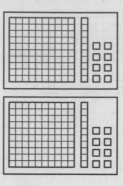

Step 6
Determine the quotient.

Each group has 1 hundred flat (100), 1 ten rod (10), and 8 units (8).
$100 + 10 + 8 = 118$

$236 \div 2 = 118$

3. Step 1
Represent 331 with base ten blocks.

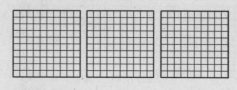

Step 2
Divide the hundreds into three equal groups (by the divisor 3).

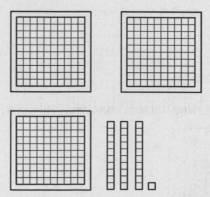

518

Step 3
Divide the tens into three equal groups.

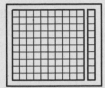 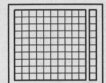

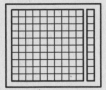

□

Step 4
Determine the quotient.
Each group has 1 hundred flat (100) and
1 ten rod (10).
100 + 10 = 110

Therefore, 331 ÷ 3 = 110 with a remainder of 1.
331 ÷ 3 = 110 R1

Lesson 2—Using Algorithms for 3-Digit by 1-Digit Division

🐝 TIME TO TRY 🐝
ANSWERS AND SOLUTIONS

1. The algorithm that uses place value would look like this:

```
     269
  2)538
     4
    13
    12
     18
     18
      0
```

538 ÷ 2 = 269

2. The algorithm that uses estimation could look like this:

```
  7)455  | 60
    420  |
     35  | + 5
     35  |
      0  | 65
```

Step 1
Estimate how many groups of seven are in 455.
Since 7 × 6 = 42, a good estimate would be 60.
7 × 60 = 420

Step 2
Subtract 420 from 455.
455 − 420 = 35

Step 3
Estimate how many groups of seven are in 35.

Since 7 × 5 = 35, there are five groups of seven in 35.

Step 4
Subtract 35 from 35.
35 − 35 = 0

Step 5
Add the estimations.
60 + 5 = 65

455 ÷ 7 = 65

PRACTICE EXERCISES
ANSWERS AND SOLUTIONS

1. The algorithm that uses place value would look like this:

```
     312
  2)624
     6
    02
     2
    04
     4
     0
```

3. The algorithm that uses estimation could look like this:

```
  7)112  | 10
     70  |
     42  | +6
     42  |
      0  | 16
```

Step 1
Estimate how many groups of seven are in 112.

Since $7 \times 10 = 70$, a good estimate would be 10.
$7 \times 10 = 70$

Subtract 70 from 112.
$112 - 70 = 42$

Step 2
Estimate how many groups of seven are in 42.

Since $7 \times 6 = 42$, there are six groups seven in 42.

Subtract 42 from 42.
$42 - 42 = 0$

Step 3
Add the estimations.
$10 + 6 = 16$

$112 \div 7 = 16$

Lesson 3—Expressing Remainders as Part of the Quotient

🐝 TIME TO TRY 🐝
ANSWERS AND SOLUTIONS

1. **Step 1**
Choose a strategy to divide 397 by 6.

This expression can be solved using an algorithm that uses estimation.

```
6)397  | 50
  300  |
  ---  |
   97  | 10
   60  |
  ---  |
   37  | + 6
   36  |
  ---  |
    1  | 66
```

Step 2
Express the remainder as part of the quotient using a whole number.
$397 \div 6 = 66 \text{ R1}$

2. **Step 1**
Choose a strategy to divide 853 by 2.

This expression can be solved using an algorithm that uses place value.

```
  426
2)853
  8
  --
  05
   4
  --
  13
  12
  --
   1
```

Step 2
Use a fraction to express the remainder as part of the quotient.

$$853 \div 2 = 426\frac{1}{2}$$

3. **Step 1**
Choose a strategy to divide 925 by 2.

This expression can be solved using an algorithm that uses place value.

```
  462
2)925
  8
  --
  12
  12
  --
  05
   4
  --
   1
```

Step 2
Express the remainder as a fraction.

$$925 \div 2 = 462\frac{1}{2}$$

Step 3
Express the fraction as an equivalent decimal.

$$\frac{1}{2} = 0.5$$

$$925 \div 2 = 462.5$$

4. **Step 1**
Write $9 as a dollar and cents amount.
$\$9 \rightarrow \$9.00$

Step 2
Divide $9.00 by 2.

```
    4.50
2)9.00
   8
  10
  10
  00
   0
   0
```

Each T-shirt costs $4.50.

PRACTICE EXERCISES
ANSWERS AND SOLUTIONS

1. **Step 1**
    Choose a strategy to divide 158 by 3.

    This expression can be solved using an algorithm that uses place value.

    ```
      52
    3)158
      15
      08
       6
       2
    ```

    Step 2
    Express the remainder as part of the quotient using a whole number.
    $158 \div 3 = 52$ R 2

3. **Step 1**
    Choose a strategy to divide 846 by 4.

    This expression can be solved using an algorithm that uses estimation.

    ```
    4)846  | 200
      800
       46  |  10
       40
        6  |  +1
        4  |
        2  | 211
    ```

    Step 2
    Express the remainder as a fraction.

    $846 \div 4 = 211\frac{2}{4}$

Express the fraction as an equivalent decimal.

$\frac{2}{4} = \frac{1}{2} = 0.5$

$846 \div 4 = 211.5$

Lesson 4—Interpreting Remainders When Solving Problems

❧ TIME TO TRY ❧
ANSWERS AND SOLUTIONS

1. **Step 1**
    Divide 278 by 7.

    ```
      39
    7)278
      21
      68
      63
       5
    ```

    Step 2
    Determine the greatest number of equal groups.

    Since the quotient is 39, the greatest number of cards each boy could have is 39 cards.

    Step 3
    Explain your answer.

    There are not enough cards to make another group of seven, so the five cards left over cannot be shared equally.

    The remainder cannot be part of the answer, so it needs to be ignored.

2. **Step 1**
    Divide 123 by 6.

    ```
      20
    6)123
      12
      03
       0
       3
    ```

    Step 2
    Determine the number of carts needed.

    If only 20 carts (the quotient) were used, three children (the remainder) would not be able to go for a cart ride at the same time as all the other children from their school.

The quotient needs to be rounded up so that all the children can travel together.

Twenty-one carts must be used. Each cart can hold six children, and the last cart will hold the remaining three children.

3. **Step 1**
Divide 163 by 5.

```
      32
  5)163
     15
     ---
     13
     10
     ---
      3
```

Step 2
Determine the number of photos on the last page.

There will be 32 pages (the quotient) that will have five photos on each page.

The remainder of 3 represents the three photos that will need to be placed on the 33rd page.

Miss Janier will place three photos on the last page.

PRACTICE EXERCISES
ANSWERS AND SOLUTIONS

1. **Step 1**
Divide 100 by 3.

```
      33
  3)100
      9
     ---
     10
      9
     ---
      1
```

Step 2
Determine the greatest number of equal teams.

Since the quotient is 33, the greatest number of teams that can be made is 33.

Step 3
Explain your answer.

There are not enough students to make another group of three, so the one student left over cannot be part of a team.

The remainder cannot be part of the answer, so it needs to be ignored.

3. **Step 1**
Divide 180 by 7.

```
      25
  7)180
     14
     ---
     40
     35
     ---
      5
```

Step 2
Determine the number of pencils that will not be put into pencil cases.

There will be 25 pencils (the quotient) placed into each of the seven pencil cases.

The remainder becomes the answer to the problem.

Five pencils will not be placed into pencil cases.

Lesson 5—Solving 3-Digit by 1-Digit Division Problems

TIME TO TRY
ANSWERS AND SOLUTIONS

1. **Step 1**
Choose a strategy to divide 244 by 4.

An example of a strategy you can use is an algorithm that uses place value. This would be a good strategy to use because 24 and 4 are compatible numbers (24 is a multiple of 4).

Step 2
Show your work.

```
      61
  4)244
     24
     ---
     04
      4
     ---
      0
```

$244 \div 4 = 61$

A total of 61 tables were used.

2. Step 1
Write a problem using the given information.

Here is an example that uses the given information:

A school bought 224 skipping ropes to be divided equally among seven classrooms. How many skipping ropes will each classroom get?

Step 2
Calculate 224 ÷ 7 using a strategy that works for you.

Here is an example of calculating using an algorithm that uses place value:

```
      32
  7)224
     21
     ──
     14
     14
     ──
      0
```

Each classroom will get 32 skipping ropes.

PRACTICE EXERCISES
ANSWERS AND SOLUTIONS

1. Step 1
Choose a strategy to divide 350 by 5.

An example of a strategy you can use is an algorithm that uses place value. This would be a good strategy to use because 35 and 5 are compatible numbers (35 is a multiple of 5).

Step 2
Show your work.

```
      70
  5)350
     35
     ──
     00
     00
     ──
      0
```

There are 70 books on each shelf.

3. Step 1
Write a problem using the given information.

Here is an example of a problem that uses the given information:

John was searching for some images on the Internet. One website listed 255 images.

Each page displayed eight images until the last page. How many images were displayed on the last page?

Step 2
Calculate 255 ÷ 8 using a strategy that works for you.

An example of a strategy you can use is an algorithm that uses place value.

```
      31
  8)255
     24
     ──
     15
      8
     ──
      7
```

The quotient tells that there were 31 pages with eight images on each page. The remainder tells that there were seven images on the last page.

Practice Test

ANSWERS AND SOLUTIONS

1. Step 1
Use an estimation algorithm.

The algorithm you use can look like this:

```
  9)936  | 100
    900  |
    ───  |
     36  | + 4
     36  |
    ───  |
      0  | 104
```

Step 2
Explain your work.

Round 936 down to 900.

Estimate how many groups of nine are in 900.
$100 \times 9 = 900$

Estimate how many groups of nine are in 36.
$4 \times 9 = 36$

Add the estimations.
$100 + 4 = 104$

$936 \div 9 = 104$

3. **Step 1**
Choose a strategy to divide 507 by 7.

This expression can be solved using an algorithm that uses place value.

$$
\begin{array}{r}
72 \\
7\overline{)507} \\
\underline{49} \\
17 \\
\underline{14} \\
3
\end{array}
$$

Step 2
Use a fraction to express the remainder as part of the quotient.

$$507 \div 7 = 72\frac{3}{7}$$

5. **Step 1**
Divide 136 by 3.

$$
\begin{array}{r}
45 \\
3\overline{)136} \\
\underline{12} \\
16 \\
\underline{15} \\
1
\end{array}
$$

Step 2
Explain your answer.

Since the quotient is 45, the coach can buy 45 hot dogs.

The remainder cannot be part of the answer, so it needs to be ignored.

The remainder tells that there is one dollar left after buying 45 hot dogs. There is not enough money to buy another hot dog.

7. **Step 1**
Divide 140 by 9.

$$
\begin{array}{r}
15 \\
9\overline{)140} \\
\underline{9} \\
50 \\
\underline{45} \\
5
\end{array}
$$

Step 2
Explain your answer.

There will be 15 pages (the quotient) with nine phone numbers written on them.

In this problem, the remainder is the answer. There will be five phone numbers written on the last page.

2-D SHAPES AND 3-D OBJECTS

Lesson 1—Identifying and Describing Line Segments in the Environment

🦋 TIME TO TRY 🦋
ANSWERS AND SOLUTIONS

1. Yes, the pattern of the bark on both trees is an example of horizontal line segments.

    The lines of the bark on both trees run side to side around the trunk of the tree, so they both show examples of horizontal line segments in the environment.

2. The lines on the parachute are all vertical lines, running up and down. The lines are actually the seams where the material is sewn together. The colours of the stripes are also following vertical lines, running up and down.

3. Yes, the fence has parallel line segments.

    Parallel lines are lines that are the exact same distance apart and will never meet.

    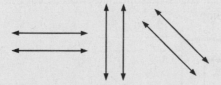

    The vertical poles are all parallel to each other. The horizontal bars are also the same distance apart from each other at all points.

4. The open scissors represent intersecting lines. Intersecting lines cross at a vertex, forming angles:

    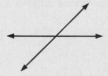

    The open blades of the scissors intersect each other at the point where the bolt fastens the two blades together. As a result, angles are formed at the vertex of intersection.

5. The roads that are perpendicular to each other are Pine Street and Maple Street.

    Perpendicular lines are formed when two lines intersect to form square corners (right angles).

    Pine Street is an example of a horizontal line. Maple Street is an example of a vertical line. The two streets form four square corners where they cross each other.

PRACTICE EXERCISES
ANSWERS AND SOLUTIONS

1. The pillars are examples of vertical lines in the environment.

    Vertical lines go straight up and down. All the pillars go up and down.

3. The Railway Crossing sign is an example of perpendicular line segments.

    Perpendicular lines are formed when two lines cross and form square corners (90°) at the vertex.

    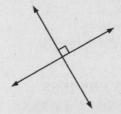

Lesson 2—Using Line Segments to Describe Sides of 2-D Shapes

🦋 TIME TO TRY 🦋
ANSWERS AND SOLUTIONS

1. There are a total of six horizontal sides, as shown.

    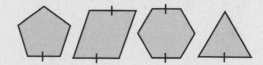

2. There are a total of three vertical sides in the given 2-D shapes, as shown.

3. There are two pairs of parallel sides, as shown.

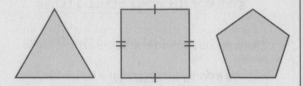

4. There are four pairs of intersecting sides.
   • Sides *BA* and *AD* intersect at vertex *A*.
   • Sides *AD* and *DC* intersect at vertex *D*.
   • Sides *DC* and *CB* intersect at vertex *C*.
   • Sides *CB* and *BA* intersect at vertex *B*.

5. There are three pairs of perpendicular sides in the given 2-D shapes, as shown.

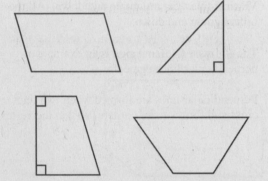

PRACTICE EXERCISES ANSWERS AND SOLUTIONS

1. There are six horizontal sides in total, as shown

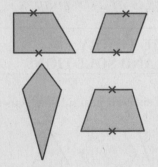

3. There are three pairs of parallel sides in total, as shown.

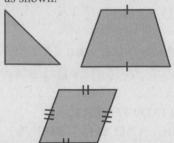

5. There are two pairs of perpendicular sides, as shown.

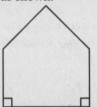

Lesson 3—Using Line Segments to Describe Edges of 3-D Objects

TIME TO TRY
ANSWERS AND SOLUTIONS

1. Four horizontal edges can be seen. Three of the horizontal edges are solid lines and one edge is a dotted line.

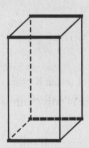

2. There are four vertical edges. Three of the vertical edges are solid lines and one vertical edge is a dotted line.

3. There are two pairs of parallel edges. Both pairs are located in the square base of the pyramid.

Your verification could look like this.

4. **Step 1**
Determine which intersecting edges you will bold and label.

Remember, any edges that meet at a vertex are intersecting edges, so there are many possibilities for you to choose from.

Step 2
The two pairs of intersecting edges could look like this.

Pyramid

5. **Step 1**
Determine which pairs of perpendicular edges you will show.
- There are four perpendicular edges on each of the three rectangular faces.
- There is one pair of perpendicular edges on each of the triangular faces.

Step 2
If you choose to show the perpendicular edges on the triangular faces, your diagram will look like this.

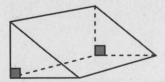

PRACTICE EXERCISES
ANSWERS AND SOLUTIONS

1. There are three vertical edges in the triangular prism.
- Edge *SW* is a vertical edge.
- Edge *XV* is a vertical edge.
- Edge *TU* is a vertical edge.

3. A rectangular prism has many pairs of parallel edges.

Three pairs of parallel edges are shown on this prism.
- Two back edges are marked with three ticks (one solid line, one dotted line).
- Two front edges are marked with two ticks (two solid lines).
- Two left-side edges are marked with one tick (one solid line, one dotted line).

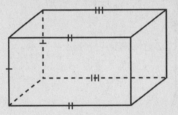

5. Recall that any horizontal edges and vertical edges that meet at a vertex are perpendicular edges. Therefore, there are many possibilities to choose from.

This diagram shows two sets of perpendicular edges.

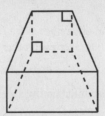

Lesson 4—Using Line Segments to Describe Faces of 3-D Objects

🦋 TIME TO TRY 🦋
ANSWERS AND SOLUTIONS

1. The horizontal edges of the shaded face run straight across. The shaded face also lies parallel with the flat surface of the floor.

    Therefore, the shaded face is a horizontal face.

2. Yes, the shaded faces are vertical faces. A face can be described as vertical if the vertical edges of the face run straight up and down.

    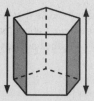

3. No, Hannah is not correct.

    The two shaded faces are identical in shape and are on opposite sides of the prism, but they are not parallel faces because they are not the exact same distance from each other at all points.

4. Yes, Amber is correct.

    The two shaded faces share an edge and two vertices. The two faces intersect each other at the shared edge and vertices.

    Therefore, the shaded faces are intersecting faces.

5. Yes, Jason is correct.

    The two faces are vertical because they run up and down. They are perpendicular because they share an edge and two vertices which form square corners.

    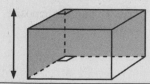

PRACTICE EXERCISES
ANSWERS AND SOLUTIONS

1. The shaded face on the rectangular prism is a vertical face because it is upright, going up and down like a vertical line.

    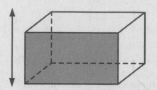

3. The two shaded faces are identical in shape, opposite each other, and are exactly the same distance apart.

    Therefore, they can also be described as parallel faces.

Lesson 5—Drawing Shapes and Objects to Illustrate Line Segments

🦋 TIME TO TRY 🦋
ANSWERS AND SOLUTIONS

1. When two sides of a triangle intersect, but not at right angles, you have a pair of intersecting sides.

    The triangle you draw could look like this.

    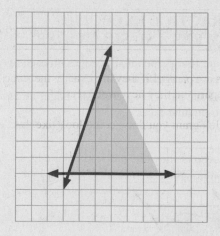

2. Horizontal edges go straight across, from side to side. The rectangular prism you draw could look like this.

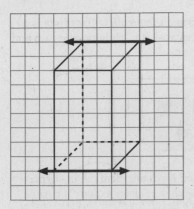

3. When two faces intersect, they share an edge and two vertices. The pyramid you draw could look like this.

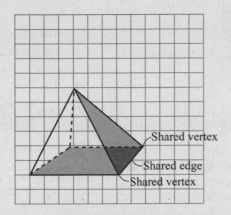

PRACTICE EXERCISES
ANSWERS AND SOLUTIONS

1. Two sides are parallel if they are exactly the same distance apart and they never intersect.

The parallelogram you draw could look like this.

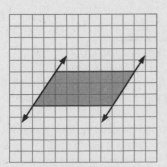

3. A horizontal face will run parallel to the horizon, in a left-right direction, like a horizontal line.

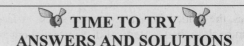

The triangle-based pyramid you draw could look like this.

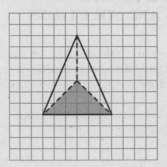

Lesson 6—Attributes of Quadrilaterals

TIME TO TRY
ANSWERS AND SOLUTIONS

1. The quadrilateral is a parallelogram because it has two pairs of sides that are opposite each other, are parallel, and are the same length. It does not have any right angles (90° angles).

Parallelogram

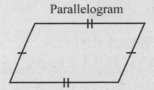

2. Rectangles are different from squares because rectangles have two sets of equal length sides but squares have all equal side lengths.

PRACTICE EXERCISES
ANSWERS AND SOLUTIONS

1. The quadrilateral shown is a trapezoid because it has only one pair of sides that are parallel. The trapezoid shown does not have any right angles, but it has one vertical line of symmetry.

3. Rectangles and rhombuses share the following similarities:
   • Both quadrilaterals have two pairs of parallel sides that are opposite each other.
   • Both quadrilaterals have two pairs of opposite sides that are equal in length.

Lesson 7—Using Attributes to Sort Quadrilaterals

🦋 TIME TO TRY 🦋
ANSWERS AND SOLUTIONS

1. **Step 1**
    Start with the first part of the sorting rule. Identify the shapes that have all equal side lengths.

    Only the rhombus has four equal side lengths. It belongs in the first group.

    Step 2
    Identify the shapes that do not have all equal side lengths.

    The parallelogram, rectangle, and trapezoid do not have four equal side lengths. They belong in the second group.

PRACTICE EXERCISES
ANSWERS AND SOLUTIONS

1. **Step 1**
    Start with the first part of the sorting rule. Identify the shapes that have parallel sides.

    The first two quadrilaterals have parallel sides. They belong in the first group.

    Step 2
    Identify the shapes that do not have parallel sides.

    The last two quadrilaterals do not have parallel sides. They belong in the second group.

3. **Step 1**
    Identify the shapes that have two pairs of equal sides.

    The rectangle and the parallelogram both have two pairs of equal sides. They belong in the first group.

    Step 2
    Identify the shapes that have all equal sides.

    The square and the rhombus have all equal sides. They belong in the second group.

Lesson 8—Determining Sorting Rules

🦋 TIME TO TRY 🦋
ANSWERS AND SOLUTIONS

1. **Step 1**
    Compare the attributes of the quadrilaterals in each group.

    In the first group, all three shapes have two pairs of parallel sides.

    In the second group, the shape has one pair of parallel sides.

    Step 2
    Determine the sorting rule used.

    The attribute that makes the two groups different from each other is the number of parallel sides.

    Therefore, the sorting rule used is "two pairs of parallel sides or one pair of parallel sides."

PRACTICE EXERCISES
ANSWERS AND SOLUTIONS

1. Compare the attributes of each group.
    - In the first group, both shapes have right angles. One shape has one pair of parallel sides and one shape had two pairs of parallel sides.
    - In the second group, neither shape has right angles. Both shapes have two pairs of parallel sides.

    The sorting rule used is "right angles or no right angles."

3. Compare the attributes of each group.
    - In the first group, both shapes have all equal sides.
    - In the second group, neither shape has all equal sides.

    The sorting rule used is "all equal sides or not all equal sides."

Practice Test

ANSWERS AND SOLUTIONS

1. There are two horizontal sides on a trapezoid, as shown on this diagram.

    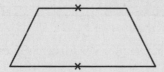

3. There are nine pairs of perpendicular sides in the given 2-D shapes.
    - Shape A has four pairs of perpendicular sides.
    - Shape B has four pairs of perpendicular sides.
    - Shape C has one pair of perpendicular sides.
    - Shape D has no perpendicular sides.

    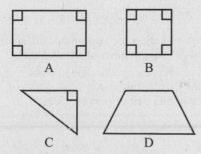

5. The two shaded faces are perpendicular faces.

    The horizontal face and the vertical face share an edge and two vertices, so the two faces intersect.

    The faces form square corners where they intersect, so they are classified as perpendicular faces.

7. Any horizontal edges and vertical edges on a cube that meet at square corners are perpendicular edges.

    This diagram shows one pair of perpendicular edges.

    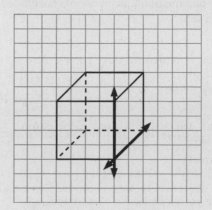

9. **Step 1**
    Identify the shapes that have parallel sides.

    The parallelogram and the last trapezoid both have parallel sides. They belong to the first group.

    Step 2
    Identify the shapes that have no parallel sides.

    The kite and the first trapezoid have no parallel sides. They belong to the second group.

    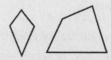

11. Parallelograms and squares share the following similarities:
    - Both quadrilaterals have two pairs of parallel sides that are opposite each other.
    - Both quadrilaterals have two pairs of opposite sides that are equal in length.

FRACTIONS AND DECIMALS

Lesson 1—Representing the Same Quantity with Equivalent Fractions

🦋 TIME TO TRY 🦋
ANSWERS AND SOLUTIONS

1. **Step 1**
    Determine one fraction that represents the shaded parts of the set.

    The fraction $\frac{3}{6}$ represents three parts shaded out of a total of six parts.

    Step 2
    Determine an equivalent fraction that has the same relationship as $\frac{3}{6}$.

    Since there are six shapes in all and three are shaded and three are not shaded, half of the set is shaded.

    Therefore, the fraction $\frac{1}{2}$ also represents the shaded parts of the set.

    $$\frac{3}{6} = \frac{1}{2}$$

    Kaylan could write the fractions $\frac{3}{6}$ and $\frac{1}{2}$ to represent the shaded parts of the given set of shapes.

2. **Step 1**
    Identify the equivalent fraction.

    The equivalent fraction shown on the fraction strip chart is $\frac{3}{4}$.

Step 2
Explain how you used the fraction strip chart.

*   Start with the fraction strip that shows eighths.

*   Count six $\frac{1}{8}$ segments.

*   Look for another strip that ends at the same place as the end of the sixth segment of $\frac{1}{8}$.

*   The strip that lines up with $\frac{6}{8}$ is the fourths fraction strip.

*   Count the number of fourths that line up. There are three $\frac{1}{4}$ segments.

$\frac{1}{4}$		$\frac{1}{4}$		$\frac{1}{4}$		$\frac{1}{4}$	
$\frac{1}{8}$	$\frac{1}{8}$	$\frac{1}{8}$	$\frac{1}{8}$	$\frac{1}{8}$	$\frac{1}{8}$	$\frac{1}{8}$	$\frac{1}{8}$

$$\frac{6}{8} = \frac{3}{4}$$

3. These two fraction strips show that $\frac{3}{5}$ and $\frac{6}{10}$ are equivalent fractions because they represent the same amount.

$\frac{1}{10}$	$\frac{1}{10}$	$\frac{1}{10}$	$\frac{1}{10}$	$\frac{1}{10}$	$\frac{1}{10}$				$\frac{6}{10}$
$\frac{1}{5}$		$\frac{1}{5}$		$\frac{1}{5}$					$\frac{3}{5}$

$$\frac{3}{5} = \frac{6}{10}$$

PRACTICE EXERCISES
ANSWERS AND SOLUTIONS

1. **Step 1**
    Determine one fraction that represents the shaded area of the figure.

    The figure is divided into 10 parts, eight of which are shaded.

    The fraction $\frac{8}{10}$ represents the shaded parts.

Step 2
Determine an equivalent fraction that also represents the shaded area.

Following is one way to determine an equivalent fraction:

Think of the same figure with the same amount of shaded area, but with only five parts instead of ten parts.

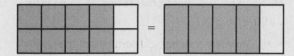

The figure is now divided into five parts, four of which are shaded. Therefore, the fraction $\frac{4}{5}$ also represents the same quantity.

One pair of equivalent fractions that represent the same shaded quantity is $\frac{8}{10} = \frac{4}{5}$.

3. One of the three parts of the wheel is shaded.
The fraction that represents the shaded part is $\frac{1}{3}$.

Following is one way to determine an equivalent fraction:

Think of the same amount of shaded area, but with the wheel having six parts (each part divided in half). Shade two of the six parts.

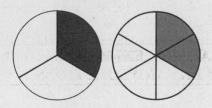

In the second wheel, two parts out of six parts are shaded. The fraction that represents the shaded part is $\frac{2}{6}$.

A fraction that is equivalent to $\frac{1}{3}$ is $\frac{2}{6}$.

Lesson 2—Rules for Developing Equivalent Fractions

PRACTICE EXERCISES
ANSWERS AND SOLUTIONS

1. Multiply the numerator and denominator by the same number to create an equivalent fraction. (You can use any number.)

Following is one example:
$$\frac{2 \times 2}{3 \times 2} = \frac{4}{6}$$
$$\frac{2}{3} = \frac{4}{6}$$

3. Divide the numerator and the denominator by the same number to create an equivalent fraction.
$$\frac{10 \div 5}{15 \div 5} = \frac{2}{3}$$
$$\frac{10}{15} = \frac{2}{3}$$

Lesson 3—Creating Sets of Equivalent Fractions

🐝 TIME TO TRY 🐝
ANSWERS AND SOLUTIONS

1. Divide the numerator and denominator by 2 to obtain an equivalent fraction. Repeat the process two more times.

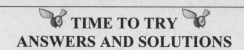

$\frac{8 \div 2}{24 \div 2} = \frac{4}{12}$	$\frac{4 \div 2}{12 \div 2} = \frac{2}{6}$	$\frac{2 \div 2}{6 \div 2} = \frac{1}{3}$

The set of equivalent fractions is given as follows:
$$\frac{8}{24} = \frac{4}{12} = \frac{2}{6} = \frac{1}{3}$$

PRACTICE EXERCISES
ANSWERS AND SOLUTIONS

1. **Step 1**
Determine the fraction that represents the shaded part of the figure.

Four of the five parts are shaded. The fraction that represents the shaded parts is $\frac{4}{5}$.

Step 2
Multiply the numerator and denominator by 3 to obtain an equivalent fraction. Repeat the process two more times.

$\frac{4\times3}{5\times3}=\frac{12}{15}$	$\frac{12\times3}{15\times3}=\frac{36}{45}$	$\frac{36\times3}{45\times3}=\frac{108}{135}$

The set of four equivalent fractions is given as follows:
$$\frac{4}{5}=\frac{12}{15}=\frac{36}{45}=\frac{108}{135}$$

3. Divide the numerator and denominator by 2 to obtain an equivalent fraction. Repeat the process two more times.

$\frac{24\div2}{40\div2}=\frac{12}{20}$	$\frac{12\div2}{20\div2}=\frac{6}{10}$	$\frac{6\div2}{10\div2}=\frac{3}{5}$

The set of four equivalent fractions is given as follows:
$$\frac{24}{40}=\frac{12}{20}=\frac{6}{10}=\frac{3}{5}$$

Lesson 4—Comparing Fractions

🦋 TIME TO TRY 🦋
ANSWERS AND SOLUTIONS

1. The comparison $\frac{3}{4}>\frac{4}{4}$ is incorrect.

   Since the denominators are the same (4), compare the numerators.
   Since $3<4$, then $\frac{3}{4}<\frac{4}{4}$.

2. **Step 1**
   Find the lowest common denominator of 3 and 5.

   Multiples of 3: 3, 6, 9, 12, <u>15</u>
   Multiples of 5: 5, 10, <u>15</u>

   Since the lowest common multiple is 15, then the lowest common denominator is 15.

Step 2
Make equivalent fractions using 15 as the new denominator.
$$\frac{2}{3}=\frac{2\times5}{3\times5}=\frac{10}{15}$$

$$\frac{2}{5}=\frac{2\times3}{5\times3}=\frac{6}{15}$$

Step 3
Now that the denominators are the same (15), compare the numerators.

Since $10>6$, then $\frac{10}{15}>\frac{6}{15}$.

Therefore, $\frac{2}{3}>\frac{2}{5}$.

PRACTICE EXERCISES
ANSWERS AND SOLUTIONS

1. Since the denominators are the same, compare the numerators.

   Since $3>1$, then $\frac{3}{7}>\frac{1}{7}$.

3. **Step 1**
   Find the lowest common denominator of 3 and 4.

   Multiples of 3: 3, 6, 9, <u>12</u>, 15, 18
   Multiples of 4: 4, 8, <u>12</u>, 16, 20

   The lowest common multiple of 3 and 4 is 12. Therefore, the lowest common denominator of 3 and 4 is 12.

Step 2
Make equivalent fractions using 12 as the new denominator.
$$\frac{2}{3}=\frac{2\times4}{3\times4}=\frac{8}{12}$$

$$\frac{3}{4}=\frac{3\times3}{4\times3}=\frac{9}{12}$$

Step 3
Now that the denominators are the same, compare the numerators.

Since $8 < 9$, then $\dfrac{8}{12} < \dfrac{9}{12}$.

Therefore, $\dfrac{2}{3} < \dfrac{3}{4}$.

Lesson 5—Ordering Fractions on Number Lines

🌿 TIME TO TRY 🌿
ANSWERS AND SOLUTIONS

1. **Step 1**
    Order the fractions from least to greatest.

    Since the denominators are the same (6), order the numerators from least to greatest.
    2, 3, 5, 6

    From least to greatest, the fractions are
    $\dfrac{2}{6}, \dfrac{3}{6}, \dfrac{5}{6}, \dfrac{6}{6}$.

    Step 2
    Order the fractions on the number line.

    The given number line is marked in sixths from 0 to 1, with $\dfrac{1}{2}$ representing the equivalent fraction $\dfrac{3}{6}$.

    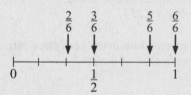

2. **Step 1**
    Determine the lowest common denominator for the fractions.

    Multiples of 2: 2, 4, 6, 8, 10, <u>12</u>,...
    Multiples of 3: 3, 6, 9, <u>12</u>,...
    Multiples of 4: 4, 8, <u>12</u>,...

    The lowest common multiple (12) is the lowest

common denominator (12).
    Step 2
    Make equivalent fractions using the common denominator of 12.
    $$\dfrac{2}{3} = \dfrac{2 \times 4}{3 \times 4} = \dfrac{8}{12}$$
    $$\dfrac{1}{2} = \dfrac{1 \times 6}{2 \times 6} = \dfrac{6}{12}$$
    $$\dfrac{3}{4} = \dfrac{3 \times 3}{4 \times 3} = \dfrac{9}{12}$$

    Step 3
    Order the equivalent fractions by the numerators.
    $\dfrac{6}{12}, \dfrac{8}{12}, \dfrac{9}{12}$

    Step 4
    Place the fractions on the number line.

    The number line is marked in twelfths from 0 to 1, with $\dfrac{1}{2}$ representing the equivalent fraction $\dfrac{6}{12}$.

    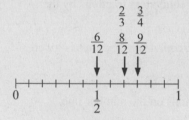

PRACTICE EXERCISES
ANSWERS AND SOLUTIONS

1. **Step 1**
    Order the fractions by the numerators.
    $\dfrac{1}{6}, \dfrac{2}{6}, \dfrac{3}{6}, \dfrac{5}{6}$

    Step 2
    Place the fractions on the number line.

    The number line is marked in sixths from 0 to 1, with $\dfrac{1}{2}$ representing the equivalent fraction $\dfrac{3}{6}$.

    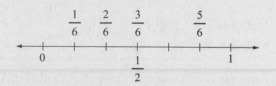

3. **Step 1**

Find the lowest common denominator of 2, 3, 4, and 6.

Multiples of 2: 2, 4, 6, 8, 10, <u>12</u>, 14,…

Multiples of 3: 3, 6, 9, <u>12</u>, 15,…

Multiples of 4: 4, 8, <u>12</u>, 16,…

Multiples of 6: 6, <u>12</u>, 18,…

The lowest common multiple (12) is the lowest common denominator (12).

Step 2

Make equivalent fractions using the common denominator of 12.

$$\frac{2}{6} = \frac{2 \times 2}{6 \times 2} = \frac{4}{12} \qquad \frac{1}{2} = \frac{1 \times 6}{2 \times 6} = \frac{6}{12}$$

$$\frac{3}{4} = \frac{3 \times 3}{4 \times 3} = \frac{9}{12} \qquad \frac{2}{3} = \frac{2 \times 4}{3 \times 4} = \frac{8}{12}$$

Step 3

Order the four equivalent fractions by the numerators.

$$\frac{4}{12}, \frac{6}{12}, \frac{8}{12}, \frac{9}{12}.$$

Step 4

Place the fractions on the number line.

The number line is marked in twelfths from 0 to 1, with $\frac{1}{2}$ representing the equivalent fraction $\frac{6}{12}$.

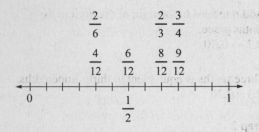

Lesson 6—Representing Decimals with Base Ten Blocks

🦋 TIME TO TRY 🦋
ANSWERS AND SOLUTIONS

1. **Step 1**
Determine the decimal number.

The number represented by the base ten blocks is two and three hundred twenty-three thousandths: 2.323

Step 2
Describe the value of each set.

- The two large cubes to the left of the decimal point represent the whole number 2 and have a value of 2.
- The three flats in the tenths place have a value of three-tenths: 0.3.
- The two rods in the hundredths place have a value of two-hundredths: 0.02.
- The three units in the thousandths place have a value of three-thousandths: 0.003.

$2 + 0.3 + 0.02 + 0.003 = 2.323$

PRACTICE EXERCISES
ANSWERS AND SOLUTIONS

1. The number represented by the blocks is 0.253.
   - The two flats in the tenths place have a value of two-tenths: 0.2.
   - The five rods in the hundredths place have a value of five-hundredths: 0.05.
   - The three units in the thousandths place have a value of three-thousandths: 0.003.

   $0.2 + 0.05 + 0.003 = 0.253$

   Remember to place a zero in the ones place if there is no whole number.

Lesson 7—Place Value in Decimal Numbers

🐝 TIME TO TRY 🐝
ANSWERS AND SOLUTIONS

1. **Step 1**
    Place the digits in their correct positions in the place value chart.

O	.	Tth	Hth	Thth
3	.	5	0	6

    Step 2
    Describe the value of the digits 5 and 6.

    The value of 5 is five-tenths: 0.5.
    The value of 6 is six-thousandths: 0.006.

2. **Step 1**
    Determine the value of each digit.
    - The number 3 represents the whole number 3 and has a value of 3.
    - The 0 represents 0 tenths. It has no value.
    - The 5 to the right of 0 represents five-hundredths: 0.05.
    - The 5 to the right of the hundredths represents five-thousandths: 0.005.

    Step 2
    Express the number in expanded notation.

    The expanded notation $3 + 0.05 + 0.005$ represents the decimal number 3.055.

PRACTICE EXERCISES
ANSWERS AND SOLUTIONS

1. **Step 1**
    Place the digits in their correct positions in the place value chart.

O	.	Tth	Hth	Thth
2	.	6	0	9

Step 2
Describe the value of each digit.
- The 2 represents the whole number 2 and has a value of 2.
- The value of 6 is six-tenths: 0.6.
- The 0 in the hundredths place has no value; there are no hundredths.
- The value of 9 is nine-thousandths: 0.009

3. **Step 1**
    Determine the value of each digit.
    - The first 0 shows that there is no whole number.
    - The second 0 has no value. It shows that there are no tenths.
    - The value of 2 is two-hundredths: 0.02.
    - The value of 3 is three-thousandths: 0.003.

    Step 2
    Express the number in expanded notation.

    The expanded form of 0.023 is $0.02 + 0.003$.

Lesson 8—Equivalent Decimal Numbers: Tenths, Hundredths, Thousandths

🐝 TIME TO TRY 🐝
ANSWERS AND SOLUTIONS

1. **Step 1**
    Express the given tenth as an equivalent hundredth.

    Add one zero to the right of the digit in the tenths place.
    $0.3 \rightarrow 0.3\underline{0}$

    Three-tenths is equivalent to thirty-hundredths.
    $0.3 = 0.30$

    Step 2
    Express the given tenth as an equivalent thousandth.

    Add two zeros to the right of the digit in the tenths place.
    $0.3 \rightarrow 0.3\underline{00}$

    Three-tenths is equivalent to three hundred-thousandths.
    $0.3 = 0.300$

2. Adding one zero to the right of the digit in the hundredths place will result in an equivalent decimal in the thousandths.
$0.09 \rightarrow 0.09\underline{0}$

Nine-hundredths is equivalent to ninety-thousandths, as shown by these diagrams.
$0.09 = 0.090$

PRACTICE EXERCISES
ANSWERS AND SOLUTIONS

1. To express a tenth as an equivalent hundredth, add a zero to the right of the digit in the tenths place.
$0.5 \rightarrow 0.5\underline{0}$

Five-tenths is equivalent to fifty-hundredths.
$0.5 = 0.50$

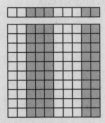

3. To express a hundredth as an equivalent thousandth, add one zero to the right of the digit in the hundredths place.
$0.47 \rightarrow 0.47\underline{0}$

Forty-seven hundredths is equivalent to four hundred seventy-thousandths.
$0.47 = 0.470$

Lesson 9—Comparing and Ordering Decimals to Thousandths

 **TIME TO TRY**
ANSWERS AND SOLUTIONS

1. **Step 1**
Compare and order the digits in the tenths places.

From least to greatest, the digits are 2, 5, 6, 9.

Step 2
Order the decimal numbers in the same order as the digits.

From least to greatest, the decimals are
$0.2, 0.5, 0.6, 0.9$.

The order can also be written as
$0.2 < 0.5 < 0.6 < 0.9$.

2. **Step 1**
Write the numbers in the place value chart.

O	.	Tth	Hth
0	.	3	6
0	.	0	7
0	.	2	8
0	.	2	5

Step 2
Compare the digits in the tenths places.

Since $0 < 2 < 3$, the number with the lowest value is 0.07, and the number with the greatest value is 0.36.

Step 3
Compare the hundredths for the two numbers that have two-tenths.

Since $5 < 8$, then $0.2\underline{5} < 0.2\underline{8}$.

From least to greatest, the decimals are
$0.07, \ 0.25, \ 0.28, \ 0.36$.

The order can also be written as
$0.07 < 0.25 < 0.28 < 0.36$.

3. **Step 1**
Write the numbers in the place value chart.

O	.	Tth	Hth	Thth
0	.	2	3	5
0	.	2	5	4
0	.	2	4	4
0	.	2	5	5

Step 2
Compare the tenths.
All the digits in the tenths place have the same value (two- tenths).

Step 3
Compare the hundredths.

Since $3 < 4 < 5$, the lowest number is 0.235, and the next lowest number is 0.244.

Step 4
Compare the thousandths for the two numbers that have two-tenths and five-hundredths.

Since $4 < 5$, $0.254 < 0.255$.

From least to greatest, the numbers are
0.235, 0.244, 0.254, 0.255.

The order can also be written as
$0.235 < 0.244 < 0.254 < 0.255$.

4. **Step 1**
    Create equivalent decimals.

    Add one zero to the right of 0.66.
    $0.66 \rightarrow 0.660$

    Add two zeros to the right of 0.6.
    $0.6 \rightarrow 0.600$

    Step 2
    Write the decimals in the place value chart.

O	.	Tth	Hth	Thth
0	.	6	6	0
0	.	6	0	0
0	.	6	3	3

    Step 3
    Compare the tenths.
    All three numbers have six-tenths.

    Step 4
    Compare the hundredths.

    Since $0 < 3 < 6$, then $0.600 < 0.633 < 0.660$

    From least to greatest, the decimals are
    0.6, 0.633, 0.66

5. **Step 1**
    Identify the tenth digits in each decimal number.
    0.395
    0.6
    0.85

Step 2
Starting at the benchmark number 0, count the number of ticks to reach the number of tenths you are working with.
- For 0.395, count to the third tick. Point the arrow between the third and fourth ticks, almost at the fourth tick.
- For 0.6, count to the sixth tick. Point the arrow right at the sixth tick.
- For 0.85, count to the eighth tick. Point the arrow halfway between the eight and ninth ticks.

Label the arrows with the numbers they represent.

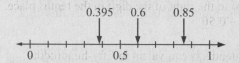

PRACTICE EXERCISES
ANSWERS AND SOLUTIONS

1. **Step 1**
    Line up the decimal points, and write the numbers in the place value chart.

O	.	Tth	Hth	Thth
0	.	4	1	3
0	.	7	3	2
0	.	4	3	1
0	.	6	3	4

    Step 2
    Compare the digits in the tenths places.

    Since $4 < 6 < 7$, the number with the greatest value is 0.732.

    The number with the second greatest value is 0.634.

    Step 3
    Compare the hundredths digits for $0.4\underline{1}3$ and $0.4\underline{3}1$.

    Since $1 < 3$, $0.4\underline{1}3 < 0.4\underline{3}1$.

    Step 4
    Order the numbers from least to greatest.

    From least to greatest, the numbers are
    0.413, 0.431, 0.634, 0.732.

3. **Step 1**
Identify the tenths place digit in each decimal number.
0.<u>4</u>27
0.<u>7</u>5
0.<u>1</u>9

Step 2
Start at the benchmark number 0, and count the ticks until you reach the required tenth.

• For 0.427, count to the fourth tick. Point the arrow between the fourth and fifth ticks, closer to the fourth tick (since the hundredths digit is 2).

• For 0.75, count to the seventh tick. Point the arrow halfway between the seventh and eighth ticks (since the hundredths digit is 5).

• For 0.19, count to the first tick. Point the arrow between the first and second ticks, almost at the second tick (since the hundredths digit is 9).

Label the arrows with the numbers they represent.

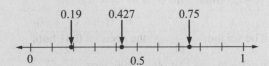

Lesson 10—Connecting Fractions and Decimals (to Thousandths)

🐝 TIME TO TRY 🐝
ANSWERS AND SOLUTIONS

1. **Step 1**
Count the number of base ten blocks in each place value.

• There are three-tenths (three flats in the tenths position).

• There are two-hundredths (two rods in the hundredths position).

• There are seven-thousandths (seven units in the thousandths position).

Step 2
Write the decimal represented by the base ten blocks.

The decimal represented by the base ten blocks is 0.327.

Step 3

Write the fraction represented by the base ten blocks.
The fraction represented by the base ten blocks is $\dfrac{327}{1\,000}$.

2. The decimal form of $\dfrac{7}{10}$ is 0.7.

The fraction $\dfrac{7}{10}$ represents seven parts out of 10 parts.

The decimal 0.7 also represents seven parts out of 10 parts.

This diagram shows how both forms represent the same quantity.

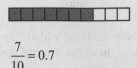

$\dfrac{7}{10} = 0.7$

3. The decimal form of $\dfrac{34}{100}$ is 0.34.

The fraction $\dfrac{34}{100}$ represents 34 parts out of a total of 100 parts.

The decimal 0.34 also represents 34 parts out of a total of 100 parts.

This diagram shows how both forms represent the same quantity.

$\dfrac{34}{100} = 0.34$

4. The equivalent decimal for the fraction $\dfrac{520}{1\,000}$ is 0.520.

The fraction $\dfrac{520}{1\,000}$ represents 520 parts out of a total of 1 000 parts.

The decimal 0.520 also represents 520 parts out of

a total of 1 000 parts.

This cube shows how both forms represent the same quantity.

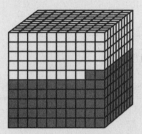

$$\frac{520}{1\ 000} = 0.520$$

5. The equivalent decimal form of $\frac{4}{100}$ is 0.04.

Since the denominator is in the hundredths, there must be two digits to the right of the decimal point in the decimal number.

Therefore, you need to place a zero to the left of the digit 4. The zero shows that there are no tenths in the number. The zero is a placeholder.

6. The decimal that is equivalent to $\frac{58}{1\ 000}$ is 0.058.

Since the denominator is in the thousandths, there must be three digits in the equivalent decimal number.

Therefore, place one zero to the left of the digit 5 in 58. The zero shows that there are no tenths in the decimal number. The zero is a placeholder.

7. The equivalent decimal form of $\frac{1}{1\ 000}$ is 0.001.

Since the denominator is in the thousandths, there must be three digits to the right of the decimal point in the equivalent decimal form.

Therefore, you need to place two zeros to the left of the digit 1.

The zeros show that there are no tenths or hundredths in the decimal number. The zeros are placeholders.

8. The equivalent fraction to 0.035 is $\frac{35}{1\ 000}$.

Since there are three digits in the decimal number, the denominator of the equivalent fraction is 1 000.

When you remove the zero in the ones place and the decimal point, you are left with 035.

Since the tenths digit is a zero, remove the zero, and you are left with 35. This is the numerator of the equivalent fraction.

$$\frac{35}{1\ 000}$$

PRACTICE EXERCISES
ANSWERS AND SOLUTIONS

1. The number represented by the base ten blocks is 0.175 or $\frac{175}{1\ 000}$.

3. The decimal equivalent of $\frac{1}{100}$ is 0.01.

The fraction $\frac{1}{100}$ and the decimal 0.01 both represent one part out of 100 parts.

5. The fraction form of 0.018 is $\frac{18}{1\ 000}$.

The decimal 0.018 and the fraction $\frac{18}{1\ 000}$ both represent 18 parts out of 1 000 parts.

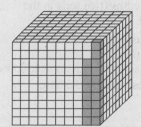

Practice Test

ANSWERS AND SOLUTIONS

1. **Step 1**
    Determine one fraction that represents the shaded area of the figure.

    Since four of the twelve parts are shaded, the fraction $\frac{4}{12}$ represents the shaded area of the figure.

    Step 2
    Determine an equivalent fraction.

    One way to determine an equivalent fraction is to think of the same figure with the same amount of shaded area, but with only six parts.

    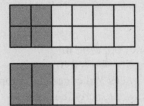

    The fraction $\frac{2}{6}$ is one equivalent fraction that represents the same shaded area.
    $$\frac{4}{12} = \frac{2}{6}$$

3. Divide the numerator and denominator by 3 to obtain an equivalent fraction. Repeat the process two more times.
    $$\frac{108 \div 3}{135 \div 3} = \frac{36}{45}$$

    $$\frac{36 \div 3}{45 \div 3} = \frac{12}{15}$$

    $$\frac{12 \div 3}{15 \div 3} = \frac{4}{5}$$

    The set of equivalent fractions is given as follows:
    $$\frac{108}{135} = \frac{36}{45} = \frac{12}{15} = \frac{4}{5}$$

    Step 4
    Place the fractions on the number line.

The number line is marked in eighteenths from 0 to 1, with $\frac{1}{2}$ representing the equivalent fraction $\frac{9}{18}$.

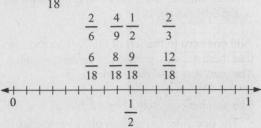

5. **Step 1**
    Describe the value of each digit.
    - The 8 represents the whole number 8 and has a value of 8.
    - The value of 4 is four-tenths: 0.4.
    - The 0 has no value. It is a placeholder for the hundredths place.
    - The value of 5 is five-thousandths: 0.005.

    Step 2
    Express the number in expanded notation.

    The expanded notation $8 + 0.4 + 0.005$ represents the decimal number 8.405.

7. **Step 1**
    Express the tenth as an equivalent thousandth.
    $0.9 \rightarrow 0.9\underline{00}$

    Step 2
    Justify your answer.

    To express a tenth as an equivalent thousandth, add two zeros to the right of the digit in the tenths place.

    Nine-tenths is equivalent to nine hundred thousandths.
    $0.9 = 0.900$

    These base ten blocks show how nine shaded parts out of 10 parts is equivalent to 900 shaded parts out of 1 000 parts.

    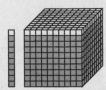

9. The equivalent decimal form of $\frac{7}{100}$ is 0.07.

Since the denominator is 100, the equivalent decimal number must have two digits to the right of the decimal point.

Add one zero to the left of the 7. The zero shows that there are no tenths in the decimal number. The zero acts as a placeholder.

11. The number represented by the blocks is 1.108.

- The one cube in the ones place represents the whole number 1 and has a value of 1.
- The one flat in the tenths place has a value of one-tenth: 0.1.
- There are no rods the hundredths place so the hundredths have no value: 0.00.
- The eight units in the thousandths place have a value of eight-thousandths: 0.008.

$$1 + 0.1 + 0.008 = 1.108$$

TRANSFORMATIONAL GEOMETRY

Lesson 1—Identifying Single Transformations

TIME TO TRY
ANSWERS AND SOLUTIONS

1. The transformation is a translation because the only thing that changed when the triangle moved was the location.

The triangle slid in a diagonal direction to a different spot. The triangle looks exactly the same in the translated position as it did in its original position.

2. Yes, Darian's drawing is correct. The two figures illustrate a reflection.

A reflection is a mirror or opposite image. Every vertex and edge of the bottom figure is directly opposite the vertices and edges of the top figure. The two figures are exactly the same distance from the line of reflection.

3. A rotation occurs when a shape turns around a point of rotation.

The figure in the first position (the left side) points upward. After the transformation, the image points to the right. Therefore, the pair of shapes illustrates a rotation.

PRACTICE EXERCISES
ANSWERS AND SOLUTIONS

1. The transformation is a translation.

A translation occurs when the shape moves to another location but looks exactly as it did in the first location. The given shape moved downward but stayed the same in every other way.

To be a reflection, the image would need to be opposite of the original shape.

3. The transformation is a rotation.

A rotation turns a shape around a vertex. In the first position (the left side), the arrow points to the bottom.

In the second position (the right side), the arrow points to the left.

Therefore, the two figures illustrate a rotation.

Lesson 2—Describing Single Transformations

TIME TO TRY
ANSWERS AND SOLUTIONS

1. Step 1
Identify the direction of the movement.

The triangle slides upward in a vertical direction to get from position 1 to position 2.

Step 2
Describe how far the triangle moves.

Each vertex of the triangle in position 1 moves four squares upward to get to position 2.

2. Step 1
Identify the line of reflection.

The line of reflection is not labelled as a line; however, the line of reflection is the *x*-axis.
The triangle is flipped over the horizontal *x*-axis.

Step 2
Describe the distance from the flip line.

Vertices *A* and *A'* are each two squares from the flip line.
Vertices *B* and *B'* are each four squares from the flip line.
Vertices *C* and *C'* are each two squares from the flip line.

Triangle *ABC* is two squares above the line.
Triangle *A'B'C'* is two squares below flip line.

3. This is one possible solution.

Step 1
Identify the direction of the turn.

Triangle 1 rotates in a clockwise direction to result in the position of triangle 2.

Step 2
Describe the angle of the turn.

Since the square corner at vertex *A* (the centre of rotation) makes a quarter turn, the rotation can be described as a 90° rotation.

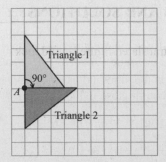

PRACTICE EXERCISES
ANSWERS AND SOLUTIONS

1. Step 1
Identify the direction of the movement.

The figure slides downward in a vertical direction to get from position I to position II.

Step 2
Describe how far the triangle moves.

Each vertex of the triangle in position I moves five squares downward to get the position II.

3. This is one possible solution.

Step 1
Describe the direction of the turn.

The triangle rotates in a clockwise direction.
The figure rotates around vertex *A*.

Step 2

Describe the angle of the turn.

The triangle in position 1 rotates a half turn (180°) to get to position 2.

Vertex *C* is on line 7 in position 1 and is still on line 7 in position 2.

Lesson 3—Drawing Images of Single Transformations

🦋 TIME TO TRY 🦋
ANSWERS AND SOLUTIONS

1. The image of the translated figure should look like this:

    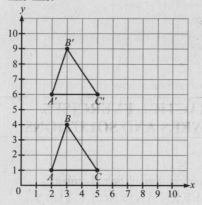

2. The image of the reflected figure should look like this:

    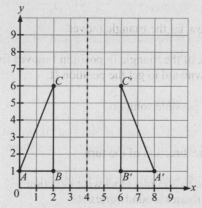

3. The image of the rotated figure should look like this:

    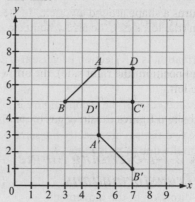

PRACTICE EXERCISES
ANSWERS AND SOLUTIONS

1. The translated image should look like this:

    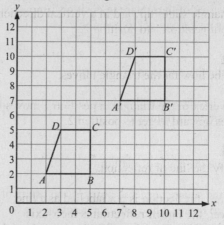

3. The reflected image should look like this:

    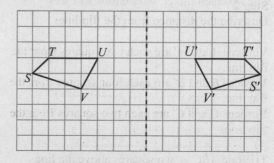

Practice Test

ANSWERS AND SOLUTIONS

1. The transformation is a reflection because it is a mirror, or opposite, image.

    Every vertex and edge of the second figure is directly opposite the vertices and edges of the first figures. The two figures are exactly the same distance from the line of reflection.

3. **Step 1**
    Identify the direction of the movement.

    The square slides upward in a vertical direction to get from position 1 to position 2.

    Step 2
    Describe how far the square moves.

    Each vertex of the square in position 1 moves six squares upward to get to position 2.

5. **Step 1**
    Describe the direction of the turn.

    Figure 1 rotates in a clockwise direction to result in the position of figure 2.

    Step 2
    Describe the angle of the turn.

    Since the square corner at point P (the centre of rotation) makes a half turn, the rotation can be described as a 180° rotation.

7. The reflected image should look like this:

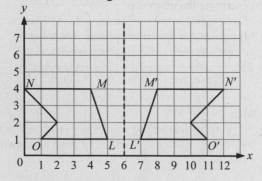

VARIABLES AND EQUATIONS

Lesson 2—Expressing Problems as Equations With One Unknown

❦ TIME TO TRY ❦
ANSWERS AND SOLUTIONS

1. The letter k represents the unknown, which is the number of red binders Kell has. The expression $k + 5$ represents the total number of binders Kell has.

    The total number of red and yellow binders that Ryan has can be represented by the expression $3 + 4$.

    Since the boys have the same number of binders, $k + 5 = 3 + 4$.

    There are variations in how you can write this equation. For example, two variations are shown as follows:
    $5 + k = 3 + 4$
    $3 + 4 = k + 5$

PRACTICE EXERCISES
ANSWERS AND SOLUTIONS

1. **Step 1**
    Identify the unknown.

    The unknown is the number that should be added to 63 to equal 100.

    Step 2
    Determine the operation.

    The clue words "if the sum is" let you know that you can use an addition or subtraction equation.

    These equations all express the problem:
    $100 - 63 = N$
    $100 - N = 63$
    $63 + N = 100$
    $N + 63 = 100$

3. **Step 1**

Identify the unknown.

The unknown is the number that 25 is multiplied by to obtain 750.

Step 2

Determine the operation.

The clue words "if the product is" let you know that you can use a multiplication or division equation.

These equations all express the problem:
$$25 \times n = 750$$
$$n \times 25 = 750$$
$$750 \div 25 = n$$
$$750 \div n = 25$$

Lesson 3—Creating Problems for a Given Equation

🦋 TIME TO TRY 🦋
ANSWERS AND SOLUTIONS

1. **Step 1**

Determine what the unknown represents.

Since subtraction can be expressed as part = whole – part, the variable r represents the whole.

It might be easier to see the whole if you reverse the two parts of the equation:
$r - 7 = 25$

Step 2

Create a problem where you do not know the whole (the total), but you know the part that is given away (7) and the part you are left with (25).

Jackie brought a bag of candies to school to share with her friends. At morning recess, she gave one candy to each of her seven best friends and had 25 candies left to share with other friends throughout the day. How many candies were in the bag before Jackie shared them?

2. **Step 1**

Determine what the unknown represents.

Since division can be expressed as total ÷ number of groups = number in each group, the variable f represents the number of groups.

Step 2

Create a problem where you know the total (20) and you know the number of items in each group (5), but you do not know the number of groups.

Hudson's mom put 20 freshly baked cookies on the counter to cool. When Hudson and some friends came into the kitchen, Hudson's mom let each child have five cookies. How many children got five cookies?

PRACTICE EXERCISES
ANSWERS AND SOLUTIONS

1. **Step 1**

Determine the unknown.

Addition can be expressed as part + part = whole. The variable represents one of the parts.

Step 2

Write a problem where you do not know the original amount but you know that 25 was added to it to result in a total of 37.

Henry had some soccer cards. After his friend gave him 25 more cards, Henry had a total of 37 cards. How many cards did Henry have originally?

3. **Step 1**

Determine the unknown.

Multiplication can be expressed as number of groups × number in each group = total. The variable h represents the total number.

Step 2

Write a problem where you have five groups with 20 items in each group, resulting in an unknown amount.

Jake had five packages of sports cards. Each package had 20 cards. How many cards were there in total?

Lesson 4—Using Inverse Operations to Solve Equations

🦋 TIME TO TRY 🦋
ANSWERS AND SOLUTIONS

1. **Step 1**
    Determine the value of f.

    If $46 = f - 13$, then $13 + 46 = f$.
    Since $13 + 46 = 59$, $f = 59$.

    Step 2
    Check your work.

    Substitute 59 for the variable f in
    the equation.
    $46 = f - 13$
    $46 = 59 - 13$
    $46 = 46$

    Since both sides of the equal sign have the same
    value (46), you know the answer is correct.

2. **Step 1**
    Determine the value of R.

    If $R + 32 = 86$, then $86 - 32 = R$.

    Since $86 - 32 = 54$, $R = 54$.

    Step 2
    Check your work.

    Substitute 54 for the variable R in the equation.
    $R + 32 = 86$
    $54 + 32 = 86$
    $86 = 86$

    Since both sides of the equal sign have the same
    value (86), you know the answer is correct.

3. **Step 1**
    Determine the value of b.

    If $88 = 4b$, then $88 \div 4 = b$.
    Since $88 \div 4 = 22$, $b = 22$.

    Step 2
    Check your work.
    Substitute 22 for the variable b in
    the equation.

$88 = 4b$
$88 = 4 \times 22$
$88 = 88$

Since both sides of the equal sign have the same
value (88), you know the answer is correct.

4. **Step 1**
    Determine the value of r.

    If $8 = r \div 9$, then $9 \times 8 = r$.
    Since $9 \times 8 = 72$, $r = 72$.

    Step 2
    Check your work.

    Substitute 72 for the variable r in the equation.
    $8 = r \div 9$
    $8 = 72 \div 9$
    $8 = 8$

    Since both sides of the equal sign have the same
    value (8), you know the answer is correct.

PRACTICE EXERCISES
ANSWERS AND SOLUTIONS

1. **Step 1**
    Determine the value of f.

    If $100 - f = 73$, then $73 + 100 = f$.
    Since $73 + 100 = 173$, $f = 173$.

    Step 2
    Check your work.

    Substitute 173 for the variable f in the equation.
    $100 = f - 73$
    $100 = 173 - 73$
    $100 = 100$

3. **Step 1**
    Determine the value of x.

    If $125 = 5x$, then $125 \div 5 = x$.
    Since $125 \div 5 = 25$, $x = 25$.

    Step 2
    Check your work.
    Substitute 25 for the variable x in the equation.
    $125 = 5x$
    $125 = 5 \times 25$
    $125 = 125$

Lesson 5—Solving Single-Variable, One-Step Problems

❦ TIME TO TRY ❦
ANSWERS AND SOLUTIONS

1. **Step 1**
Identify the unknown.

The unknown is the number of cookies that Jordan took to school.

Step 2
Write an equation to express the problem.

One equation you can use to solve the problem is $30 + C = 75$.

Step 3
Solve the equation.

If $30 + C = 75$, then $75 - 30 = C$.
Since $75 - 30 = 45$, $C = 45$.

Jordan took 45 cookies to school.

Step 4
Check your work.

Substitute 45 for the variable C in the equation.
$$30 + C = 75$$
$$30 + 45 = 75$$
$$75 = 75$$

Since both sides of the equal sign have the same value (75), you know your answer is correct.

2. **Step 1**
Identify the unknown.

The unknown is the number of children on each team.

Step 2
Write an equation to express the problem.

One equation you can use to solve the problem is $54 = 6s$.

Step 3
Solve the equation.

If $54 = 6s$, then $54 \div 6 = s$.
Since $54 \div 6 = 9$, $s = 9$.

There were nine children on each team.

Step 4
Check your work.

Substitute 9 for the variable s in the equation.
$$54 = 6s$$
$$54 = 6 \times 9$$
$$54 = 54$$

Since both sides of the equal sign have the same value (54), you know your answer is correct.

PRACTICE EXERCISES
ANSWERS AND SOLUTIONS

1. **Step 1**
Identify the unknown.
The unknown is the number of cupcakes Stephanie baked.

Step 2
Write an equation to express the problem.
One equation you can use to solve the problem is $C - 83 = 17$.

Step 3
Solve the equation.

If $C - 83 = 17$, then $17 + 83 = C$.
Since $17 + 83 = 100$, $C = 100$.

Stephanie baked 100 cupcakes.

Step 4
Check your work.

Substitute 100 for the variable C in the equation.
$$C - 83 = 17$$
$$100 - 83 = 17$$
$$17 = 17$$

3. **Step 1**
Identify the unknown.

The unknown is the total number of boxes ordered.

Step 2
Write an equation to express the problem.
One equation you can use to solve the problem is $P \times 8 = 120$.

Step 3
Solve the equation.

If $P \times 8 = 120$, then $120 \div 8 = P$.
Since $120 \div 8 = 15$, $P = 15$.

Mr. Friss ordered 15 boxes of paper.

Step 4
Check your work.

Substitute 15 for the variable P in the equation.
$P \times 8 = 120$
$15 \times 8 = 120$
$120 = 120$

Practice Test

ANSWERS AND SOLUTIONS

1. **Step 1**
Identify the unknown.

The unknown is the number of medals that were not silver.

Step 2
Determine the operation.

The clue words "were not silver" let you know that you can use a subtraction or addition equation.

These equations all express the problem:
$45 - 19 = G$
$45 - G = 19$
$19 + G = 45$
$G + 19 = 45$

3. **Step 1**
Determine the unknown.

Addition can be expressed as part + part = whole. The variable k represents one of the parts.

Step 2
Write a problem in which you do not know the original amount, but you know that 18 was added to it to result in a total of 40.

Melody had some soccer cards. After her friend gave her 18 more cards, Melody had a total of 40 cards. How many cards did Melody have originally?

5. **Step 1**
Determine the value of N.

If $83 + N = 150$, then $150 - 83 = N$.
Since $150 - 83 = 67$, $N = 67$.

Step 2
Check your work.

Substitute 67 for the variable N in the equation.
$83 + N = 150$
$83 + 67 = 150$
$150 = 150$

7. **Step 1**
Identify the unknown.

The unknown is the number of pennies that still need to be rolled.

Step 2
Write an equation to express the problem.

One equation you can use to solve the problem is $T + 370 = 1\,000$.

Step 3
Solve the equation.

If $T + 370 = 1000$, then $1\,000 - 370 = T$.
Since $1\,000 - 370 = 630$, $T = 630$.

Six hundred thirty pennies still need to be rolled.

Step 4
Check your work.

Substitute 630 for the variable T in the equation.
$T + 370 = 1\,000$
$630 + 370 = 1000$
$1\,000 = 1\,000$

9. **Step 1**
Determine the value of P.

If $P \div 11 = 11$, then $11 \times 11 = P$.
Since $11 \times 11 = 121$, $P = 121$.

Step 2
Check your work.
Substitute 121 for the variable P in the equation.
$P \div 11 = 11$
$121 \div 11 = 11$
$11 = 11$

CAPACITY AND VOLUME

Lesson 1—Relationships Between Millilitres and Litres

PRACTICE EXERCISES ANSWERS AND SOLUTIONS

1. A bottle of syrup could have a capacity of 725 mL.

3. A cup of hot chocolate could have a capacity of 200 mL.

Lesson 2—Using Appropriate Referents for Millilitres and Litres

🐝 TIME TO TRY 🐝 ANSWERS AND SOLUTIONS

1. Yes, Laramy chose an appropriate referent.

   The size of the lid is a reasonable size compared to the size of the thermos being measured. The lid is about the size of a small cup that could hold about 200 mL of liquid.

2. No, using a 100 mL cup was not an appropriate choice.

   Since the laundry sink is large and deep, it would have been more appropriate to use a referent for litres instead of a small referent like a 100 mL cup.

PRACTICE EXERCISES ANSWERS AND SOLUTIONS

1. No, the eyedropper is not an appropriate referent.

   A drop of water is about 1 mL. Since the liquid in the beaker is at the 300 mL mark and the beaker is not yet half full, it would take a very long time to fill the beaker drop by drop. An eyedropper is much too small a referent to measure a capacity in the hundred millilitres.

Lesson 3—Estimating Capacity Using Referents

🐝 TIME TO TRY 🐝 ANSWERS AND SOLUTIONS

1. **Step 1**
   Determine the estimated capacity of the large pail.

   The big pail has a capacity of about 880 mL.

   Step 2
   Explain how the referent was used.

   The markings on the big pail show that four of the small pails would equal the capacity of the big pail.

   Since the small pail has a capacity of about 220 mL, the big pail will have a capacity that is four times greater than 220 mL.
   220 mL × 4 = 880 mL

2. **Step 1**
   Estimate the capacity of the large pail.

   The capacity of the large pail is a little more than 32 L.

   Step 2
   Explain how the referent can be used to estimate the capacity of the large pail.

   You can fill the small pail and then pour it into the big pail. Repeat this until the large pail is full.

   Draw lines on the large pail to show the water level after each small pail was poured into the large pail.

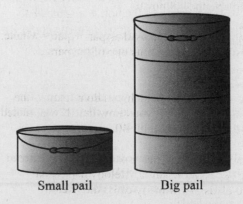

Small pail   Big pail

Since a little more than 8 L fills the small pail, the capacity of the large pail is about four times greater.
$8 \times 4 = 32$

Since the capacity of the small pail is a little more than 8 L, the capacity of the large pail is a little more than 32 L.

PRACTICE EXERCISES
ANSWERS AND SOLUTIONS

1. **Step 1**
    Estimate the capacity of the bottle.
    The bottle has a capacity of about 700 mL.

    Step 2
    Explain your answer.

    The first arrow on the bottle shows the level of water after 2 cups have been poured into the bottle.
    2 cups $= 100 + 100 = 200$ mL

    The other arrows show where the level would be when the bottle is two-thirds and three-thirds full.

    Each successive marking will be another 200 mL.
    $200 + 200 + 200 = 600$
    Since the bottle has more room above the third arrow, the capacity of the bottle is somewhat greater than 600 mL. A good estimate could be 700 mL.

Lesson 4—Measuring and Recording Capacity

🦋 TIME TO TRY 🦋
ANSWERS AND SOLUTIONS

1. Larger unit to smaller unit → think multiplication.

    Since 1 L = 1 000 mL, convert 4 L into millilitres by multiplying 4 by 1 000.

    $4 \text{ L} \times 1\ 000 = 4\ \underline{000}$ mL
    $4 \text{ L} = 4\ 000$ mL

2. Smaller unit to larger unit → think division.

    Since 1 000 mL = 1 L, to convert 1 520 mL to litres, divide 1 520 mL by 1 000.

    $1\ \underline{520} \div 1\ 000 = 1.52$
    $1\ 520$ mL $= 1.52$ L

    There are 1.52 L of milk in the bowl.

3. **Step 1**
    Determine the number of litres equal to 28 one-quarter litre cartons.

    The students drank a total of 7 L of milk.

    Step 2
    Explain your answer.

    Four one-quarter litre cartons equals 1 L.
    250 mL $\times 4 = 1\ 000$ mL

    Since 28 students each drank a carton of milk, divide 28 by 4.
    $28 \div 4 = 7$

4. **Step 1**
    Order the millilitre capacities first.

    Since all the millilitre capacities are less than 1 000 mL (1 L), you do not need to convert the litre capacities to millilitre capacities.

    Since 454 < 544, 454 mL < 544 mL.

    Step 2
    Order the litre capacities.

    Since 4 < 4.5, 4 L < 4.5 L.

552

Step 3
Write the millilitre capacities, followed by the litre capacities.

From least to greatest, the capacities are 454 mL, 544 mL, 4 L, 4.5 L .

5. **Step 1**
Change the litres to millilitres.

Since one of the millilitre measurements is greater than 1 000 mL (1 L), you need to change the litres to millilitres before you can compare the capacities.
$2 \text{ L} \times 1\ 000 = 2\ 000 \text{ mL}$
$1 \text{ L} \times 1\ 000 = 1\ 000 \text{ mL}$

Step 2
Place the numbers from greatest value to least value.
$2\ 000 > 1\ 200 > 1\ 000 > 950$

$2\ 000 \text{ mL} > 1\ 200 \text{ mL} > 1\ 000 \text{ mL} > 950 \text{ mL}$

From greatest to least, the capacities are 2 L, 1 200 mL, 1 L, 950 mL.

PRACTICE EXERCISES
ANSWERS AND SOLUTIONS

1. **Step 1**
Determine the capacity of one bottle.

Larger unit to smaller unit → think multiplication.
$1 \text{ L} = 1\ 000 \text{ mL}$
$2 \text{ L} = 1\ 000 \times 2 = 2\ 000 \text{ mL}$

Each bottle has a capacity of 2 000 mL.

Step 2
Determine the capacity of three bottles.

Multiply 2 000 mL by 3.
$2\ 000 \text{ mL} \times 3 = 6\ 000 \text{ mL}$

The three bottles have a combined capacity of 6 000 mL.

3. **Step 1**
Change the litre capacities to millilitre capacities.

$$1 \text{ L} = 1\ 000 \text{ mL}$$
$$1\frac{1}{2} \text{ L} = 1\ 000 + 500\ = 1\ 500 \text{ mL}$$
$$4\frac{1}{2} \text{ L} = 4\ 000 + 500 = 4\ 500 \text{ mL}$$

Step 2
Order the numbers from least to greatest.

$250 < 1\ 000 < 1\ 200 < 1\ 500 < 4\ 500$

From least to greatest, the capacities are

$250 \text{ mL}, 1\text{L}, 1\ 200 \text{ mL}, 1\frac{1}{2}\text{L}, 4\frac{1}{2}\text{L}$.

Lesson 5—Understanding Volume of Prisms

PRACTICE EXERCISES
ANSWERS AND SOLUTIONS

1. **Step 1**
Count the number of cubes that fill the box.

There are five cubes in each row. There are four rows of cubes.
$5 \times 4 = 20$

There are 20 cubes filling the box.

Step 2
Determine the volume.

Each cube represents one cubic unit.
The volume of the box is 20 cubic units. This is written as 20 units^3.

Lesson 6—Using Appropriate Referents for Cubic Centimetres and Cubic Metres

PRACTICE EXERCISES
ANSWERS AND SOLUTIONS

1. Marina should use the set of dice that have square corners.

Cubic units are the most appropriate unit to use for estimating volume because cubes fit side by side without leaving spaces or gaps. Cubes can also be layered without spaces or gaps.

2. Sam made a good decision when he chose to use a large referent to estimate the volume of a large space. The estimated volume will be a smaller number and will be easier to work with.

    A 1 cm^3 box would be so small that it would fit into Sam's hand. It would not be practical to estimate the volume of such a large space with such a small referent. The estimated volume would be in the millions.

Lesson 7—Estimating Volume Using Referents

🐝 TIME TO TRY 🐝
ANSWERS AND SOLUTIONS

1. **Step 1**
    Estimate the volume of the box.
    The volume of the box is around 24 cm^3.

    Step 2
    Explain your answer.

    Four cubes should fit side by side for the length of the box.
    Two rows of cubes should cover the base of the box.

    The bottom layer would then have eight cubes.

Three cubes should fit one above the other.

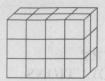

Twenty-four cubes would fill the box.
$8 + 8 + 8 = 24$

PRACTICE EXERCISES
ANSWERS AND SOLUTIONS

1. **Step 1**
    Estimate the volume.
    The volume of the cube is around 27 cm^3.

    Step 2
    Explain your answer.

    Since the figure is a cube, it has the same length, width, and height. Each side is 3 cm.

    Since each die is 1 cm^3, three rows with three dice in each row would be needed to cover the base of the cube.
    $3 + 3 + 3 = 9$
    Three layers of dice would be needed to fill the cube.
    $9 \times 3 = 27$

3. **Step 1**
    Estimate the volume.
    The volume of the crate is around 96 m^3.

    Step 2
    Explain your answer.

    Since there are eight cubes representing the length and three cubes representing the width, you would need 24 cubes to cover the base of the crate.
    $8 + 8 + 8 = 24$ or $8 \times 3 = 24$

    Since there are four cubes representing the height, you would need four layers of cubes to fill the crate.
    $24 \times 4 = 96$

Lesson 8—Measuring and Recording Volume

🐛 TIME TO TRY 🐛
ANSWERS AND SOLUTIONS

1. **Step 1**
   Count the number of cubes used to make the length (6) and width (3) of the base layer.

   Step 2
   You can multiply them to find the number of cubes in the base layer.
   $6 \times 3 = 18$

   Step 3
   Count the number of layers (5) to see how high the prism is.

   Step 4
   Multiply the number of cubes in the base layer (18) by the number of layers (5) to find the volume.
   $18 \times 5 = 90$ units^3

2. **Step 1**
   Identify the volume formula.

   The formula for determining the volume of a rectangular prism is $V = l \times w \times h$.

   Step 2
   Show your work.

   Substitute the numbers for the length (15 cm), the width (7 cm), and the height (8 cm) into the formula.
   $$V = l \times w \times h$$
   $$= 15 \times 7 \times 8$$
   $$= 840 \text{ cm}^3$$

   The volume of the prism is 840 cm^3.

PRACTICE EXERCISES
ANSWERS AND SOLUTIONS

1. **Step 1**
   Count the number of cubes that make up the length and the width of the base of the box.

   length: 5 cubes
   width: 4 cubes

   Step 2
   Calculate the number of cubes that cover the base layer.
   $5 \times 4 = 20$ or $5+5+5+5 = 20$

   Step 3
   Count the number of cubes that make up the height of the box.
   height 6 cubes

   Step 4
   Calculate the number of cubes in the six layers.
   $20 \times 6 = 120$
   or
   $20 + 20 + 20 + 20 + 20 + 20 = 120$

   The volume of the box is the total number of cubes in the six layers. The volume of the box is 120 cm^3.

Lesson 9—Constructing or Drawing Right Rectangular Prisms

🐛 TIME TO TRY 🐛
ANSWERS AND SOLUTIONS

1. **Step 1**
   Identify three numbers that equal 27 when multiplied by each other.

   $3 \times 3 \times 3 = 27$

   The prism could have a length of three cubes, a width of three cubes, and a height of three cubes.

   Step 2
   Construct or draw the prism.

   The prism will be a cube because the length, width, and height will all be represented with three cubes.

Each layer will be made out of nine cubes.

2. Step 1
Determine which three numbers multiplied by each other will equal 8.

One set of numbers is $4 \times 2 \times 1 = 8$.

The prism you construct or draw could have a length of four cubes, a width of two cubes, and the height of one cube.

Step 2
Choose another three numbers that equal 8 when multiplied by each other.

$2 \times 2 \times 2 = 8$

This rectangular prism will be a cube because the length, width, and height will be represented by the same number of cubes (2).

PRACTICE EXERCISES
ANSWERS AND SOLUTIONS

1. Step 1
Identify three numbers that equal 24 when multiplied by each other.

One set of numbers is $4 \times 2 \times 3 = 24$.

Step 2
Construct or draw the prism.

Let four cubes represent the length.
Let two cubes represent the width.
Let three cubes represent the height.

The prism you make could look like this:

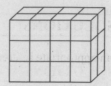

2. Step 1
Identify three numbers that equal 12 when multiplied by each other.

One set of numbers is $4 \times 1 \times 3 = 12$.

The prism you draw could look like this:

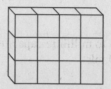

Step 2
Identify three other numbers that equal 12 when multiplied by each other.

One set of numbers is $12 \times 1 \times 1 = 12$.

The prism you draw could look like this:

Step 3
Identify another three numbers that equal 12 when multiplied by each other.

One set of numbers is $3 \times 2 \times 2 = 12$.

The prism you draw could look like this:

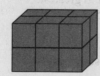

Practice Test

ANSWERS AND SOLUTIONS

1. No, the eyedropper is not an appropriate referent.

   Cups come in many sizes, but most regular-sized cups have a capacity of at least 200 mL.

   A drop is about 1 mL, so an eyedropper is much too small a referent to use when measuring a capacity in the hundred millilitres.

   It would take a long time to fill the cup drop- by- drop.

3. **Step 1**
   Change the litre capacities to millilitre capacities.
   $1.5 \text{ L} = 1.5 \times 1\,000 = 1\,500 \text{ mL}$

   $0.5 \text{ L} = 0.5 \times 1\,000 = 500 \text{ mL}$

   Step 2
   Order the numbers from greatest to least.
   1 500, 1 005, 1 000, 500

   Step 3
   Order the capacities from greatest to least.

   1 500 mL > 1 005 mL > 1 000 mL > 500 mL

   1.5 L > 1 005 mL > 1 000 mL > 0.5 L

5. **Step 1**
   Change the litre capacities to millilitre capacities.
   $1 \text{ L} = 1\,000 \text{ mL}$
   $2 \text{ L} = 2\,000 \text{ mL}$
   Step 2
   Order the numbers from least to greatest.
   950, 1 000, 1 200, 2 000, 2 050

   Step 3
   Order the capacities from least to greatest.

   950 mL, 1 L, 1 200 mL, 2 L, 2 050 mL

7. **Step 1**
   Determine the volume.
   The volume of the box is 98 units^3.

   Step 2
   Explain how you can use the blocks.

Count the number of blocks that represent the length of the box. (7)

Count the number of blocks that represent the width of the box. (2)

Determine the number of blocks in the base layer.
$7 \times 2 = 14$

Since there are seven layers (the height), multiply 14 by 7 to determine the volume.
$14 \times 7 = 98$

9. **Step 1**
   Identify three numbers that equal 18 when multiplied by each other.

   One set of numbers is $3 \times 2 \times 3 = 18$.

   The prism you make could have a length of three cubes, a width of two cubes, and a height of three cubes.

   Step 2
   Identify three other numbers that equal 18 when multiplied by each other.

   One set of numbers is $9 \times 1 \times 2 = 18$.

   The prism you make could have a length of nine cubes, a width of one cube, and a height of two cubes.

   Step 3
   Identify another three numbers that equal 18 when multiplied by each other.

   One set of numbers is $18 \times 1 \times 1 = 18$.

   The prism you make could have a length of 18 cubes, a width of one cube, and a height of one cube.

ADDITION AND SUBTRACTION OF DECIMALS

Lesson 1—Estimating Sums and Differences to Thousandths

❦ TIME TO TRY ❦
ANSWERS AND SOLUTIONS

1. Step 1
Use front-end estimation.
$120.005 \rightarrow 120$
$12.1 \rightarrow 12$
$0.016 \rightarrow 0$
$24.02 \rightarrow 24$

Step 2
Calculate the estimated sum.
$120 + 12 + 24 = 156$

Step 3
Describe the sum of
$120.005 + 12.1 + 0.016 + 24.02$.

Although all the numbers were rounded down, the rounded numbers were very close in value to the original numbers.

Therefore, you can describe the sum of
$120.005 + 12.1 + 0.016 + 24.02$ as being about 156.

2. Step 1
Use front-end estimation.
$163.983 \rightarrow 163$
$10.981 \rightarrow 10$

Step 2
Calculate the estimated difference.
$163 - 10 = 153$

Step 3
Describe the difference of $163.983 - 10.981$.

Since the tenths and the hundredths digits are the same (98) and the thousandths digits are so close in value (3 and 1), the estimated difference will be almost the same as the actual difference.

Therefore, you can describe the difference of
$163.983 - 10.981$ as being about 153.

3. Step 1
Round the decimal numbers.
$14.\underline{7}35 \rightarrow 15$ because $7 > 5$
$0.\underline{1}09 \rightarrow 0$ because $1 < 5$
$363.\underline{5} \rightarrow 364$ because $5 = 5$

Step 2
Add the rounded numbers.
$364 + 15 = 379$

The estimated sum of
$14.735 + 0.109 + 363.5$ is 379.

4. Step 1
Round the decimal numbers.
$605.\underline{3}5 \rightarrow 605$ because $3 < 5$
$295.\underline{6}89 \rightarrow 296$ because $6 > 5$

Step 2
Subtract the rounded numbers, regrouping where necessary.
$605 - 296 = 309$

The estimated difference of
$605.35 - 295.689$ is 309.

PRACTICE EXERCISES
ANSWERS AND SOLUTIONS

1. Step 1
Start with front-end estimation.
$173.123 \rightarrow 173$
$0.27 \rightarrow 0$
$236.051 \rightarrow 236$

Step 2
Calculate the estimated sum.
$173 + 236 = 409$

Step 3
Describe the actual sum.

Although the numbers were rounded down, the estimated numbers were very close in value to the original numbers.

Therefore, the sum of $173.123 + 0.27 + 236.051$ can be described as being close to 409.

3. **Step 1**
Round the decimal numbers.
398.<u>9</u>03 → 399 because 9>5
172.<u>9</u>99 → 173 because 9>5
18.<u>0</u>5 → 18 because 0<5

Step 2
Calculate the estimated sum.
398 + 173 + 18 = 589

The estimated sum of 398 + 173 + 18 is 589.

Lesson 2—Calculating Sums and Differences to Thousandths

❦ TIME TO TRY ❦
ANSWERS AND SOLUTIONS

1. Remember to line up the decimals and the place values when you write the numbers.

$$\begin{array}{r} 17.503 \\ +52.096 \\ \hline 69.599 \end{array}$$

Remember to put the decimal point in the answer, between the ones digit and the tenths digit.

2. **Step 1**
Add zeros to make equivalent decimals.
34.52 → 34.520
1.8 → 1.800

Step 2
Show your work.

Remember to line up the decimals and the place values when you write the numbers.

$$\begin{array}{r} ^{1\ 1\ 1} \\ 34.520 \\ 176.409 \\ 1.800 \\ \hline 212.729 \end{array}$$

Remember to put the decimal point in the answer, between the ones digit and the tenths digit.

3. Remember to line up the decimals and the place values when you write the numbers.

$$\begin{array}{r} ^{5\ 10} \\ 83.7\cancel{6}\cancel{0} \\ -2.145 \\ \hline 81.615 \end{array}$$

Remember to put the decimal point in the answer, between the ones digit and the tenths digit.

4. **Step 1**
Make an equivalent decimal for 38.96.
38.96 → 38.960

Step 2
Show your work.

Remember to line up the decimals and place values.

$$\begin{array}{r} ^{5\ 10} \\ 38.9\cancel{6}\cancel{0} \\ -7.832 \\ \hline 31.128 \end{array}$$

Remember to put the decimal in the answer, between the ones digit (1) and the tenths digit (1).

PRACTICE EXERCISES
ANSWERS AND SOLUTIONS

1. **Step 1**
Add two zeros to make an equivalent decimal.
165.5 → 165.500

Step 2
Line up the decimal points and calculate.

$$\begin{array}{r} ^{1} \\ 83.409 \\ +165.500 \\ \hline 248.909 \end{array}$$

3. **Step 1**
Add two zeros to make an equivalent decimal.
14.5 → 14.500

Step 2
Line up the decimal points and calculate.

$$\begin{array}{r} 426.663 \\ -14.500 \\ \hline 412.163 \end{array}$$

Lesson 3—Solving Problems Involving Decimals to Thousandths

✿ TIME TO TRY ✿
ANSWERS AND SOLUTIONS

1. **Step 1**
   Determine the operation that will solve the problem.

   The words "total weight" are a clue that you need to add.

   Step 2
   Add the two given weights to determine the total weight.

   $$
   \begin{array}{r}
   \overset{1}{5}.\overset{1}{3}56 \\
   +1.786 \\
   \hline
   7.142
   \end{array}
   $$

   The total weight of the papers and flyers is 7.142 kg.

PRACTICE EXERCISES
ANSWERS AND SOLUTIONS

1. **Step 1**
   Determine the operation.

   The clue words "total time" let you know you need to add.

   Step 2
   Make equivalent decimals.
   73.5 → 73.500
   70.09 → 70.090

   Step 3
   Line up the decimals, and calculate.

   $$
   \begin{array}{r}
   \overset{1}{7}\overset{1}{3}.\overset{1}{5}00 \\
   70.090 \\
   +69.445 \\
   \hline
   213.035
   \end{array}
   $$

   The total time of the practice race was 213.035 s.

3. **Step 1**
   Determine the operation.

   The clue words "in all" let you know that you need to add.

Step 2
Make equivalent decimals.
5.8 → 5.800
9.25 → 9.250

Step 3
Line up the decimals, and calculate.

$$
\begin{array}{r}
\overset{1}{}\overset{1}{5}.\overset{1}{8}00 \\
9.250 \\
+12.459 \\
\hline
27.509
\end{array}
$$

Mrs. Mullen bought 27.509 m of material in all.

Practice Test

ANSWERS AND SOLUTIONS

1. **Step 1**
   Start with front-end estimation.
   37.56 → 37
   1.392 → 1
   146.5 → 146

   Step 2
   Calculate the estimated sum.
   $37 + 1 + 146 = 184$

   Step 3
   Describe the actual sum.

   Since all three numbers were rounded down, the sum of $37.56 + 1.392 + 146.5$ is greater than 184.

3. **Step 1**
   Add zeros to make equivalent decimals.
   120.5 → 120.500
   1.25 → 1.250

   Step 2
   Line up the decimal points and calculate.

   $$
   \begin{array}{r}
   \overset{1}{1}20.\overset{1}{5}00 \\
   87.061 \\
   +1.250 \\
   \hline
   208.811
   \end{array}
   $$

5. **Step 1**

Start with front-end estimation.

198.903 → 198

72.919 → 72

Step 2

Calculate the estimated difference.

198 − 72 = 126

Step 3

Describe the actual difference.

Since the numbers were rounded down about the same amount, the difference for 198.903 − 72.919 is close to 126.

7. **Step 1**

Add a zero to make an equivalent decimal.

27.45 → 27.450

Step 2

Line up the decimals points and calculate.

$$\begin{array}{r} \overset{2\ \ \ 9\ \ 15\ \ \ 4\ 11}{3\ 0\ 5\ .\ 5\ 1\ 6} \\ -2\ 7\ .\ 4\ 5\ 0 \\ \hline 2\ 7\ 8\ .\ 0\ 6\ 6 \end{array}$$

PROBABILITY

Lesson 1—Likelihood of a Single Outcome

🦋 TIME TO TRY 🦋
ANSWERS AND SOLUTIONS

1. No, Pascal is not correct.

For an outcome to be certain, it must happen every time.

There is no possibility that another outcome could occur. That is not the case with the two-sided coin.

Since the coin has two sides (white and brown), there is a possibility that the coin could land on either white or brown. Therefore, the outcome of landing on white for 10 flips may be possible, but it is not absolutely certain.

2. It is impossible for Joannie to pull out a pink gumdrop.

An impossible outcome is one that will never happen.

Since there are no pink gumdrops in the bag, it is impossible to pull a pink gumdrop out of the bag. It is only possible to pick a colour that is in the bag (purple, red, or blue).

3. It is possible that the spinner will land on yellow.

There are three possible outcomes.

It is possible for the spinner to land on each colour on the wheel: red, orange, or yellow. Even though yellow is the smallest part of the wheel, it is still possible for the spinner to land on it.

PRACTICE EXERCISES
ANSWERS AND SOLUTIONS

1. The outcome is certain.

    The numbers 1, 2, 3, 4, 5, and 6 are all single-digit numbers. Therefore, the number cube will always land on a single-digit number.

3. It is impossible for the outcome to occur.

    The numbers on the cube only go up to 6. Although 6 is greater than 5, it is not an odd number. The next odd number greater than 5 is 7. It is impossible to roll a 7 when there is no 7 on the number cube.

Lesson 2—*Comparing the Likelihood of Two Possible Outcomes*

❧ TIME TO TRY ❧
ANSWERS AND SOLUTIONS

1. The most likely outcome is that the student will pick a card with the number 2 on it.

    The most likely outcome will be the one that has the most cards with the same number on them.
    - Three cards have the number 1.
    - Five cards have the number 2.
    - One card has the number 3.
    - One card has the number 4.

    Since there are more 2s than any other number, the most likely outcome is to pick a card with a 2.

2. Emma is correct when she says that it is less likely that the spinner will stop on yellow than on red.

    There is only one part labelled yellow on the wheel. There are two parts labelled red on the wheel.

    Since 1 is less than 2, it is less likely that the spinner will stop on yellow than on red.

3. Ryan is correct when he says the spinner is not fair.

    The spinner is not fair because the outcomes (grey and white parts) are not equally likely. Since five out of the eight parts of the spinner are white, Jason has more chances of winning.

    To be fair, both boys should have an equal chance of winning. There should be four grey parts and four white parts on the spinner for the outcomes to be equally likely.

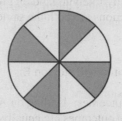

PRACTICE EXERCISES
ANSWERS AND SOLUTIONS

1. No, the outcomes are not equally likely.

    Since there are more blue tiles (6) than green tiles (5), the two colours do not have an equal chance of being pulled.

3. Spinner A has the least likely chance of stopping on 3. Each spinner has a different number of equal parts.
    - Spinner A has eight equal parts.
    - Spinner B has five equal parts.
    - Spinner C has four equal parts.
    - Spinner D has six equal parts.

    The spinner with the least likely chance of stopping on 3 is the spinner with the most parts, which results in the smallest-sized parts.

Practice Test

ANSWERS AND SOLUTIONS

1. The students are more likely to land on green than on blue on Spinner H.

On spinner H, the green part is larger than the blue part, so there is a greater chance of landing on green than blue.

On spinner G, it is equally likely to land on green or blue because these sections are both the same size.

3. It is possible that the spinner will stop on E.

There are five possible outcomes: landing on A, B, C, D, and E. All of the outcomes are equally likely because the five sections are equal in size. Even though the spinner has not yet stopped on E in 14 spins, it is still a possible outcome.

5. Following are some descriptions of the outcomes:

- The spinner is more likely to land on a 2 than on 1 because there are two equal spaces labeled 2 and only one equal space labeled 1.

- The spinner is less likely to land on 1 than on a 2 because there is only one equal space labeled 1 and there are two equal spaces labeled 2.

- The spinner is not equally likely to stop on a 1 or 2 because there are more equal spaces labeled 2 than 1.

- The spinner is equally likely to stop on a white 2 or a shaded 2 because the two spaces are an equal size.

7. Yes, the spinner is drawn correctly.

- Since the spinner is most likely to land on a 6, the 6 part must be the largest part.

- Since the spinner is least likely to land on a 2, the 2 part must be the smallest part.

- Since it is possible to land on a 4, the 4 part must be larger than the 2 part and smaller than the 6 part.

Credits

Every effort has been made to provide proper acknowledgement of the original source and to comply with copyright law. However, some attempts to establish original copyright ownership may have been unsuccessful.

If copyright ownership can be identified, please notify Castle Rock Research Corp so that appropriate corrective action can be taken.

Some images in this document are from www.clipart.com, copyright (c) 2009 Jupiterimages Corporation.

ORDERING INFORMATION

SCHOOL ORDERS

Please contact the Learning Resource Centre (LRC) for school discount and order information.

THE KEY Study Guides are specifically designed to assist students in preparing for unit tests, final exams, and provincial examinations.

THE KEY Study Guides – $29.95 each plus G.S.T.

SENIOR HIGH		JUNIOR HIGH	ELEMENTARY
Biology 30	Biology 20	English Language Arts 9	English Language Arts 6
Chemistry 30	Chemistry 20	Math 9	Math 6
English 30-1	English 20-1	Science 9	Science 6
English 30-2	Mathematics 20-1	Social Studies 9	Social Studies 6
Applied Math 30	Physics 20	Math 8	Math 4
Pure Math 30	Social Studies 20-1	Math 7	English Language Arts 3
Physics 30	English 10-1		Math 3
Social Studies 30-1	Math 10 Combined		
Social Studies 30-2	Science 10		
	Social Studies 10-1		

Student Notes and Problems (SNAP) Workbooks contain complete explanations of curriculum concepts, examples, and exercise questions.

SNAP Workbooks – $29.95 each plus G.S.T.

SENIOR HIGH		JUNIOR HIGH	ELEMENTARY
Biology 30	Biology 20	Math 9	Math 6
Chemistry 30	Chemistry 20	Science 9	Math 5
Applied Math 30	Mathematics 20-1	Math 8	Math 4
Pure Math 30	Physics 20	Science 8	Math 3
Math 31	Math 10 Combined	Math 7	
Physics 30	Science 10	Science 7	

Visit our website for a tour of resource content and features or order resources online at
www.castlerockresearch.com

#2340, 10180 – 101 Street   **Phone:** 780.448.9619
Edmonton, AB Canada T5J 3S4   **Toll-free:** 1.800.840.6224
e-mail: learn@castlerockresearch.com   **Fax:** 780.426.3917

CASTLE ROCK
RESEARCH CORP

ORDER FORM

THE KEY	QUANTITY
Biology 30	
Chemistry 30	
English 30-1	
English 30-2	
Applied Math 30	
Pure Math 30	
Physics 30	
Biology 20	
Social Studies 30-1	
Social Studies 30-2	
Biology 20	
Chemistry 20	
English 20-1	
Mathematics 20-1	
Physics 20	
Social Studies 20-1	
English 10-1	
Math 10 Combined	
Science 10	
Social Studies 10-1	
English Language Arts 9	
Math 9	
Science 9	
Social Studies 9	
Math 8	
Math 7	
English Language Arts 6	
Math 6	
Science 6	
Social Studies 6	
Math 4	
English Language Arts 3	
Math 3	

Student Notes and Problems Workbooks	QUANTITY	
	SNAP Workbooks	Solution Manuals
Math 31		
Biology 30		
Chemistry 30		
Applied Math 30		
Pure Math 30		
Physics 30		
Biology 20		
Chemistry 20		
Mathematics 20-1		
Physics 20		
Math 10 Combined		
Science 10		
Math 9		
Science 9		
Math 8		
Science 8		
Math 7		
Science 7		
Math 6		
Math 5		
Math 4		
Math 3		

TOTALS
KEYS
SNAP WORKBOOKS
SOLUTION MANUALS
SOLUTION MANUALS

Learning Resources Centre

Castle Rock Research is pleased to announce an exclusive distribution arrangement with the Learning Resources Centre (LRC). Under this agreement, schools can now place all their orders with LRC for order fulfillment. As well, these resources are eligible for applying the Learning Resource Credit Allocation (LRCA), which gives schools a 25% discount off LRC's selling price. Call LRC for details.

Orders may be placed with LRC by
Telephone: 780.427.2767
      Fax: 780.422.9750
Internet: www.lrc.education.gov.ab.ca
Or mail: 12360 – 142 Street NW
      Edmonton, AB T5L 4X9

Learning Resources Centre

PAYMENT AND SHIPPING INFORMATION

Name: _____
School Telephone: _____
SHIP TO
School: _____
Address: _____
City: _____ Postal Code: _____
PAYMENT
☐ by credit card
VISA/MC Number: _____
Expiry Date: _____
Name on card: _____
☐ enclosed cheque
☐ invoice school   P.O. number: _____

CASTLE ROCK
RESEARCH CORP

#2340, 10180 – 101 Street, Edmonton, AB T5J 3S4   **Phone:** 780.448.9619   **Fax:** 780.426.3917
Email: learn@castlerockresearch.com   **Toll-free:** 1.800.840.6224
www.castlerockresearch.com